Religion and Democratic Citizenship

Religion and Democratic Citizenship

Inquiry and Conviction in the American Public Square

J. CALEB CLANTON

LEXINGTON BOOKS

A division of
ROWMAN & LITTLEFIELD PUBLISHERS, INC.
Lanham • Boulder • New York • Toronto • Plymouth, UK

LEXINGTON BOOKS

A division of Rowman & Littlefield Publishers, Inc.
A wholly owned subsidiary of The Rowman & Littlefield Publishing Group, Inc.
4501 Forbes Boulevard, Suite 200
Lanham, MD 20706

Estover Road
Plymouth PL6 7PY
United Kingdom

Copyright © 2008 by Lexington Books

All rights reserved. No part of this publication may be reproduced,
stored in a retrieval system, or transmitted in any form or by any
means, electronic, mechanical, photocopying, recording, or otherwise,
without the prior permission of the publisher.

British Library Cataloguing in Publication Information Available

Library of Congress Cataloging-in-Publication Data

Clanton, J. Caleb, 1978–
　Religion and democratic citizenship : inquiry and conviction in the American public square / J. Caleb Clanton.
　　　p. cm.
　Includes bibliographical references and index.
　ISBN-13: 978-0-7391-2080-4 (cloth : alk. paper)
　ISBN-10: 0-7391-2080-8 (cloth : alk. paper)
　ISBN-13: 978-0-7391-2081-1 (pbk. : alk. paper)
　ISBN-10: 0-7391-2081-6 (pbk. : alk. paper)
　1. Religion and politics—United States. 2. Democracy—United States. I. Title.
　BL65.P7.C53 2008
　322'.10973—dc22　　　　　　　　　　　　　　　　　　　2007038883

Printed in the United States of America

♾™ The paper used in this publication meets the minimum requirements of American National Standard for Information Sciences—Permanence of Paper for Printed Library Materials, ANSI/NISO Z39.48–1992.

For my mother, whose strength is matched only by her nurturing compassion.

For my father, who taught me as much about inquiry as he did about conviction.

Contents

Acknowledgments		ix
1	Tension in Our American Public Philosophy	1
2	William James and That Old-Time Religion: The Jamesian Roots of the Reconstructivist Strategy	15
3	Questionable Neo-Pragmatic Proposals Concerning Religion's Role in the Public Square	39
4	Silence and Neutrality: Liberalism's Public Reason	63
5	Liberalism's Hidden Garments: A Multidimensional Response to the Naked Public Square	85
6	Public Deliberation After Rawls: Stout's Contribution and Instructive Shortcoming	107
7	Speculations on an Open Socratic-Peircean Public Square	123
Conclusion		149
Bibliography		151
Index		159
About the Author		163

Acknowledgments

A number of people have been very helpful in the completion of this book, and I owe them an enormous debt of gratitude. I would like to thank John Lachs, Michael Hodges, Henry Teloh, Michael Sandel, Richard Gale, and Wilfred McClay for their helpful comments on various parts of this book. I have benefited greatly from my interactions with these men and am honored to have had them consider my arguments. I am particularly indebted to Robert Talisse, who as a friend, colleague, and teacher has greatly influenced, challenged, and sharpened my thoughts.

Many of the arguments contained in this book have been informed, in part, by a series of discussions that I have had with a number of my friends and colleagues over the last few years. I am especially grateful to Scott Aikin, Josh Crites, Aaron Simmons, Mason Marshall, and Ben Jordan for their friendship and conversation. The dialectical resistance provided by these men has resulted in the formation and correction of many of the ideas in this book.

I am especially grateful to Jonathan Melton who provided not only a wonderful philosophical sounding board but also crucial assistance in the preparation of the manuscript. I would also like to thank the wonderful students in my Religion in the Democratic Public Square seminar at Vanderbilt for their helpful remarks and keen insights.

Lastly, I would like to thank my family, whose love and support for me as a son and brother has been an anchor in still and choppy waters alike.

Chapter One

Tension in Our American Public Philosophy

An interesting and problematic tension haunts our American public philosophy.[1] This tension stems from the fact that we conceive ourselves in two different and, at times, conflicting ways. The United States, like many modern industrialized states, is at once both *liberal* and *democratic*. We understand ourselves as being liberal to the degree that we maintain that citizens should not be required to submit to any one particular religious, moral, or philosophical authority.[2] Our liberal aim motivates our public urge to accommodate a wide range of difference, allowing citizens to pursue various goods and ends consistent with individual choice and conscience. Alongside this liberal aim stands our democratic ambition. Roughly put, this democratic ambition motivates our felt need to seek political legitimacy by means of consent among those governed. Integral to this notion of self-government is the idea that citizens should be free to voice their concerns, beliefs, and preferences, as they understand them in the political sphere. What falls out of this democratic aspiration is the need for the pursuit of common goods and ongoing public dialogue about matters of shared interest in which citizens engage even at fundamental levels.

Traditionally, this liberal aim—or more generally, liberalism—has been understood by many as being not only consistent with but a necessary supplement to democracy itself. At least since John Stuart Mill, political theorists have argued that democracy should be kept in check by certain institutional limits so as to prevent the tyranny of the democratic majority over individual citizens. Mill writes:

> Protection, therefore, against the tyranny of the magistrate is not enough; there needs protection also against the tyranny of the prevailing opinion and feeling, against the tendency of society to impose, by other means than civil penalties,

> its own ideas and practices as rules of conduct on those who dissent from them; to fetter the development and, if possible, prevent the formation of any individuality not in harmony with its ways, and compel all characters to fashion themselves upon the model of its own. There is a limit to the legitimate interference of collective opinion with individual independence; and to find that limit, and maintain it against encroachment, is as indispensable to a good condition of human affairs as protection against despotism. (Mill 1859, 933)

The concern that Mill aptly expresses here is that without some constraints in place, the democratic ambition can get out of hand, and democracy runs the risk of collapsing into mob rule. Thus, individuals stand in need of a set of rights and liberties invulnerable to the changing tides of prevailing majoritarian opinion. Only when our democratic ambition is so limited can we expect to protect the value of the freedom to choose and follow one's own good in one's own way, which, according to Mill, is the "only freedom which deserves the name" (1859, 937). And, it is only when the exercise of this individual freedom brings harm upon others that it can be justifiably encroached by the democratic majority.

Contemporary liberals like John Rawls argue similarly concerning the fit between liberalism and democracy. According to Rawls, liberalism is a type of constraint upon democracy that allows it to function properly. This constraint manifests itself as a conception of political legitimacy—what Rawls calls the "liberal principle of legitimacy"—according to which, "the exercise of political power is proper only when we sincerely believe that the reasons we offer for our political action may reasonably be accepted by other citizens as a justification of those actions" (Rawls 1996, xlvi). Individual citizens are then effectively guarded against oppression by means of the installation of a higher standard of political legitimacy than mere majority opinion can achieve. As such, an individual is free to pursue her own conception of the good life unless prohibitions can be justified to that individual in terms which she can be expected to endorse. That is, only when the use of coercive state power is justified to "every last individual"—even those individuals who differ from the prevailing opinion—is it legitimate (Waldron 1993, 37). And, only when this liberal principle of legitimacy is met, so it is thought, is our democratic ambition safeguarded from tyranny.

But, while this liberal aim and democratic ambition stand side by side in our public philosophy, they are not always entirely compatible. Hence the tension of concern to this book.[3] On the one hand, our liberal aim prompts us to pursue neutralist types of constraints within the public square so that the actions of the government can be justified to all individuals, despite disagreement concerning religious, moral, and philosophical doctrines. Under this view, political decisions should be made in such a way as to prevent any one particular doctrine from dominating the public sphere. Thus, only reasoning and decision-making which are neutral among competing and conflicting doctrines will sufficiently reflect our urge to afford individuals enough space to march to the beat of their own drummers, thereby muting any would-be oppressive and homogenizing cadence. On the other hand, our democratic ambition promotes the notion that "We the People" are sovereign. As such, this democratic ambition prompts us to think that the commitments, convictions, and the voices of the citizens should be taken and heard as they stand. Among other things, this means that citizens should not have to bracket their doctrines when entering the public square.

It is an uncontroversial, sociological fact that citizens disagree about religious, moral, and philosophical authority. This sociological fact of pluralism, when fully acknowledged, pushes to the surface the tension latent in our liberal democratic public philosophy. We want the actions of the state to be justifiable to citizens, thereby satisfying the conditions for legitimacy. But, these comprehensive doctrines about which citizens disagree are themselves visions of ultimate value, of final goods, and so are not easily compromised for the sake of political values. It seems inevitable, then, that justifications in the public square will need to engage these comprehensive religious, moral, and philosophical doctrines. So, the question emerges: Given the sociological fact of pluralism, how are we to achieve the sort of justification and legitimacy required by our democratic ambition? On what grounds can the actions of the state be justified to citizens who are so divided? Restated just a bit, how are citizens to govern themselves when those very citizens do not share fundamental religious, moral, and philosophical commitments? Unchecked majoritarianism threatens to lead into a baser mob rule, as Mill contends, potentially undermining our liberal aims. But, it seems that if we impose the sort of neutralist constraints required by our liberal aims when thinking about the public square, we find it increasingly difficult to prop up our democratic aspirations which allow citizens to come as they are to the public square, complete with their comprehensive doctrinal commitments concerning ultimate value and final goods. Consequently, the tension between our liberal aim and our democratic ambition fully emerges, thrusting upon us difficult questions that continue to vex our public philosophy in America.

It is unlikely that we will be able to make much progress in answering these questions without taking significant moment to figure out exactly what the role of religious, moral, and philosophical doctrines in public political discourse—and matters of the public square more generally—should be. Why is this? We are trying to figure out how self-government is possible for a citizenry that is divided on fundamental commitments. Consequently, it makes sense to consider what role those fundamental commitments about which the citizenry is so divided should play in the public political arena.

Perhaps it goes without saying that those fundamental commitments in question are going to be chiefly religious within the American context. We are, no doubt, a religious people. According to Jean Bethke Elshtain, "some 95 percent of Americans claim belief in God and fully 70 percent membership in a church, synagogue, or mosque" (2000, 14). This is not to say that Americans are all religious in the same sense—some are Christian, some Jewish, some Muslim, and so forth. However, it remains a sociological fact that many, indeed most, Americans believe that they are answerable to some religious source of ultimate authority. And, it is not uncommon that these religiously committed Americans believe that their moral and social commitments—ranging from their views on abortion to what they think of welfare and homosexuality—follow either directly or indirectly from these religious sources. Again the tension between the liberal urge and the democratic ambition emerges: Must we allow the religious commitments of the majority to take precedence in the political sphere? If so, our liberal aims are seriously crippled and the specter of an oppressive mob rule looms large, for religious reasons are not acceptable as reasons to all citizens. Yet, are we simply to suppress those religious commitments/reasons in order to accommodate our liberal aims, thereby potentially squashing our democratic ambitions? The tension in our American public philosophy between the liberal aim and the democratic ambition articulates itself particularly as a question concerning the role of religion in the public political arena. This is, at present, a major issue of concern in contemporary political philosophy.[4]

Of course, this issue is not a new one to us. Since Thomas Jefferson,[5] our American tradition has continually struggled to understand the proper role of religion in affairs of the state. It would perhaps be difficult to decide—one way or another—as to whether the founders meant America to be a religious nation. Consider the voluminous arguments on either side of the issue. A brief look at the writings of the founders reveals much inconsistency among and even within individuals. Jefferson is often cited with the view that church and state should be separated by a "high and insurmountable wall." James Madison, though at times very sympathetic to the Jeffersonian view, seems to waver a bit. He is quoted as saying, for instance, that "religion is the basis and foundation of government." One can find in Patrick Henry, George Washington, and William Penn views that advocate a role for religion in the affairs of the state. And, of course, one can find a number of other founders who, like Jefferson, express considerable suspicion about religion in the public square. My point here is simply that there remains some confusion about the relationship between religion and public life intended by the founders. That is, no one, single, and unproblematic intent can be accredited collectively to "The Founders," as such. And so, the stage has been set for various attempts within the American tradition of public philosophy—a tradition itself containing various sub-traditions ranging from pragmatism to analytic political theory to political theology—to settle the question of how religion should relate to the American public square.

Moreover, the issue concerning religion's role in the public square has practical importance outside of academic or intellectual circles. This issue impacts nearly every aspect of our American public life—from the way that we design forums of public deliberation like town hall meetings to the way that election campaigns are run to how we as individual citizens vote. Moreover, our thoughts about how religion should play into the public domain affects in some way or another our decisions on many, if not most, of the controversial issues currently gripping us as a nation—from our decisions about school prayer, school vouchers, public Ten-Commandments displays, welfare assistance, and blood transfusions to our decisions about abortion, right-to-die, the death penalty, environmental issues, animal rights, and so forth. In fact, it is difficult to locate any substantive issue on the American political landscape that in some way does not, either directly or indirectly, involve at some level the question of how religion should relate to the public square.

If there was any suspicion that this issue was not important to us as a nation, I think it is safe to say it too perished on September 11, 2001. The horrible terrorist attacks of 9/11 clearly mark the most important event in recent American history. No event since then has contributed as much to the formation and justification of public policy, both foreign and domestic. While its magnitude is agreed upon, we do not collectively know yet how to interpret this defining moment in American public life. This confusion about how to read the events that took place on and after 9/11 reveal an underlying confusion that we maintain concerning our own public life. The question of religion's role in the public square was once again thrust upon us. On the one hand, religion—or least some articulation of it, namely Islamic fundamentalism—is often blamed for the motivation behind the terrorist attacks. On the other hand, religion is often touted by many as the only viable way out of the troubles thrust upon us. Where we eventually come down on this issue in particular will contribute greatly to what we understand the proper relation between religion and public life to be. Of course, this cuts both ways: our understanding of the relationship between religion and public life will greatly contribute to our understanding and interpretation of 9/11. It is likely that the answers to these and other important questions then pivot upon what we mean by "religion." Perhaps religion should play a role in public life—but what *kind* of religion and what *kind of role*?

1.1 A Question of Good Citizenship

In August 2004, several Roman Catholic bishops announced that they would deny communion to those public officials who consistently support abortion rights.[6] They claimed that politicians who support abortion rights are at odds with the fundamental moral principles of the Catholic Church, and, as such, should not be allowed to participate in the sacraments. This announcement raised a number of eyebrows at the time, especially given that the 2004 Democratic presidential hopeful, John Kerry, was both Catholic and pro-choice.

Liberals claim that these bishops are stepping outside their proper role as clergymen when they expect Catholic politicians to formulate their political opinions according to Catholic teaching.[7] Religious authorities—and religions in general—have no business in the political realm, liberals contend. For, one's religious faith is a personal matter, and thus does not provide the proper sort of public reasoning for deciding matters of politics. Political matters—like how politicians decide policy issues or how citizens vote in an election—should be decided on the basis of those reasons which can be recognized by all citizens as reasons, and not just according to those reasons (e.g., the Catholic doctrine of ensoulment) acceptable only to citizens of a particular religious persuasion. Thus, when political matters are at stake, politicians and citizens should restrict themselves to deliberating, voting, and legislating according to reasons which are neutral with respect to one's religious doctrine. So liberals argue, when bishops attempt to penalize those politicians and citizens who do not decide on the basis of Catholic teaching, they effectively attempt to influence politicians and citizens by means of religious threat to violate the liberal principle of political legitimacy. On this view, citizens who vote in obedience to the religious authority are failing at proper democratic citizenship.

But this liberal view confronts a difficulty. It seems clear that Catholic citizens and politicians are going to feel some sort of obligation to avoid sin, as defined by Catholic teaching. And, this religious obligation will often entail action and decision on the part of citizens within the political domain, and not just the private domain. However, liberals tell religious citizens that their religious convictions should not be a determining force in the political sphere. Yet, to be told to bracket one's religious obligations is itself a form of coercion. And, liberals argue that coercive power ought to be justified to every last citizen. But, how are the liberal constraints upon Catholic citizens going to be justified to Catholic citizens?

Although the above issue is particularly interesting, it is by no means the only example of a controversial mix of religion and politics in the context of American democracy. Consider the following examples:

- In March 2005, the Colorado Supreme Court threw out a death penalty in a gruesome rape-and-murder case because several of the jurors had distributed and discussed Bible passages such as "eye for eye, tooth for tooth" while deliberating the sentence behind closed doors. Defense attorneys learned of the deliberation process and argued that these jurors were making illegitimate appeals beyond the scope of the law. The U.S. Supreme Court effectively upheld this decision in October 2005 by refusing to hear the case.

- In August 2005, a group of Tennessee citizens opposing cuts in the state's public health-care budget (TennCare) staged public protests at the state capitol. Several voiced their concerns about the thousands of Tennesseans who would effectively lose health care coverage by asking, "Who would Jesus cut?"

- A student activist at Vanderbilt University publicly argues that his university has a moral responsibility to pay a living wage to all of its employees, not just the faculty. He unapologetically claims that his living-wage campaign is fundamentally motivated by his Christian convictions to help the poor.

According to polls, nearly 75 percent of Americans seek religious guidance in day-to-day living,[8] which as it turns out, *includes* political action and decision. According to other recent polls, 48 percent of Americans think of themselves as a member of a particular religion when it comes to political matters.[9] Roughly 44 percent of Americans admit that their religious belief plays a role in deciding which candidates to support.[10] Some 49 percent of Americans say that their religious beliefs affect how they vote in an election.[11] And, interestingly, these trends do not seem to be on the decline in more recent years. Approximately 61 percent of Americans said that their religious beliefs and faith would be an important factor when it came to deciding how to vote in the 2004 presidential election.[12]

What these data suggest is that nearly half of all Americans—in some cases more—allow their religion to play some role in their public lives as citizens, from how they formulate political opinions to political advocacy to voting behavior. But, are these citizens failing to be good democratic citizens by not bracketing their religious beliefs when entering the public square? Most of the leading mainstream liberal political theorists of our day think so. The claim is that these religious citizens are violating the liberal principle of legitimacy by allowing reasons which are not acceptable to all as reasons (i.e. religious reasons) to carry coercive force in the political domain.

But, can a compelling case be made that says that nearly one out of two Americans are, in fact, *bad* citizens? Are citizens out of order when they cite Jeremiah 1:5 or Psalms 139:13–16 in support of anti-abortion policies that aim to govern other citizens who reject the normative authority of Jewish and Christian scriptures? Stated more generally, the question becomes this: in a religiously and morally pluralistic society such as ours, are citizens wrong to ground their political behavior on the basis of sectarian religious reasons? These are the sorts of questions I take up in this book. Note that the issue is *not* whether these citizens have the *right* to vote as they vote or to participate in public deliberation as they do. Even adamantly anti-religious democratic thinkers avoid making these sorts of arguments against such *rights* to religious liberty and freedom of expression. And, indeed, it is highly likely in America that religious citizens will continue to allow their legal rights to be influenced by their respective religions in the course of public deliberation, political advocacy, and voting. The issue, instead, is whether the involvement of religion in matters of the public square violates what we might think of as the ethics or moral duties of good democratic citizenship (Wolterstorff 1997, 67–69; cf. Rawls 1996, 213; Eberle 2002, 21–22).

1.2 What is the Public Square?

Terms like "public square," "public life," "political domain," and "political sphere," are, no doubt, rather broad terms and can be used to indicate a number of different things. I intentionally mean to employ these terms broadly so as to indicate more than other narrowly construed terms allow.[13] We often think of the public square or the political sphere as merely including the matters of governmental institutions or agencies. I do not wish to so limit the concept of the American public square. Our pubic square spans everything from citizen protests at the local grocery store to neighborhood sporting events to town hall meetings to state election campaigns to national debates on affirmative action. Essential to this concept of the public square is the manner in which individuals are brought together in a space that is inherently non-private, where other individuals are addressed, engaged, and affected. Hence, I will be employing the terms "public square," "public life," "political sphere," "political domain," and the like to indicate this conceptual space where citizens participate in a number of activities *as citizens affecting other citizens*. These activities include (but are not necessarily limited to) deliberation about public policy, advocacy of candidates, election campaigns, and voting by individual citizens. Consequently, when a citizen participates in any of these activities, that citizen can be said to have entered the public square.

Some may initially find it a bit strange to talk about voting behavior as belonging to the public square. Voting, so one might suppose, is a private, personal matter—when I close the curtain, no one else besides me determines what lever I shall pull. Thus, unlike, say, public deliberation, no one else is present and involved when an individual citizen votes. But, we should be careful not to conflate secrecy with privacy. Although citizens might use secret ballots, a citizen's voting behavior clearly has an impact on other citizens. Surely, when a citizen votes according to one's comprehensive doctrine, one is attempting to coerce others, as voting is directly causally connected to what the government does. In fact, voting is, in many cases, *the* deciding factor concerning how other citizens are to be affected. Recognizing voting as an activity of the public square has interesting implications. If we think that a citizen violates the moral duties of good democratic citizenship when she employs religious reasons in public deliberation, we must also conclude that that citizen violates the same ethics of citizenship when she votes in accordance with those religious reasons. Otherwise, as Rawls rightly points out, we run the risk of being "hypocritical": we commit ourselves to saying that citizens have to "talk before one another one way" and yet can still "vote another" (1996, 215). Of course, to say that one ought to vote in a certain fashion (by, say bracketing her religious convictions) may settle uneasily with us. However, when considering the role of religion in the public square, we are right to think of voting behavior as falling within the domain of relevance.

1.3 Outlining My Investigation

In this book, I critically examine a number of proposals within the tradition of American public philosophy to deal with the problem of religion in democracy, that is, the question of how religion should factor into the American public square. Inasmuch as the "classical" American philosophical tradition projects itself as a fully engaged public philosophy that is concerned, as John Dewey put it, with the "problems of men" as opposed to the "problems of philosophers," my investigation begins there precisely because, with respect to this self-image, that tradition is due some criticism. Subsequently, I move into a consideration of more contemporary efforts in neo-pragmatism and more mainstream analytic political theory to the address the issue. As I see it, there are essentially three main types of strategies that emerge: separatist, reconstructivist, and integrationist proposals.[14] Separatist proposals generally suggest that religion should stand outside the realm of the political sphere—religion and politics should remain two separate enterprises. Reconstructivist proposals usually allow space for religion within the public square, as long as certain *qualitative* semantic adjustments are made to the religion in question. Integrationist views usually recommend that religion in its unaltered form should be integrated into political life. While it appears that flatly integrationist views, which insist upon a particular religious source for all normative authority, are not workable in a democratic context such as ours,[15] I show that the separatist (seen particularly in Rawls) and reconstructivist (seen particularly as emerging from pragmatists) proposals likewise seem doomed.

In Chapter Two, I critically examine William James's defense of religious belief. The purpose of this examination is to highlight the religious reconstructivism employed by both James and a significant representation of the classical American pragmatist tradition. The concern is that the reconstructivist conception of religion defended by pragmatists like James is neither sufficiently pluralistic nor pragmatically potent. This discussion is significant insofar as it identifies the historical precursor to various contemporary political proposals to negotiate the role of religion in the public square.

In Chapter Three, I turn our attention toward various appropriations of this Jamesian religious reconstructivism within the political sphere. I examine several neo-pragmatic attempts to formulate what I call reconstructivist strategies to negotiate the role of religion in the public square. This prompts me to discuss the work of both Richard Rorty and Cornel West. In examining Rorty's neo-pragmatism, I highlight the two divergent interpretations of his position concerning religion in the public square. First, I identify a view I call the Rortyan Reconstructivist Allowance, which states that religion can properly factor into the public square as long as religious claims are interpreted symbolically. I show that this sort of reconstructivist proposal, while promising on the surface, is ultimately insufficiently inclusive of religious voices. Next, I consider Rorty's more explicitly separatist view, which stems from his belief that religion is a conversation-stopper. I show that his pragmatic argument for separatism fails for pragmatic reasons. In the second part of Chapter Three, I focus upon the reconstructivist strategy implicit in West's prophetic pragmatism. I argue that such a strategy fails to the degree that ethically suspicious relationships underwrite the practical success of such a reconstructivist strategy.

Chapter Four shifts into an examination of the separatist strategy to conceptualize the proper role of religion in the public square, which is found in the work of Rawls. I take up a discussion of Rawls's view of public reason in order to expose the separatism implicit therein. While this chapter focuses primarily upon Rawls, I show that the Rawlsian view of public reason—and hence Rawls's separatism—is essentially the view held by most leading contemporary liberals. Underwriting this separatist proposal is what I call the doctrine of neutrality: that citizens must employ reasons which are neutral among comprehensive doctrines.

I take up a direct consideration of this doctrine of neutrality in Chapter Five. I ask if the neutrality required by Rawls is 1) ever achieved in practice; 2) possible; 3) desirable. Following the work of many of the leading critics of liberalism, I argue that we have reason to suppose that the answer to each of these question is, in fact, "no."

Given the failure of Rawlsian separatism, I shift in Chapter Six into a discussion of political theologian Jeffery Stout's recent attempt to address the issue of religion's role in the public square. Stout attempts to go beyond the failures of Rawls's separatist view of public reason and offers an alternative, one which, on the surface, appears more elastic and inclusive of the religious voice within the political arena. I show that, on closer reading, Stout's proposed new view of public reason falls short of pushing us entirely past the predicament he means to avoid.

Given the failure of both the reconstructivist and the separatist approaches to thinking about this issue, in the last chapter I draw upon the influence of Socrates and C.S. Peirce to sketch out an open model of the democratic public square designed to accommodate as many democratically predisposed citizens as possible, religious or not. I argue that, if a religious citizen holds her religious lines of reasoning with respect to particular political matters in a manner that recognizes the risk of deliberative defeat and is thus open to inquiry and deliberation, then she thereby meets the minimal requirements of deliberative democracy. Thus, if a religious citizen can meet this modest fallible inquiry requirement, the ethics of democratic citizenship do not require religious citizens to bracket religious lines of reasoning. I try to map out several strategies for religious citizens in the face of deliberative defeat. Also, I attempt to sketch out a strategy for orchestrating temporary *modus vivendi* arrangements in the face of what I call act-now deliberative stalemates.

It may very well be the case that my proposal here does not *per se* solve the problem of religion in the public square in some ultimate sense. However, I think that my investigation will prove useful to the extent that it shows more clearly what is at stake in the issue at hand and what proposals advanced thus far are not going to work. Perhaps at best, my hope is to move us in the right direction by initiating and staging the framework for further discussion and inquiry, wherein we might eventually come to some conclusive resolution concerning this important and pressing issue. What makes this book a distinctive contribution in the ever growing body of literature pertaining to the intersection of religion and politics is that it provides a typology of the three broad categories of approaches to thinking about the issue, a detailed critique of various contemporary and historical treatments of religious participation in politics, and a unique proposal for thinking about religious reasoning in the public square. To the extent that most authors writing on this issue tend to focus their discussions on the advantages and/or criticisms of either separatist or integrationist proposals, most authors fail to pay much if any (useful) attention to the more middle-ground, compromise strategies of the reconstructivist proposals found in the American pragmatist tradition. My suspicion is that this neglect stems from a tendency on the part of some writing in contemporary political theory to overlook (and hence fail to engage) the various streams of thought stemming from the classical American pragmatist tradition. This is unfortunate not only because it fails to give us the "full picture" wherein the various perspectives on this debate can be viewed side-by-side and assessed accordingly, but also because it prevents us from learning from some of our past mistakes. In an effort to remedy this problem, I approach the issue of religion in politics by means of a critical engagement of both the classical American (and neo-pragmatist) tradition and mainstream analytic liberal political theory. On the flip side, what I seek to offer in this book is a strategy to accommodate religious participation in the activities of the democratic public square—a strategy that enables citizens to employ religious reasoning *and* meet the epistemic obligations of good deliberative democratic citizenship. My goal in this respect will seem to some to be overly ambitious, especially in light of the apparent tensions between religious conviction and the role of collective, open inquiry in the process of achieving a healthy, stable, just, and competent democracy. In any case, I will leave it to the reader to decide whether the arguments advanced in the following chapters succeed.

Notes

1. By "public philosophy" I mean roughly what Sandel (1996) means by the term. He defines it as "the political theory implicit in our practice, the assumptions about citizenship and freedom that inform our public life" (4). Commenting upon this definition, Sandel claims that "a public philosophy is an elusive thing, for it is constantly before our eyes. It forms the often-unreflective background to our political discourse and pursuits. In ordinary times, the public philosophy can easily escape the notice of those who live by it. But anxious times compel a certain clarity. They force first principles to the surface and offer an occasion for critical reflection" (4). Sandel is right about this point. My conten-

tion is that there is a tension in our public philosophy which prompts our need to revisit basic questions concerning the role of religion in public life. Cf. Yoder 1997, esp. chap.

2. There are, of course, several different senses of the term "liberal." Here, I refer to the sense of "liberal" that is associated with the dominant version of liberalism currently afloat in contemporary political theory, which may be characterized as "right-over-the-good" liberalism (Sandel 1998a).

3. Pointing out the tension between liberal and democratic elements in American culture is a common way of discussing contemporary public philosophy. See, for instance, Barber 1999; Dahl 1998; Dryzek 1996; MacPherson 1965; Mansbridge 1983. While I set up the issue a bit differently, in part I take cues from Mouffe (2000), who identifies this tension present in liberal democracies as a tension between universalist tendencies of our liberal aims and particularist tendencies of our democratic aspirations.

4. It would be impossible to give an exhaustive list here, so I will merely present a sampling of the recent literature concerned with the role of religion in public life. See, for instance, Audi and Wolterstorf 1997; Audi 2000; Barry 2001; Dombrowski 2001; Eberle 2002; Elshtain and Beem 1998; Elshtain 2000; Fish 1999; George 2001; George and Wolfe, eds. 2000; Mendus 2000; Neuhaus 1984; Rawls 1996 and 1999; Rorty 1999, 2003, and 2005; Rosenblum 1998; Stout 2004a; Greenawalt 1988 and 1995; Carter 1993.

5. This statement could, of course, be accurately extended well beyond Jefferson. It is possible to describe the history of the American colonies as having been initiated and orchestrated in large part by this same quest to understand the proper role of religion in the life of the state.

6. See Wyatt 2004.

7. To the degree that these bishops are imposing communion sanctions for purposes which are internal to the church organization, perhaps Rawlsian liberals would have no objection. However, many take these bishops to be aiming at influencing policy decisions and voting behavior as these bishops make politicians, as opposed to church members more generally, targets of their sanctions.

8. 2002 Poll. Data provided by National Election Studies, Center for Political Studies, University of Michigan. The NES Guide to Public Opinion and Electoral Behavior. (http://www.umich.edu/~nes/nesguide.htm). Ann Arbor, MI: University of Michigan, Center for Political Studies [producer and distributor], 1995–2000. Downloaded on September 6, 2004.

9. September 2000 Harris Poll. Data provided by the Roper Center for Public Opinion Research, University of Connecticut. (http://www.roperweb.ropercenter.uconn.edu/cgi-bin/hsrun.exe/Roperweb/iPoll). Downloaded September 6, 2004.

10. September 2003 Time/CNN/Harris Interactive Poll. Data provided by the Roper Center for Public Opinion Research, University of Connecticut. (http://www.roperweb.ropercenter.uconn.edu/cgi-bin/hsrun.exe/Roperweb/iPoll). Downloaded September 6, 2004.

11. June 2003 Religion and Public Life Survey by Pew Research, Pew Forum on Religion and Public Life. Data provided by the Roper Center for Public Opinion Research, University of Connecticut. (http://www.roperweb.ropercenter.uconn.edu/cgi-bin/hsrun.exe/Roperweb/iPoll). Downloaded September 6, 2004.

12. November 2003 Gallup Poll. Data provided by the Roper Center for Public Opinion Research, University of Connecticut. (http://www.roperweb.ropercenter.uconn.edu/cgi-bin/hsrun.exe/Roperweb/iPoll). Downloaded September 6, 2004.

13. My use of the terms "public square," etc. in the manner here described is not unique but is a fairly standard use. See, for instance, Taylor 2004, esp. chap. 6.

14. I have set up the three main strategies here in a, more or less, logical order—separatist, reconstructivist, and integrationist proposals. At present, this is a more abstract view of organizing the issue. However, in the chapters that follow, I will *not* proceed in this order. Rather, I will allow these model types to emerge along more organic and chronologically oriented lines.

15. To the degree that the flatly integrationist proposal is implemented and thereby at all possible it is oppressive; to the degree that it is not oppressive, it is unrealistic; cf. Stout (2004a).

Chapter Two

William James and That Old-Time Religion: The Jamesian Roots of the Reconstructivist Strategy[1]

The classical American pragmatist tradition has projected itself as one poised to tackle the problems relevant to everyday folks—as John Dewey put it, the "problems of men" as opposed to the "problems of philosophers."[2] Attempting to heed the challenges set forth by Ralph Waldo Emerson,[3] this tradition has attempted to evade the long-standing and fruitless metaphysical and epistemological puzzles of European philosophers and instead focus upon matters which are important to the lives of Americans. Perhaps more than any other, William James understood that this call to relevance trumpeted by pragmatism's prophets forces attention to fall upon the role that religion is given within the scope of experience. Throughout the corpus of his writings, James recognized that practical benefits could be drawn from religion, ultimately leading him to defend religious belief and contend that such belief should be tolerated within intellectual circles.

Integral to this defense of religious belief is a reconstructivist move indicative of the pragmatist urge to dissolve conflict by semantically recasting religion such that it can meet the epistemic demands of the community. Some contemporary political theorists thinking within the vein of the pragmatist tradition have moved toward appropriating James's religious reconstructivism as the means through which to negotiate the proper role of religion in the public square. Extending the work of James, these thinkers advocate what I shall call a *reconstructivist strategy* for understanding the proper role of religion in the public square: given sufficient semantic adjustments, religion can be integrated into the political sphere. In the next chapter, I shall examine various articulations of this reconstructivist strategy. For now, I want to focus our attention specifically upon James's defense of religious belief, which can be read as a conceptual (as well as historical) precursor to this reconstructivist strategy in contemporary political discourse. The point of doing this is to try to determine whether James's reconstructivist view of religion provides a good strategic backdrop against which to formulate a view concerning the role of religion in the American public square. It will be useful, then, to take up an examination of James's philosophy of religion as it stems from his overall pragmatic project.

James's pragmatist treatment of religion is the focus of renewed interest because it appears to many scholars to be a good resource when thinking through some of the present difficulties related to religious diversity. Because he is often thought to be a pluralist,[4] many pragmatist thinkers are hopeful that, by following James's cues, we can begin to design religious communities that are more tolerant, politically progressive, and compatible with a democratic body politic whose citizens remain divided on fundamental religious doctrine. Cornel West even goes as far as to suggest that reshaping the identity of religious communities along these lines is "central to democracy matters" in America (2004, 159). I certainly agree that questions related to religious pluralism, diversity, and tolerance are important and even vital to the health of our democracy. But, unlike many contemporary interpreters of James, I am no longer quite so optimistic that Jamesian pragmatism can actually provide the conceptual tools we need to construct a religious pluralism robust enough to address the texture of our situation in this day. In this chapter, I trace the trajectory of my waning confidence in Jamesian pragmatism by first examining some of the reasons why James appears to have provided the scaffolding for thinking about religious pluralism. Subsequently, I show why James falls short of producing a useful framework for conceptualizing religious pluralism and tolerance. What warrants the most concern is the manner in which James semantically reconstructs religion into something quite foreign to the ears and hearts of common, everyday, traditional religious believers—those whom we might call "old-time religionists." By doing so, James leaves little, if any, room for the traditional believer to claim ownership of either James's picture of religion or the defense of that religion put forth by him. Primarily, this is because the more traditional religious believer maintains a conception of religion underwritten by a metaphysical realism from which James purposefully distances himself. I consider this difference between the religion of James and that of the old-time religionist in light of Ellen Suckiel's defense of James against objections leveled by Bertrand Russell. Ultimately, I mean to raise the suspicion that, given the fundamental disparity between the traditional religious believer's conception of religion and the manner in which James defines religion consistent with his pragmatic theories of truth and meaning, James's depiction and subsequent defense of religion may not be as pluralistic as it first appears, at least when viewed from the perspective of the traditional religious believer. Likewise, I mean to consider the possibility that James's philosophy of religion may be more pragmatically impotent than he would like to admit. The implication of this chapter's investigation is that, given the suspicions raised concerning the narrowness of James's religious pluralism and the impotence of his religious pragmatism, the Jamesian reconstructivist approach to religion, when employed as a political strategy to negotiate the relationship between religion and the public domain, is rendered highly problematic for roughly Jamesian reasons. In other words, the reconstructivist strategy in the political sphere can be seen as problematic precisely because the root of the strategy is problematic on its own pragmatic terms.

2.1 James's Pragmatic Religion

The thrust of James's pragmatic philosophy is to develop a philosophical method that incorporates both theory and practice in such a way that allows for momentary concreteness, while providing some temporary canopy of constancy and thus meaning to experience. However, the reality of this marriage between the theoretical and practical, as James acknowledges, is the remainder of at least some uncertainty within our overall account of experience. Namely, this uncertainty is introduced by the on-going, evolutionary, and incomplete nature of experience itself. As such, the future always holds in store some aspect of uncertainty with which we must deal. With this in mind, James turns his attention to bridling that uncertainty. In his "Sentiment of Rationality," he argues that perhaps the chief task of philosophy is, in some way, to define expectancy and thereby "banish uncertainty from the future" (WWJ, 326).[5] By banishing this uncertainty associated with the future, a sentiment of rationality can be attained such that we are freed to act in the world of ongoing experience. The problem, of course, is wrapped up in exactly how we aim to accomplish this. Descartes, recall, made provisions for action (outlined in his *Discourse on Method*) by insulating the context in which such action could emerge from the context of philosophical inquiry and skepticism introduced in the *Meditations on First Philosophy*. Descartes recognized that his methodological skepticism would render him utterly incapable of action, at least *during* the meditation process. James's method, though, is quite different. By utilizing philosophical inquiry *within* the context of ongoing experience and action (as opposed to abstracting philosophy from experience, as does Descartes), one can be afforded the tools with which to confront and bridle the uncertainty of the future—all in such a way that marries philosophical inquiry with action itself.

In order to accomplish this goal, James thinks we must employ *faith*. He defines faith as a "belief in something concerning which doubt is still theoretically possible; and as the test of belief is willingness to act, one may say that faith is the readiness to act in a cause the prosperous issue of which is not certified to us in advance" (WWJ, 333). Faith *allows one to act* in the face of the inevitable uncertainties affiliated with the future that is always streaming into the ongoing process of experience. Of course, James must explain why faith is justifiable with respect to providing room or courage for action. But, his defense of faith is actually just that: that faith, as "synonymous with working hypothesis," allows for the very possibility of action (WWJ, 336). That is, faith is actually justified in the sense that it allows expectancy to be defined insofar as it projects the desires of the subject (in terms of what one would hope to be true) onto experience. As such, this defining of expectancy allows one to bridle uncertainty, thereby allowing one to take action. And, according to James, there is a class of truths in which faith is "not only licit and pertinent, but essential and indispensable" inasmuch as those "truths cannot become true till our faith has made them so" (WWJ, 337).

James bids us to consider an example to illustrate his point. We are led to imagine a man who has to make a huge leap in order to survive. On the one hand, the man has no evidence that he can actually make the huge leap, but projects an image of hope or faith that he, in fact, can land the jump successfully. In turn, because of the man's faith, he makes the jump and lives. On the other hand, we are told to imagine a man, who, by requiring evidence of his ability to jump successfully (which is simply unavailable given the uncertainty associated with the future at that moment), remains skeptical concerning his ability to land the jump and hesitates in a state of exhaustion and fear. As a result, he ends up falling to his death. James writes:

> In this case (and it is one of an immense class) the path of wisdom is clearly to believe what one desires; for the belief is one of the indispensable preliminary conditions of the realization of its object. *There are then cases where faith creates its own verification.* (WWJ, 337)

The significance of faith, then, is its ability to provide a useful avenue of action for the individual. Inasmuch as faith provides this useful avenue of action, faith verifies itself. James argues that to say a belief is true is to say that it will lead to a particular course of action and that that course of action is successful. In this sense, the true is a subset of the good. As James puts it, "Truth happens to an idea. It becomes true, is made true by events" (WWJ, 430). Understood in this way, James's conception of truth differs from the more traditional correspondence theory of truth, which says that an idea (or proposition) is true to the extent that it corresponds to the external, objective reality of the world or something-in-itself.[6] Rather, under James's view, truth is conceived in terms of an idea's "cash-value in experiential terms," where an idea is verified in experience to the degree that it leads to a state of satisfaction and away from frustration. James writes,

> You can say of it [an idea] then either that "it is useful because it is true" or that "it is true because it is useful." Both these phrases mean exactly the same thing, namely that here is an idea that gets fulfilled and can be verified. True is the name for whatever idea starts the verification-process, useful is the name for its completed function in experience. (WWJ, 431)

Consistent with—though conceptually prior to—such a pragmatic conception of truth is James's theory of meaning whence his theory of truth is derivable. This theory states that a belief's meaning can be determined by looking at how that belief causes us to act, i.e. how that belief terminates in practical experience. Consequently, a belief can only be said to be different from another belief—and, hence, come to have distinct meaning—to the degree that the belief results in a different line of action. Thus, James argues, "There can be no difference which doesn't make a difference—no difference in abstract truth which does not express itself in a difference of concrete fact, and of conduct consequent upon the fact, imposed on somebody, somehow, somewhere, and somewhen" (WWJ, 349). So, for instance, imagine Adam says he believes X, while Betty says she believes Y. Yet, if there is no difference in action consequent upon X and Y, then we have no way of claiming that there is any difference in meaning between X and Y, insofar as the meaning of a belief is ultimately judged in terms of action.

Given the way that these pragmatic theories of meaning and truth operate, James contends that "on pragmatic principles we cannot reject any hypothesis if consequences useful to life flow from it" (WWJ, 461). If a hypothesis (or belief) leads us to a successful course of action, then that hypothesis can be said to be true according to the pragmatist conception of truth. And, as it turns out, according to James, religious belief can satisfy this condition for truth. Thus, religious belief is justified precisely because it can provide a useful way of approaching the world. In "Some Metaphysical Problems Pragmatically Considered," James contends that the theistic or spiritualistic (religious) world-view, while perhaps "inferior . . . in clearness to those mathematical notions" proves itself to be practically advantageous in comparison with its materialist counterpart (WWJ, 398).[7] But what are these opposing world-views? On the one hand, materialism stipulates that the "laws of physical nature are what run things" (WWJ, 393). Thus, James writes,

> The highest production of human genius might be ciphered by one who had complete acquaintance with the facts, out of their physiological conditions, regardless whether nature be there only for our minds, as idealists contend, or not. (WWJ, 393)

The key element to this view, as James suggests, is that nature is objective, somehow detached from the influence of our subjectivity. As a result, our minds have the task of simply recording what that objective nature does, and "write it down as operating through blind laws of physics" (WWJ, 393). Theism or spiritualism, for James, stands in opposition to this materialism or naturalism insofar as theism positions some non-physical mind as an active element in the make up and orchestration of the world. According to James, "Spiritualism says that mind not only witnesses and records things, but also runs and operates them: the world being thus guided, not by its lower, but by its higher element" (WWJ, 393). A significant aspect of this spiritualist view, as presented by James, is that it posits the universe to be, at least to some degree, subjectively conditioned.

In an attempt to illustrate how the religious worldview is pragmatically advantageous over the materialist worldview, James presents us with an interesting thought-experiment wherein we are to imagine ourselves at the final point of the world's existence reflecting back over the past. The theists will contend that the world was driven by the hand of God in a purposeful, ordered, and meaningful way. Materialists, on the other hand, will say that the course of events was merely a mechanical operation carried out by matter and physical laws. Despite their verbal dissimilarities, according to James, there would be no difference in meaning between these two theories insofar as there would be no future experience in which any real difference that makes a difference could be spelled out. James explains,

> And since there is to be no future; since the whole value and meaning of the world has been already paid in and actualized in the feelings that went with it in the passing, and now go with it in the ending; since it draws no supplemental significance (such as our real world draws) from its function of preparing something yet to come; why then, by it we take God's measure, as it were. (WWJ, 395)

Insofar as no future course of action could follow in accordance with either view, there is, for the Jamesian pragmatist, simply no way of judging which view is true or even if there is a meaningful difference between the two. According to James, something can be said to be true insofar as it can be verified and proven useful in experience, primarily by way of guiding one's course of action successfully. Still, this requires that there be future experience in which those actions could be played out. So, to say that one worldview is better or truer than another at this last moment, for James, misses the mark. "When a play is once over, and the curtain down," James says, "you really make it no better by claiming an illustrious genius for its author, just as you make it no worse by calling him a common hack" (WWJ, 395).

But, as James quickly reminds us, the fat lady has not sung just yet. And insofar as the world is incomplete and unfinished, the worldview we choose now, together with how we settle the religious question, is in fact a matter of great practical importance; our "outlooks on experience" and, in turn, the quality of our practical lives, hang in the balance (WWJ, 397). Ultimately, what tilts

James's scales in the direction of defending religious belief is that the materialist view is simply not as desirable as the theistic outlook insofar as it is "not a permanent warrant for our more ideal interests, not a fulfiller of our remotest hopes" (WWJ, 398). Concerning the materialist view, James quotes a Mr. Balfour, who in James's opinion captures the negative finality associated with the materialist view:

> I cannot state it better than in Mr. Balfour's words: "The energies of our system will decay, the glory of the sun will be dimmed, and the earth, tideless and inert, will no longer tolerate the race which has for a moment disturbed its solitude. Man will go down into the pit, and all his thoughts will perish. The uneasy consciousness which in this obscure corner has for a brief space broken the contended silence of the universe will be at rest. Matter will know itself no longer. 'Imperishable monuments' and 'immortal deeds,' death itself, and love stronger than death, will be as if they had not been. Nor will anything that is, be better or worse for all that the labor, genius, devotion, and suffering of man have striven through countless ages to effect." (WWJ, 397)

This materialist view, given that it ultimately projects what James describes as an eschatological "wreck and tragedy," denies the eternality of the continuation of development, of evolution, of progress, and of the possibility of possibility itself (WWJ, 398).

By contrast, the theistic view ensures hope insofar as it "guarantees an ideal order that shall be permanently preserved," where "tragedy is only provisional and partial, and shipwreck and dissolution not the absolutely final things" (WWJ, 398). In other words, because this view denies that Mr. Balfour's final dark moment will come crashing down upon us, the religious view promises a future and thus possibility within experience. And, insofar as such a possibility of the future is provided by this religious outlook, it is to our advantage to adopt such a worldview, according to James. By promising future experience, the religious outlook motivates us to choose with care the course of action we take now. And, insofar as such a course of action is required, a moral order is instantiated by this worldview. For, the possibility of a future prompts us to recognize the differences that we can make in that world to come and that we have a moral duty to try to make it a better place. Of course, as James notes, neither this nor any future world is governed by guarantees: that there will be future *possibilities* does not entail that the future will necessarily turn out better; nor, does it mean that the world will turn out worse. Things can go either way, so it matters what we do *now*. Thus, we must be committed morally to making tomorrow better than today. Consequently, James's defense of the religion hinges upon how well that religious outlook promotes this meliorism. That is, the theistic view affirms and reinforces the possibility that the world *could* be made better because of the role that we play in how it is both constructed and developed. And, this meliorism acts as the overarching value for James—everything else is interpreted in its light.

James is particularly adept at using colorful and imaginative examples to make his points compelling. Yet, it is worth noting the peculiar manner in which this above thought-experiment positions religion to be something that, regardless of any other theological importance, always opens up space for future possibility and hence the possibility of a moral order. This expresses something crucial about James's view of religion. For, as it turns out, only insofar as the religious outlook has such a defining characteristic is it at all distinguishable semantically from the materialistic view. But, this implies that religion only has one essential and relevant difference from materialism: that it is conducive to the growth of possibility and the instantiation of a moral order within experience by means of positing a future in which our present actions can practically unfold.

Much the same point is articulated more explicitly elsewhere in the Jamesian corpus, including his most famous essay, "The Will to Believe," in which he defends religious belief to the degree that it calls upon us to enter into a commitment to this melioristic attitude concerning the world. James argues that, while the Cliffordian evidentialist is inclined to disbelieve religion on the grounds that there is not sufficient evidence to support it, the benefits of avoiding error (by not believing in a potential untruth) do not outweigh the opportunity costs of foregoing the goods of religious belief "if *it be true*" (WWJ, 732). Such evidentialism causes one to act as if religion were not true, thereby effectively committing the evidentialist to a modified materialist outlook on experience that prevents one from acting in accordance with the possibility that future experience will be permanently preserved. According to James, though, it is better to act as if religion were true, even when available evidence has not yet settled the matter. For, such religious belief causes us to act such that we are committed to making the world a better place, motivated by the melioristic attitude. And so, James writes,

> If religion be true and the evidence for it be still insufficient, I do not wish, by putting your extinguisher upon my nature . . . to forfeit my sole chance in life of getting upon the winning side,—that chance depending, of course, on my willingness to run the risk of acting as if my passional need of taking the world religiously might be prophetic and right. (WWJ, 732)

For James, this "winning side" clearly means the melioristic attitude that stipulates moral involvement in the development of an incomplete world. And, insofar as a belief can be said to be true to the extent that it proves useful and beneficial for guiding one's action, James earnestly champions one's right to believe religion, as long as doing so results in a course of action committed to the hopeful and positive development of the world.

Interestingly absent in James's defense of religion is any call for us to decide upon the metaphysical existence of God. In fact, there is sufficient textual evidence to support the view that James intentionally rejects a more traditional, metaphysical approach to thinking about religion. And, in general, James's pragmatism—as well as his treatment of religion—can be characterized as an attempt to evade and/or dissolve the seemingly endless debate surrounding metaphysical problems by focusing on the practical meaning of an idea within experience. This orientation prompts James to claim that theology of the sort that is concerned with the metaphysical attributes and questions concerning the objective existence of God are a "matter of small practical moment" (WWJ, 357). Rather, James simply asks us to consider the extent to which religion serves our practical human needs within concrete experience. James's defense of religion hinges upon what he sees as a simple recognition of what religion *means* in practical terms—its so-called cash-value—which James thinks ultimately boils down to a melioristic outlook that stipulates moral action. The "real" meaning of religion, James explains, is found simply in the "emotional and practical appeals, in these adjustments of our concrete attitudes of hope and expectation and all the delicate consequences" implied by religious belief—not in the "hair-splitting abstractions about . . . the metaphysical attributes of God" (WWJ, 398) Pragmatically interpreted, religion simply "means the affirmation of an eternal moral order and the letting loose of hope" (WWJ, 398) The meaning of religion is simply that practical outlook on experience, and religion's truth can be judged according to how successful that outlook is for us. "After all," James says, even religion's postulation of a deity "serves *only to let loose in us the strenuous mood*" (WWJ, 628, emphasis added). The usual dealings of theology, according to James, are abstracted from any actual foot-hold in experience and are thus pointless insofar as the "conglomeration of attributes" spilled over by theology "awakens no responsive active feelings and calls for no particular conduct of our own" (WWJ, 356). And, to this degree James deems much, if not *all*, of theological metaphysics to be "nothing but a shuffling and matching of pedantic dictionary-adjectives, aloof from morals, aloof from human needs" (WWJ, 356). Thus James footnotes in the conclusion to his "The Will to Believe,"

> The whole defense of religious faith hinges upon action. If the action required or inspired by the religious hypothesis is in no way different from that dictated by the naturalistic hypothesis, then religious faith is pure superfluity, better pruned away, and controversy about its legitimacy is a piece of idle trifling, unworthy of serious minds. (WWJ, 734, footnote)

Ultimately, what we see in James's writings is a defense of religion only insofar as it serves to provide and facilitate practical results within the realm of action and concrete experience, i.e. morality. Given his pragmatism, of course, that might very well be the best defense he can muster. However, James asserts with confidence nonetheless that, to the extent that the religion in question remains non-theological and "merely melioristic in type," his pragmatism can remain religious (WWJ, 472).

That pragmatism's conception of religion remains "merely melioristic" introduces an apparent pluralism into pragmatism's range of allowable religious systems, seemingly attaching Jamesian pragmatism and religious pluralism at the hip. For, James's defense of religion seems to accommodate a variety of religious systems insofar as that defense does not require or presuppose any particular, sectarian metaphysical or theological doctrine which could be used as a fulcrum point upon which to exclude and/or oppress other religious systems. Because the essence of the religious hypothesis, according to James, centers on the motivational potential of religious belief in the practical life of believers, the metaphysical and theological differences among different religious systems can be deemed unessential, important only in the private realm of one's own preferred religious stylizing and "over-belief" (WWJ, 771). Thus, according to James, pragmatism acts as a hotel corridor with "innumerable chambers open[ing] out of it," presumably including, on this view, a multiplicity of different religious chambers (WWJ, 380).

2.2 What About That Old-Time Religion?

One wonders, though, if the expectation that pragmatism's conception of religion remains "*merely* melioristic in type" puts the pragmatist in conflict with the conception of religion actually held by most traditional religious believers such that they would be denied entrance into the Jamesian hotel. If so, then it seems that James's well intentioned pragmatism can only accommodate a regrettably small circle of religious believers like himself, crippling his notion of religious pluralism considerably. Consider, for instance, the difference between traditional religious believers and pragmatists, like James, when it comes to how each understands religious belief. One way of making this difference explicit is by considering Ellen Suckiel's defense of James in light of objections leveled against him by Bertrand Russell. Russell objects to James's defense of religion in the following way:

> The advantage of the pragmatic method is that it decides the question of the truth of the existence of God by purely mundane arguments, namely by the effects of belief in His existence upon our life in this world. But unfortunately this gives a merely mundane conclusion, namely, that belief in God is true, i.e. useful, whereas what religion desires is the conclusion that God exists, which pragmatism never even approaches. (Russell 1968, 125)

Russell here essentially takes James to be advocating belief in God on the grounds that such a belief will lead to desirable results in one's life. However, Russell contends, to believe that God exists means to take the proposition "God exists" to be true, where the term "God" has objective reference. Thus, unless some evidence for God's existence can be given, "it is irresponsible. . . to recommend that we should believe in Him" (Suckiel 1996, 82).

Suckiel contends that Russell's seemingly destructive epistemological objection is actually not harmful to James insofar as Russell's argument presupposes both metaphysical realism and a correspondence theory of truth. According to Suckiel, Russell "rejects James's pragmatic analysis of religious truth because it contradicts his requirement that true propositions have objective reference" (1996, 83). She contends that James intentionally rejects such a realist model of truth in which Russell's would-be-fatal objections are rooted. And, given that James rejects such a theory of truth, objections built upon such a theory are unsuccessful at ruining his argument. According to Suckiel, James's rejection of such a realism comes with his denial "that knowing is a static copying or representational relation between the knower and the known, one which excludes consideration of the knower's purposes and interests" (1996, 83). Suckiel suggests that, for James, the knower participates in the makeup of the known and is not merely a passive gatherer of knowledge. "For James," Suckiel writes, "the desire to fulfill our interests provides both the motivation for cognition and the ultimate criterion for its success" (1996, 83). Given the role that James places upon the subjective agent in the construction of knowledge, according to Suckiel, Russell's objection simply fails insofar as it is based upon a misguidedly presupposed notion of objective reference.

It is not my intention to decide here whether Suckiel's argument can defeat Russell's objections, or *vice versa*. I simply recount this exchange because it is useful in pointing out the differences between traditional religious believers and the Jamesian pragmatist when it comes to religious belief. Whereas the Jamesian view of religion presupposes the pragmatic theories of meaning and truth, the traditional religious believer maintains a view of religion that presupposes metaphysical realism and the correspondence theory of truth. Religious faith for the traditional religious believer, as Russell indicates, is not merely a melioristic hope, but is also propositional in makeup and metaphysical in character. To claim that human interests and purposes contribute to the truth of religious belief or the very conception of God smacks of idolatry and narcissism to traditional religious believers. For, to adopt the pragmatic view of meaning and truth is to betray their religious view, which prescribes certain epistemological and metaphysical doctrines that are inconsistent with pragmatism.

2.3 Good Pluralism? Good Pragmatism?

It seems, then, that we are left with a perhaps unbridgeable gap between the traditional religious believer's view of religion as based upon metaphysical realism and a correspondence theory of truth, and the Jamesian reconstructed conception of religion based upon a pragmatic conception of meaning and truth and the anti-theological metaphysical schema implied therein.[8] Depending upon one's starting place, i.e. one's operative theory of truth, conclusions concerning religion follow accordingly. What is particularly tricky, though, is that it *seems* as though James is posing his pragmatic defense of a pragmatic conception of religion as a pragmatic defense of religion in general. And, certainly, various readings and retold versions of the "Will to Believe" argument are often presented as such. However, what I mean to have pointed out is that James, given the manner in which he defines religion in accordance with his pragmatic conception of meaning and truth, ends up *not defending* traditional conceptions of religion at all. In fact, it may be correct to say that James, knowingly or otherwise, actually lays down the groundwork for exclusionary attitudes toward more traditional religious belief.[9] For, if James is defending one type of religious belief and not another, we might suppose that he is doing so because he is dismissing the one type of religious belief as unworthy of intellectual defense and thus tolerance by anyone other than the feebleminded. Richard Gale seems to agree when he contends that,

> Whereas James's Will to Believe doctrine concerns only cases in which one is morally *permitted* to believe (or continue believing) without sufficient epistemic warrant, it quite plausibly can be extended to cases in which one is morally *forbidden* to believe. (2005, 167)

Gale goes on to say that "James firmly believed that the case of an exclusivist religious belief is a suitable target for this extended version of the Will to Believe" (2005, 167). Notice that, if Gale is correct, then James's pragmatism must exclude traditional conceptions of religious belief insofar as their presupposition of metaphysical realism and a correspondence theory of truth render them monistic. Thus, to label James's view of religion as pluralistic would clearly be at odds with the fact that his very defense of religion requires the exclusion of traditional religious believers.

Of course, to suggest that James advocates a certain sort of religious intolerance *seems* to fly in the face of much of what he explicitly says. In fact, James's "The Will to Believe" might, on some accounts, easily be renamed "The *Right* to Believe," especially given the extent to which he defends one's right to maintain religious belief even in light of certain evidentialist objections presented by Clifford, et al. James, indeed, concludes the following in that essay:

> No one of us ought to issue vetoes to the other, nor should we bandy words of abuse. We ought, on the contrary, delicately and profoundly to respect one another's mental freedom: then only shall we bring about the intellectual republic; then only shall we have that spirit of inner intolerance without which all our outer tolerance is soulless. . . . (WWJ, 734)

So, clearly, James intends to advocate some notion of tolerance based, in part, upon the notion of religious pluralism many scholars want to pull out of his work. Such a Jamesian notion of religious pluralism seems, on the surface, maximally inclusive of a variety of religious beliefs insofar as all religious systems are reducible, for James, to the indeterminate essentials portrayed in the religious hypothesis—i.e., that the most perfect things are eternal and that one is better off believing that the most perfect things are eternal (WWJ, 731).[10] And, given the extent to which this picture of religion seems inclusive of a multiplicity of religious beliefs, a "spirit of inner tolerance" is achieved.

But, that "spirit of *inner* tolerance" can only come, as per the Jamesian defense, when a religious belief fits comfortably within the parameters of James's melioristic conception of religion. This leaves us with a telling question: what about religious beliefs that simply are not compatible with this pragmatic conception of religion that seeks to remain "merely melioristic in type"? Should they be tolerated by anyone other than the feebleminded? Given the prompts from Russell, there are legitimate concerns that the traditional religious believer will find the pragmatic conception of religion to stand quite far away from her own. So, what about religious systems of belief that are established upon monistic, metaphysical realist conceptions of truth, which thereby deny the truth of other religions? Are *these* types of religious beliefs, these more traditional—and, clearly, more widely held—religious beliefs being defended by James? The answer is that he is *not* defending these more traditional types of religious belief inasmuch as they fall outside of what he both defines and defends as religious belief. In fact, to the degree that such traditional religious beliefs are incompatible with his own definition of religious belief, James seems unable to promote, ironically enough, some lofty "spirit of *inner tolerance*" with regard to more traditional conceptions of religion. Perhaps concerning traditional religious belief, James can at best only advocate a spirit of "soulless" *outer* tolerance. Of course, exactly why such *outer* tolerance is pejoratively deemed "soulless" would be an interesting question for Jamesian scholars to address.

As the exchange between Suckiel and Russell shows, James's defense of religious belief makes sense only against the backdrop of the more fundamental metaphysical premises of pragmatism. This raises the question of whether James is actually at all a religious pluralist in any sense beyond name only for most religious systems in currency actually oppose the metaphysical premises upon which James's picture of religion rests. Insofar as James moves to reinterpret all religious language into his meliorism (by means of boiling all religions down to their essentials in his religious hypothesis), tolerance is achieved—but only because there is nothing about which to disagree anymore. That is, all religious claims, for James, *mean* the same thing, viz. hope. Different religions are merely different expressions of the same hope. But, if all religions mean the same thing, are they not simply *the same* at that point (post-reconstruction) for James? It seems so. And, if so, where is the tolerance? Where is the pluralism? It appears that James's "pluralism" is effectively circumscribed within the parameters of his exclusivist monism, one that rejects traditional religion and imposes an artificial homogeneity on religious diversity.

Tolerance, in any robustly meaningful sense, requires *real* conflict and *real* disagreement. As James Rachels rightly points out,

> a tolerant person is willing to live in peaceful cooperation with those who see things differently. But there is nothing in the nature of tolerance that requires you to say that all beliefs, all religions, and all social practices are equally admirable. On the contrary, if you did not think that some were better than others, there would be nothing for you to tolerate. (2003, 29)

Of course, the problem is that, when interpreted pragmatically, all religious beliefs effectively mean the same thing. But, if it turns out that a Muslim and a Catholic are really up to the same thing with their respective religious belief, then what does it mean to say that the one is tolerant of the other? Sure, James might *say*, they have a "spirit of inner tolerance." But, is this "spirit of inner tolerance" not merely recognition of sameness? One wants to ask, though: how this is at all tolerance? Sameness does not afford enough space for tolerance to emerge meaningfully as a possibility, as tolerance is conceptually tied to difference. Accordingly, religious pluralism would have to require *real* difference in meaning, i.e. a plurality of religious meanings. And, James's view of religion cannot produce this. So, while perhaps James can let a thousand religious flowers bloom, it appears that they will all have to be the same color. And, it turns out that brushstrokes which paint James as religiously pluralistic will have, at best, a queer hue.

One way of responding on James's behalf is by claiming that just because he is not giving a defense of a certain sort of religion (i.e., traditional religious belief) does not necessarily entail that he is intolerant toward that sort of religion or those who practice it. It may be the case, so one might claim, that James is not intolerant of traditional religious believers, just that he has given up the project of trying to find and present objective evidence for their sort of religious belief. Along these lines, the issue is really not about intolerance at all, but rather the sort of audience to which James is addressing himself. In order to better understand this sort of defense of James—let us call it the "appeal to audience" defense—it is necessary to recognize the relevant historical and biographical background. James was writing at the turn of the Twentieth Century when religion in general was on the intellectual retreat given the advent of Darwinism and the widespread notoriety of certain scientific and technological advances. Consequently, James, as an individual torn between the spirituality of his youth and the science of modernity, was attempting to reconcile religion with an otherwise dismissive, scientifically-minded intelligentsia. Some scholars and biographers speculate that this reconciliatory attempt is due to some urge in James to somehow save his father, a theologian, from falling into the category of the intellectually ridiculous.

Bearing all of this in mind helps to shed some light on those whom James takes his audience to be. Insofar as James is attempting to reconcile religion with science, James clearly understands his audience to be those individuals who *already* find religion problematic given a modern worldview.[11] James's audience is comprised of those individuals who cannot get past the grip of the epistemic problems surrounding religious claims like the Virgin Birth, or that water was turned into wine. It is this sort of person gripped by these sorts of epistemic concerns to whom James is addressing his defense of religion. In this sense, James's motivation might initially seem quite laudable from the standpoint of the religious. His attempt is to champion religion by making it defensible and thus tolerable to an educated community of scientifically minded intellectuals who are seeking some way to render it respectable. Consequently, so the story might go, James is not actually addressing an audience that does not already find problematic certain religious claims about, say, the Virgin Birth.[12] Thus, my claim that James is intolerant toward traditional religious believers is misguided because I fail to recognize that he is simply not addressing himself to a certain sort of crowd: it is not that he is intolerant, it is just that he does not care to give a defense of religion that would carry weight with the pre-modern mind of the traditional religionist.

But, it is not clear to me that this sort of "appeal to audience" defense can get James off the hook here. Granted, James may be targeting an audience that already finds the claims of religion to be epistemically problematic. But, even if we allow for this, it is not clear that any and all suspicion surrounding James's treatment of religion is removed. Admittedly, it is difficult to locate some place in the Jamesian corpus that directly articulates intolerance or exclusivity (and hence monism) concerning matters of religion. However, I think that the attitude of intolerance is expressed nonetheless. Consider James's essay "What Makes Life Significant," where James suggests that part of what contributes meaning to one's life is struggle and the attempt to overcome that struggle. To live in a place of utter "charm and ease" like the campgrounds at Chautauqua Lake, to live in some "middle-class paradise, without sin, without a victim, without a blot, without a tear" (as James describes life at the campgrounds) is to miss out on those non-placid elements of extremity that contribute to life's significance (WWJ, 647). Commenting on his stay at Chautauqua Lake, James writes,

> But in this unspeakable Chautauqua there was no potentiality of death in sight anywhere, and no point of the compass visible from which danger might possibly appear. The ideal was so completely victorious already that no sign of any previous battle remained, the place just resting on its oars. But what our human emotions seem to require is the sight of the struggle going on. The moment the fruits are being eaten, things become ignoble. Sweat and effort, human nature strained to its uttermost and on the rack, yet getting through alive, and then turning its back on its success to pursue another more rare and arduous still—

this is the sort of thing the presence of which inspire us, and the reality of which it seems to be the function of all the higher forms of literature and fine art to bring home to us and suggest. At Chautauqua there were no racks, even in the place's historical museum; and no sweat, except possibly the gentle moisture on the brow of some lecturer, or on the sides of some player in the ball field. Such an absence of human nature *in extremis* anywhere seemed, then a sufficient explanation for Chautauqua's flatness and lack of zest. (WWJ, 648)

Even if we provisionally grant that those who do not feel the grip of traditional religion's problematic epistemology are not among those to whom James addresses his defense of religion, this reflection on Chautauqua indicates something significant about the Jamesian attitude concerning those who are *not* in his audience: that they somehow lack a certain quality that makes life significant. They live, under James's view, insignificant lives, at least to some degree. This, of course, does not mean that James wishes violence upon them. But, this analysis does gesture toward the claim that James sees traditional conceptions of religion as rooted in a way of thinking which is both intellectually unsophisticated (and indefensible) and not worthy of being adopted by those that would choose to live significant lives marked by intellectually modern epistemic struggles (e.g., religion vs. science) and reconstructivistic reconciliatory attempts (e.g., pragmatically reconstructed religion) to overcome those struggles. What this means, of course, is that James is implicitly suggesting that, in an world comprised of modern, significant lives seeking to be intellectually respectable and responsible—what James hopes will be *our* world—only one form of religion is tolerable: religion *qua* pragmatic meliorism.

Of course, we can couch James's view in as gentle language as we like; but such a rhetorical strategy alone will not ultimately salvage his view from the legitimate suspicions concerning his ability to motivate a robust religious pluralism and tolerance. It remains the case that James severs his own pragmatic conception of religion from the more widely held, traditionalist view of religion. In this sense, James drives a wedge between himself as a philosopher and traditional religious believers who knowingly or otherwise presuppose metaphysical realism and a correspondence theory of truth with respect to their religious beliefs. Thus far, I have only argued that this distance compromises the sense in which James's treatment of religion can be accurately described in the language of pluralism. But, there is an additional concern that emerges which I only briefly sketch out below. The chasm between James and traditional religious believers with respect to interpretation of religious belief should be the source of some concern to the pragmatist because it seriously threatens the ability of Jamesian pragmatists to develop and maintain influential relationships with traditional religious believers. And, this shoots straight to the heart of pragmatism's ability to get anything done at the practical level. In theory, pragmatism's inspiration is ordinary life and ordinary language as it attempts to resolve ordinary problems of ordinary people or, as Dewey put it, "the problems of men" as opposed to the "problems of philosophers." Yet, the manner in which James reconstructs his religion—clearly one of the hallowed and central components to many if not most of everyday Americans—is anything but ordinary to most religious believers. What this entails is that, if and when religious language is employed by the pragmatist, one of two things will occur: Either, it will fall flat; or it will become the tool for ethically problematic manipulation.

Concerning the former, imagine a case where a pragmatist and a traditional religious believer fully understand each other's interpretation of religious beliefs. The traditional religious believer will have little choice but view the pragmatist's use of religious language as unacceptably reductive. What the pragmatist means when using the term "God" is *not* what the traditional religious believer takes the term to mean. For the pragmatist, belief in God is interpreted in light of its effect upon human behavior. As far as the traditional religious believer is concerned, belief in God is a belief that the term "God" somehow corresponds to some objective referent. As it turns out, of course, the myriad traditional religious believers disagree about the name, quality, nature, etc. of the objective referent(s) in question. Yet, James's attempt to "resolve" these religious differences amounts to nothing more than, as Richard Rorty would have it, "changing the subject" of discussion; we are no longer discussing anything beyond *our* needs, interests, and so forth (1982, xiv). But, upon changing the subject, the sort of religious belief James ultimately defends is wholly lacking in religious content as far as the traditional religionist is concerned; and, therefore, it simply is not religion anymore. From the perspective of the traditionalist, the Jamesian interpretation of religion has, as Dewey puts it, "cut the vital nerve of the religious element itself in taking away the basis upon which traditional religions . . . have been founded" (1957, 2). Thus, when the Jamesian utters religious language before the ears of traditional religious believers, it is heard as something unfamiliar, not unlike a foreign language. What is more, James's reconstructed religion is not only foreign to traditional religious believers, but it also lacks a certain psychological "ummmph" factor (Aikin and Hodges 2006, 12ff). For, it is highly doubtful that the invocation of such religion will bring about a successful course of action for traditional religious believers (or even for the pragmatist that utters it), which is the very reason James sees religion as defendable in the first place. Admittedly, pragmatically interpreted religious claims may be psychologically motivating for *pragmatists* themselves. But, even at their very best, pragmatic interpretations of religious claims are less motivationally powerful than traditional interpretations. At the end of the day, it is difficult to imagine that religious claims can stir us as forcefully when they are interpreted pragmatically as when they are interpreted along metaphysical realist lines—that metaphorical interpretations afford the same potency as literal interpretations do. Scott Aikin and Michael Hodges hit the nail on the head when they argue:

> Once we commit to the pragmatic second-order interpretation, we cannot help but look upon much of our religious life as mere ritual, powerful but senseless emoting, or worse, mere play-acting. When we do that, we do not get the edification religious life affords . . . we live a lie. There is a great distance between the kind and the degree of psychological benefit we get from viewing a passion play, say, as existential metaphor and as the story of the death of humanity's savior. One is of a mild, mollifying nature. The other is of a violent, passionate, and emphatic nature. Naturalism just does not stir us the way super-naturalism does. (2006, 12–13)

What this means, then, is that a Jamesian treatment of religion renders itself pragmatically impotent with respect to influencing traditional religious believers (where matters of religion are involved) precisely because the pragmatist's use of religious language, when properly understood by the traditionalist, has no purchase. Hence, pragmatism's failure to generate a religious pluralism broad enough to include traditional religious believers has the result of crippling the extent to which their pragmatisms are practically effective.

The only way around this problem of pragmatic impotence is by means of deception in the form of equivocation used to mimic a sense of pluralism. Imagine a case where a pragmatist's use of religious language is effective in stirring traditional religionists, thereby preserving its pragmatic utility. It is not difficult to see, though, that the efficacy of religious language in question would stem from the fact that the traditional religious believer does not understand what the pragmatist means by the religious language employed. In this case, clarifying the interpretation of the religious language employed would only diminish its motivational force and humiliate the traditional religionist. As such, it would remain to the practical advantage of the pragmatist to evade such clarification and thereby bank upon the robust motivational force of an interpretation of religious belief the pragmatist finds intellectually immature—i.e. an interpretation that presupposes both metaphysical realism and a correspondence theory of truth. (I take up an examination of exactly this sort of strategy in the next chapter).

Thus, the Jamesian pragmatist treatment of religion faces a difficult dilemma. Were pragmatists to bite the bullet and accept that pragmatism must exclude traditional religious belief, they must also confront the severely diminished capacity with which to have any practical impact. Or, if pragmatists seek to preserve solidarity with and influence upon traditional religious communities by means of the employment of religious language, they run the risk of compromising themselves ethically.

2.4 Other Classical Pragmatist-Reconstructivists

So far, I have focused my examination upon James and the reconstructivism that pervades his defense of religious belief. In this section, I want to highlight very briefly the manner in which the reconstructivist treatment of religion is advocated by other leading figures in the classical American pragmatist tradition. Emerson, for instance, clearly promotes a similar reconstructivism in his famous "Divinity School Address" (1838). There, Emerson urges his audience to rework religion such that it becomes something that allows for the growth and cultivation of the evolving human spirit. According to Emerson, the "evils of the church" (1838, 115) are wrapped up in the "stationariness of religion" (1838, 112). He writes,

> [T]he assumption that the age of inspiration is past, that the bible is closed; the fear of degrading the character of Jesus by representing him as a man—indicate with sufficient clearness the falsehood of our theology. (1838, 112)

Rather than view religion in this stationary way, Emerson argues that we should reconstruct it in such a way that acknowledges that the "office of the true teacher [is] to show us that God is, not was; that He speaketh, not spake" (1838, 112). Religion, then, loses its staleness and becomes malleable enough to address the problems faced by us now, in this age and generation. But, this means religion as it was held formerly must be altered. "[L]et the breath of new life be breathed by you through the forms already existing," Emerson writes—"For if once you are alive, you shall find they shall become plastic and new" (1838, 115).

George Santayana advocates a similar reconstructivist approach by recommending that religion be understood as a sort of poetry (1962; cf. 1957). Understood in this way, religion will be less likely to "arrogate to itself literal truth and moral authority" (1962, 13). Taken literally, the importance of religion becomes "intelligible no less than its contradictions and practical disasters" (1962, 13). Consequently, Santayana urges us to view religion in all its "fineness and significance" by acknowledging the "truth of religion" which "comes from its interpretation of life, from its symbolic rendering of that moral experience which it springs out of and which it seeks to elucidate" (1962, 13–14). Religion properly reconstructed becomes a poetical device capable of explaining and sculpting our moral experience.

Likewise, in his *A Common Faith,* Dewey explicitly advocates the reconstruction of religion such that it can be separated "from the supernatural and the things that have grown up about it" (1957, 2). In doing so we can come to understand the religious as the attitude which accompanies "any activity pursued in behalf of an ideal end against obstacles and in spite of threats of personal loss" (1957, 27). As such, even the very concept of "God" undergoes alteration. No longer is "God" to be understood as some supernatural being. Rather, for Dewey, "God" comes to mean the "active relation between ideal and actual" (1957, 51). Religion thus reconstructed can become the object of "the common faith of mankind," thereby aiding us in our "responsibility of conversing, transmitting, rectifying and expanding the heritage of values we have received that those who come after us may receive it more solid and secure, more widely accessible and more generously shared than we have received it" (1957, 87).

It is clearly not my intention to explain at any depth the views of Emerson, Santayana, and Dewey. Admittedly, there are certainly nuances to each view held by these prominent classical pragmatists that I do not speak to here. However, I merely wish to point out that several other major classical pragmatist figures who, like James, advocate a similar story concerning the semantic reconstruction of religion. The commonality of these classical views is that religion should be semantically reconstructed *so that* it can properly play a role in the lives of people. But notice that such reconstruction comes at a cost. The pragmatist/reconstructivist religion—whether that be religion *qua* meliorism (as in James) or religion *qua* poetry (as in Santayana)—is severed from the conception of religion held by traditional religious believers to the extent that metaphysical realism and correspondence theories of truth are rejected by these reconstructivists. And, this leaves the pragmatist views of Emerson, Santayana, and Dewey susceptible to all the problems facing James's view of religion: it is neither robustly sensitive to pluralism nor fully pragmatically potent.

Consider Dewey's reconstructivist concept of God, for instance. Sidney Hook, who assisted Dewey in the preparation of his *A Common Faith*, criticized Dewey's use of the word "God" on the grounds that the reconstructivist concept employed by Dewey was nothing like the concept of God most commonly found in Western thought.[13] Michael Eldridge (1998) notes Hook's commentary on Dewey in the following way:

> According to Hook, Dewey gave four reasons for using the term *God*:
> One, "the term had no unequivocal meaning in the history of thought." Two, "there was no danger of its being misunderstood," presumably because Dewey would specify the sense in which he was using the term. Three, "there was no reason why its emotive associations of the sacred, profound, and ultimate should be surrendered to the supernaturalist." Four, "Besides there are so many people who would feel bewildered if not hurt were they denied the intellectual right to use the term 'God'." (Hook quoted in Eldridge 1998, 155–156)

Extending Hook's objection to Dewey's use of the term "God," Eldridge points out that the first three reasons given by Dewey stand in conflict with one another. "To the extent that there are specified 'emotive associations,' there is not the desired latitude implied in the lack of an unequivocal meaning," Eldridge argues. "It is because of the connotations of sacredness, profoundness, and ultimacy in the various meanings that some read into Dewey's use what he thought his specified meaning prohibited" (1998, 156).

Hook's (and Eldridge's) criticism of Dewey seems correct to me. That is, Dewey's "God" is no God in any sense a traditional religious believer would recognize. While Hook is correct to advise against Dewey's "bait-and-switch," I disagree with Hook about religion in general, as Hook advocates an adamantly anti-religious view. However, I agree with Hook concerning pragmatism's character as anti-religious as far as the traditional religious believer is concerned. After all, pragmatism is a kind of naturalism, and most religions in currency are decidedly anti-naturalist. So, whereas pragmatists can call something "religion," they cannot embrace traditional religious systems on their own terms and are not pluralists in this way. The main point of this brief—perhaps too brief—discussion is simply to point out that the reconstructivist approach seen in James is likewise taken up by several of his fellow classical pragmatists (with Hook being the notable exception here). This means, among other things, that if I am right in my criticism of James, the suspicions raised against James likewise haunt a significant representation of the classical American pragmatist tradition.

2.5 Conclusion

Whether or not James himself meant to utilize (or to have others utilize) his reconstructivist approach to religion as a strategy for understanding the proper relationship between religion and the political domain is a question that I will leave for someone else to decide. Clearly, though, the reconstructivist strategy employed by James for the purposes of defending religious belief can be (and has been) adopted and appropriated for understanding what the relationship between religion and public life ought to be. In this sense, James manufactures the tools for the expression of such a politic. The Jamesian view might run as follows: given that religion must be reconstructed in order to be intellectually respectable and defensible, likewise religion must be reconstructed in order to gain proper admittance into the public domain, e.g. in public deliberation, political advocacy, and voting.

I suggested that James's religious reconstructivism distances his conception of religion from the traditional religious believer (2.2). This poses serious concerns as to whether James's view of religion is pluralist and whether it is pragmatically potent (2.3). But precisely because of these concerns, the political appropriations of Jamesian reconstructivism, if adopted as a strategy for the purposes of articulating a view of the proper role of religion in the political domain, fall flat. In the next chapter, I turn our attention toward the views of two notable, politically-minded neo-pragmatist thinkers, both of whom work within this pragmatist tradition and employ this sort of Jamesian reconstructivism within their own consideration of the proper role of religion in the public square. As I shall show, the branches of this pragmatist family tree are as weak as its root.

Notes

1. An adaptation of portions of this chapter appears in Clanton 2006.
2. See, for instance, Stuhr 1997, ix–x.
3. See Emerson's "American Scholar." There Emerson maintains: "Each age, it is found, must write its own books; or rather, each generation for the next succeeding. The books of an older period will not fit this" (1837, 67).
4. See, for instance, Stuhr 1997, 75 and 2003, 184; O'Shea 2000, 17; Parker 1999, 212. For a recent discussion concerning whether pragmatists more generally can be pluralists, see Talisse and Aikin 2005 and the various responses by Eldridge 2005; Jackman 2005; Misak 2005; Sullivan and Lysaker 2005.
5. All references to the Jamesian corpus will be made to the essays compiled in John J. McDermott's anthology, *The Writings of William James: A Comprehensive Edition* (Chicago: Univ. of Chicago Press, 1977). Hereafter, citations will be made in the following form: (WWJ, p. x).
6. I have only quickly, and perhaps *too* quickly, presented James's conception of truth here. To be fair, James's conception of truth is far too robust and sophisticated to be understood merely and solely in contradistinction to a correspondence theory of truth. I do not mean to suggest that James's view of truth occupies one side of a dichotomy. It seems appropriate to expect that James would be uncomfortable with such a dichotomy in the first place. Rather, James's view of truth, I think, moves in the direction of deconstructing such a dichotomy. James readily admits, for instance, that in certain scenarios, the context is set and in place such that certain statements are either true or false and that the procedures are in place to make such determinations. However, some contexts remain wherein such procedures are not in place and hence one's passions and desires are operative and relevant to the truth of the matter (e.g. belief in god). An extremely careful treatment of James's theory of truth would have to note that James sees that these contexts are different but not hermetically sealed. Perhaps the language of foreground/background would be helpful.
7. In this particular essay, James uses the terms "spiritualism" and "theism" interchangeably. Elsewhere, e.g. in "The Will to Believe," James uses the term "religious" to indicate essentially the same thing. Following James, I use the words "spiritualism," "theism," and "religion" all interchangeably throughout this chapter.
8. There may be some dispute with the claim that traditional religious believers are metaphysical realists and correspondence theorists consistent with the Russellian objection to James. This is, of course, a difficult claim to verify conclusively with sociological data, given that available polling questions seem not to touch directly upon this sort of issue. However, some data are consistent with this claim. According to public opinion polls, 70 percent of Americans think that God is personally concerned with every human (Mitchell 2000, 290); 72 percent believe in a life after death (292); 72 percent believe in religious miracles (298); 31 percent think that the Bible is to be taken literally, word for word, while 49 percent think that the Bible is God-inspired, not necessarily to be taken literally word for word and only 16 percent think that the Bible is an ancient book of fables, legend, history, and moral precepts recorded by men (300). Note, though, that even if it cannot be conclusively shown that, sociologically speaking, most religious believers presuppose metaphysical realism and a correspondence theory of truth, the point against James sticks the same: James's view of religion is inconsistent with those conceptions of religion that presuppose metaphysical realism and a correspondence theory of

truth. Cf. Yoder 1964.

9. See, for instance, Richard Rorty's appropriation of Jamesian pragmatism when he characterizes the traditional religious believer by considering her to be analogous to a "primitive culture" that eventually gets conquered by a "more advanced one" (1989, p. 90).

10. See Gale (2002) for an interesting discussion about an apparent tension in James concerning the essentials of religion. On the one hand, the essence of religion for James seems to be wrapped up in the religious experience itself, as opposed to, say, theological doctrine. However, as Gale points out, James claims in his *Varieties of Religious Experience* that "'the most interesting and valuable things about a man are usually his over-beliefs', an over-belief being a philosophical theory about the nature of the apparent object of a religious experience" (32).

11. Textual evidence for this sort of claim emerges all over the corpus of James's texts, most notably perhaps in his *Pragmatism* where he repeatedly makes reference to himself and his audience as a "we" and an "us." He describes that "we" or "us" when he says, for instance, "*Our* children, one may say, are almost born scientific" (WWJ, 366, emphasis added).

12. Clearly, more could be said about those who do not find certain religious claims like Virgin Birth (when taken literally) as epistemically problematic. This is an area of some intrigue, particularly within philosophy of religion and religious epistemology. One might claim that, as an involuntarily encumbered self located within a particular religious tradition, to raise questions concerning the epistemic feasibility of the Virgin Birth is to raise questions that, given one's existential makeup, cannot be recognized as problematic without sacrificing the very nature of one's own self-identity. Thus, to register certain religious claims as problematic is to risk literally going insane. Paul Tillich opens an interesting analysis of just these sorts of issues in his discussion of the two "literalisms" in his *Dynamics of Faith*. He calls the one who is not gripped by the epistemic problem of certain religious claims (like the Virgin Birth) a person who has an "unbroken myth" or a "natural literalism." If the full thrust of the problematic is ever recognized, Tillich argues, the religious believer only has two possibilities: replace unbroken myth with a Jamesian reconstructed myth (or "broken myth") or to maintain what Tillich calls a conscious literalism "with repression of and aggression toward autonomous thought." (1957, 52–53).

13. Cf. MacIntyre's criticism of Tillich's conception of God (MacIntyre and Ricoeur 1969, 53).

Chapter Three

Questionable Neo-Pragmatic Proposals Concerning Religion's Role in the Public Square

In the preceding chapter, I outlined the manner in which William James's famous defense of religion operates by means of employing a reconstructivist conception of religion. In this chapter, I examine various contemporary attempts to adopt and appropriate this reconstructivist conception of religion for purposes of articulating proposals concerning the role of religion in the public square. Doing so requires consideration of the work of two of the most notable neo-pragmatists, Richard Rorty and Cornel West. Both thinkers, though differently, provide a way for us to extend the religious reconstructivism of James into reconstructivist strategies to negotiate the proper role of religion in the political domain such that, given certain qualitative adjustments, religion can be properly allowed into the public square. In the last chapter, I showed that there are problems facing the sort of reconstructivist view of religion held by James. The suspicion is that similar problems face reconstructivist strategies within the political sphere.

3.1 A Rortyan Reconstructivist Strategy

Since the publication of his *Philosophy and the Mirror of Nature* in 1979 and the subsequent publication of his *Consequences of Pragmatism* in 1982, Richard Rorty has been among those responsible for a considerably renewed examination of the classical American philosophers. He is heralded by many as *the* continued voice of James and Dewey, though this is certainly disputed by notable pragmatist scholars.[1] In any case, Rorty's views are often harshly criticized from all angles, including those sympathetic to his aspirations for pragmatic renewal.[2] Certainly, Rorty sees himself as attempting to continue a line of thought that he sees as praiseworthy in the likes of Emerson, James, and Dewey. I consider here how Rorty's neo-pragmatism, taking cues from James's philosophy of religion, provides the groundwork for a reconstructivist strategy in the political sphere. In this section, I briefly extract this view latent in Rorty's neo-pragmatism (1997; 2003; 2005) and critically assess it. My aim is to show that a Rortyan reconstructivist strategy in the political domain faces problems similar to those confronting James's view of religion, and, as such, effectively excludes those religious citizens it purports to include in the public square.

In his "Religious Faith, Intellectual Responsibility, and Romance" (1997), Rorty argues that James's "Will to Believe" specifically addresses the question of what to do with a belief—in particular, religious belief—that cannot be justified to other people insofar as the evidence just is not forthcoming. Rorty argues that the fundamental question lurking around in that essay should have been explicitly phrased by James in the following way: "What sort of belief, if any, can I have in good conscience, even after I realize that I cannot justify this belief to others?" (1997, 9). James's evidentialist foil, W. K. Clifford, maintains that we ought not hold a belief if evidence sufficient to justify that belief cannot be provided. James, on the other hand, thinks that it is acceptable to formulate certain beliefs, the most important of which is the religious hypothesis, even in the face of insufficient evidence—evidence that could otherwise be presented in a public forum. Rorty adopts the Jamesian position with modifications: as long as those beliefs which fail the epistemic requirements of the community are private matters—that is, as long as those beliefs have no impact or entailment within the public forum—there will be no question concerning whether one has the right to them.

By carving a safe place for religious belief within the private sphere, Rorty contends that religious belief is made compatible with the political agenda of his pragmatism, namely democracy. Notice that, under Rorty's view, religious beliefs must be privatized precisely because, on his view, they are unable to meet the epistemic requirements of the public community; meeting these requirements is the condition for a belief's publicity. But, notice too that meeting this condition for publicity does not necessarily require that the public use of religious language be altogether prohibited. For, what if religious language could be semantically reconstructed in such a way that evades any violation of the justificatory demands of the public square? Following Rorty here, we might claim that religious vocabulary can come out of the private closet of the believer and be properly employed within the public forum (say, perhaps for the purposes of political advocacy or deliberation), as long as elements of that vocabulary are altered in order to meet the epistemic requirements imposed by the public community into which the believer is now advancing.

What this means, then, is that religious terms must either be dropped when a believer steps into a public forum or those terms must be redescribed in such a way as to meet the epistemic requirements of the public space. And, while Rorty seems instinctively to favor the former, he does not explicitly deny the latter as a possibility. He contends, after all, that the pragmatist can still be religious, but she will "have to get along without Personal Immortality, Providential Intervention, the efficacy of sacraments, the Virgin Birth, the Risen Christ, the Covenant with Abraham, the authority of the Koran, and a lot of other things which theists are loath to do without" (1997, 10). Presumably, such metaphysical tenants of the theist's faith, when brought to the public forum, stand in violation of the epistemic standards of intellectual responsibility within that democratic social arrangement. So, if such religious terms are going to be advanced in the public forum, they will need to be semantically reworked and stripped of metaphysical substance. The religious pragmatist, Rorty says, "will have to interpret [religious terms] 'symbolically'" (1997, 10). Doing so allows him to see explicitly religious texts like, say, I Corinthians 13 to be "an equally useful text for both religious people . . . whose sense of what transcends our present condition is bound up with a feeling of dependence [upon God], and for nonreligious people like myself, for whom this sense consists simply in hope for a better human future" (Rorty 2005, 40). Taken symbolically, religious beliefs are not interpreted as *beliefs that* something exists in some literal sense. Rather, the belief is seen more like a *belief in* something. As Scott Aikin and Michael Hodges point out, religious beliefs construed in this Wittgensteinian way "are not epistemological but practical" (Aikin and Hodges 2006, 5). They go on to note that, "if religious utterances are no longer interpreted as expressing propositions [that somehow correspond with some historical event or metaphysical object], they are no longer in conflict with our epistemic standards" (2006, 16). This is of course the sort of deflated religious terminology that a good Rortyan might allow in the public domain, precisely because the semantically reconstructed religious terminology no longer stands in violation of the epistemic standards of the community.

This anti-metaphysical move is the stamp of the pragmatist in many ways, following closely behind in the footsteps of James. For Rorty, this anti-metaphysical move is the only one that we can make once we fully recognize the contingency of our language, selfhood, and community. In *Contingency, Irony, and Solidarity,* Rorty argues that:

> [S]ince truth is a property of sentences, since sentences are dependent for their existence upon vocabularies, and since vocabularies are made by human beings, so are truths. For as long as we think that "the world" names something we ought to respect as well as cope with, something personlike in that it has a preferred description of itself, we shall insist that any philosophical account of truth save the "intuition" that truth is "out there." (1989, 21)

Once we come to terms with the fact that we cannot somehow get outside of language, we become thoroughly Wittgensteinian, and we thereby "de-divinize the world," Rorty says (1989, 21). When we give up the notion that there is something beyond how we describe things, we must give up the sort of metaphysical vocabulary that gestures to such a beyond, or rework this vocabulary (or "de-divinize" it) so as to make it no longer perniciously metaphysical.

This has important ramifications for the Rortyan when it comes to understanding the religious pragmatist, as he must become thorough-goingly anti-metaphysical in his employment of religious terminology in the public domain. For the Rortyan that means that the religious pragmatist must be even more anti-metaphysical than even James's religious hypothesis allows. According to Rorty, James's religious hypothesis is haunted by some affiliation with something non-human or beyond-human that can bring us good, given his reference to the albeit nebulous "eternal." This sort of reference comes a little too close to being metaphysical for Rorty. Instead, the pragmatist's religious belief should emphasize the hope "that we ourselves will do such good" (1997, 14). Only when religious belief can fully emphasize this proper sort of humanistic hope will it be sufficiently anti-metaphysical and thus sufficiently modified to accommodate the pragmatic political agenda of democracy. Rorty writes,

> The kind of religious faith which seems to me to lie behind the attractions of both utilitarianism and pragmatism is . . . a faith in the future possibilities of mortal humans, a faith which is hard to distinguish from love for, and hope for, the human community. I shall call this fuzzy overlap of faith, hope and love "romance." Romance, in this sense, may crystallize around a labor union as easily as around a congregation, around a novel as easily as around a sacrament, around a god as easily as around a child. (1997, 14)

We are now in a position to extract what I shall call the Rortyan Reconstructivist Allowance.[3] Basically, this view does not necessarily prohibit religious terminology from entering the public domain. As long as religious terminology is sufficiently reconstructed semantically—that is, as long as the religious is recast as the romantic or some such—it can be introduced into the public square. For, such semantic reconstruction poises that religious terminology such that it can evade the epistemic requirements which would otherwise necessitate the prohibition of religious terminology in the first place. With this reconstructivist allowance in hand, we can extract from Rorty's neo-pragmatism a reconstructivist strategy to negotiate the role of religion in the public square. Roughly, the strategy is to provide space for religion in the public square by semantically reconstructing it in such a way as to filter out contentious metaphysical claims that might violate the epistemic standards of a modern, democratic community. Religious claims are semantically translated into humanistic romance and social hope and are given full admittance into the public square.

At the outset, it appears as though the Rortyan Reconstructivist Allowance gives us a rather inclusive and pluralistic view with respect to public deliberation. That is, it seems as though this reconstructivist allowance facilitates the participation of religious citizens (speaking in their *own* voices) in matters of public concern. Not only can religious voices be included, but a seemingly wide range of religious voices can also be included under such a Rortyan view. For, as long as religious terminology is employed symbolically, religious citizens of all varieties can employ their particular religious vocabulary when involved in public deliberation. Employing a particular religious vocabulary symbolically acts to neutralize it within the public square so that others of different religious persuasions can access that terminology usefully during the course of public deliberation.

But, one wonders: Does this reconstructivist arrangement actually *include* religious citizens? As the discussion in the last chapter indicates (2.2), there are sufficient reasons to suppose that the reconstructed religion of pragmatists like James (and now Rorty) stands at odds with the religion held by traditional religious believers. This is because traditional religious believers presuppose metaphysical realism and a correspondence theory of truth. As such, religious terminology employed by the traditional religious believer is exactly *not* understood/intended/interpreted in the way required by the pragmatist like James or Rorty. Thus, when advanced by the traditional religious believer, religious terminology does not meet the symbolic "romanticizing"/neutralizing requirements of the Rortyan Reconstructivist Allowance.

Fair enough, we might say: in order to employ religious terminology in the public square, the traditional religious believer must pay the entrance fee to the public domain, so to speak, by recasting her religious terminology in such a way as to meet the demands of the allowance. But, notice that this is precisely to say that the traditional religious believer can no longer speak in her *own* voice. Sure, the traditional religious believer can employ some of the same words. However, those words can no longer carry the *meaning* that the traditional believer takes them to have.

Let us consider an example in order to clarify this point. In a forum of public deliberation, a traditional religious believer might propose a certain policy *P* to give aid the poor. When asked for the reasons why he supports *P*, the traditional believer might respond: "Jesus commands us to feed the poor." The question now is this: What do the words "Jesus commands us" mean for this traditional believer? In short, this traditional believer means that those words correspond to the actual historical event of an incarnate god who made certain authoritative normative commands. But, notice that the Rortyan Reconstructivist Allowance requires those words to be interpreted differently in order to avoid all of the metaphysical implications of such an interpretation. Under such a Rortyan re-interpretation, "Jesus commands us" means roughly something like, "our human purposes are well served if we do so." The religious terminology is semantically translated into neutralized/secularized vocabulary. Words like "Jesus" and "command" are simply romantic words used to gild the lily.

But, of course, we can see how the traditional believer might object. His actual reasons for advocating the policy are not humanistic in nature. Rather, they are precisely theological in nature. It is precisely because the traditional religious believer thinks that an actual Jesus wants him to feed the poor that the religious believer supports the policy *P*—not because it serves our collective human purposes.

The point here is simply that a Rortyan Reconstructivist Allowance is hardly as inclusive in the course of public deliberation as it might project itself to be. For, if the concept of inclusion is going to mean much, it has to involve *real* difference in meaning. If it turns out that the religious claims allowed by such a reconstructivist strategy are simply those claims that (when taken symbolically) mean something roughly equivalent to secularized, humanistic claims, then there is no semantic difference allowed in the forum of public deliberation at hand. For, where is the inclusion of the traditional religious believer who interprets his religious terminology consistent with metaphysical realism and a correspondence theory of truth? Under the Rortyan reconstructivist strategy, these religious citizens cannot be allowed to speak in their own voices because they do not interpret their religious terminology symbolically; hence they should simply privatize their religious claims so as to avoid violating what Rorty sees to be the epistemic standards of the community.[4]

This means that the Rortyan view simply pans out to be a collective agreement in meaning on all the important matters. Difference in word choice (e.g. words like "Jesus" as opposed to "human purposes") is simply deemed irrelevant and unimportant, and hence allowable or includable. But, the problem is this: such a reconstructivist strategy is not *really* inclusive of religious citizens speaking in their own voice (i.e. those who refuse to "change the subject" along Rortyan lines) insofar as the price for their inclusion is precisely to surrender the meaning of the voice which is supposed to be accommodated. It seems highly problematic to label this Rortyan reconstructivist strategy inclusive if the price for inclusion is the abandonment of the very thing to be included in the first place. Robust models of inclusion would have to be more costly to the party doing the including, not to those being included.

It should be noted that Rorty himself does not unambiguously advocate what I have called the Rortyan Reconstructivist Allowance. Unlike James and a host of other pragmatists, Rorty has given up all nostalgia for religion, as he "find[s] it merely confusing to talk about God" (1997, 17). And perhaps for this reason Rorty does not feel compelled to try to argue for any such allowances in the public square. That being said, Rorty's position on the role of religion in the public square seems to have tended over the last decade in the direction of the reconstructivist strategy discussed above, and clearly his neo-pragmatism provides the groundwork for such a politic. And, at least in this lesser sense, the reconstructivist allowance is very Rortyan in nature. We might think that Rorty is actually warming up to the reconstructivist strategy, given the view expressed very recently. Rorty says, for instance: "I have come to think that Nicholas Wolterstorff is largely right and Robert Audi largely wrong about whether it is

OK for religious believers to offer religious reasons for their political opinion" (2003, No page; cf 2005, 40). Note that Wolterstorff (1997) argues, contra Audi (1997), that it is permissible for citizens to offer religious reasons in the public square. However, Rorty continues: "I persist in thinking that non-theists make better citizens of democratic societies than theists" (2003, No page; cf. 2005, 40). With this qualification, though, Rorty seems to retract that agreement. For, the issue at hand is precisely this: does a citizen violate the duties of good democratic citizenship when she offers religious reasons in the public square? So, even while his own neo-pragmatism seems to be moving in the direction of the reconstructivist strategy, Rorty seems to be a bit confused on where he wants to come down on the issue, and he shirks away from fully embracing a reconstructivist position. Maybe this is because Rorty cannot quite overcome his older position on the issue: that even if religious claims are semantically reconstructed and thereby made fit for public deliberation, the lingering suspicion is that religious language tends to be a "conversation-stopper" (Rorty 1994, 171). According to Rorty, religion in all forms (pre- and post-reconstruction) is a little like bad etiquette and puts a downer on conversation within a democratic community. As such, religion most properly ought to ride the pine when it comes to matters of public life. I shall now turn our attention to consider this view, and thereby elucidate the tension present within Rorty's thinking about the proper role of religion within the public square.

3.2 Rorty as Conversation-stopper

In his essay, "Religion As Conversation-stopper," Rorty contends that, roughly since 1910, intellectuals have confidently adopted a this-worldly world-view (1994, 168). As such, intellectuals no longer place much stock in talk about souls and the like, insofar as they became sold on the idea that "human beings had only bodies" (1994, 168). The consequence of this confidently developed "this-worldliness" Rorty argues is that appeals to religion in intellectual discussions about public matters employ premises and appeals to authorities, the sources of which are rejected by intellectuals. When religion surfaces in intellectual discussions about public matters, it tends to prevent discussions from moving forward precisely because religious premises are not acceptable to intellectual interlocutors who reject the source of the premises in question. Thus, the introduction of religious premises into public deliberation is, according to Rorty, "far more likely to end a conversation than to start an argument" (1994, 171). Rorty says,

> The same goes for telling the group, "I would never have an abortion" or "Reading pornography is about the only pleasure I get out of life these days." In these examples, [as in cases involving religious premises], the ensuing silence masks the group's inclination to say, "so what?" We weren't discussing

your private life; we were discussing public policy. Don't bother us with matters that are not of concern. (1994, 171)

Religious language, then, is both silly and irrelevant—a conversation-stopper—when it comes out in public. Rorty wonders how we are to respond when such appeals to religion are introduced.

> [A]re we atheist interlocutors supposed to try to keep the conversation going by saying, "Gee! I'm impressed. You must have a really deep, sincere faith"? Suppose we try that. What happens then? What can *either* party do for an encore? (1994, 171)

Given this apparent conversational impasse caused by religion we ought to "enforce Jefferson's compromise": religion ought to be privatized in exchange for the "guarantee of religious liberty" (1994, 169; cf. 1988, 175). Public discussions should be carried out in secular terms, by "dropping reference to the source of the premises of the arguments" (1994, 173). Meanwhile, religion should remain a matter of private concern. Of course, the problem that many religious folks have with this proposal, according to Rorty, is that they think, following Stephen Carter,[5] that privatization entails the trivialization of religion. Rorty responds:

> Carter's inference from privatization to trivialization is invalid unless supplemented with the premise that the non-political is always trivial. But, this premise seems false. (1994, 170)

Family life, love, poetry—these things are private matters, Rorty contends. And, they are hardly trivial to us, as they "give meaning to individual human lives" and aid us toward personal perfection (1994, 170). But, while important for personal projects, religious premises, at least in a pluralist democracy, are not "relevant to public policy" and "public-spirited adults are quite right in not attempting to use them as a basis for politics" (1994, 170).

What Rorty gives us here (1994) is his separatist-leaning view. Rorty explicitly advocates the view that religion and politics should remains entirely separate enterprises. At least in this respect, Rorty's view resembles that of Rawlsian liberal theorists, which I shall examine in the next chapter. For now, let us consider Rorty's separatist-leaning view: that religion ought to be excluded from the political domain—particularly in public deliberation—on the grounds that it tends to act as a conversation-stopper. This is essentially a pragmatic argument. Let us explicitly summarize Rorty's Pragmatic Argument for Separatism in the following way:

> 1) Religious authorities are not universally recognized;
> 2) Religious premises depend upon particular sources of religious authority;
> 3) Hence, religious premises stop conversation because they appeal to sources of authority not shared by all interlocutors;

4) Therefore, religious separatism should be implemented by means of Jefferson's compromise—i.e., religion should be privatized.

For the sake of conversation, let us grant Rorty's conclusion that religion tends to be a sort of conversation-stopper in the political arena. But, we should ask the following question: Is this *necessarily* a bad thing all of the time? Rorty contends that religious premises in public deliberation evoke the "so what?" response from the deliberating group. I want to turn this question back on Rorty and ask him in turn: So what?

Let us imagine a forum of public deliberation where religious premises act as a conversation-stopper. Clearly, if Rorty is correct, this is not hard to imagine. But, we can also imagine how religious premises might actually stop what many take to be a horribly *bad* conversation. Take, for instance, public deliberation concerning abortion. If coined exclusively in secular terms in accordance with Rorty's vision,[6] many feel passionately that *that sort* of conversation about abortion may, in fact, need to be halted. They may come to think this precisely because they feel that the established parameters of the discussion systematically tend to exclude considerations which should be recognized as relevant to the debate at hand. Such exclusions, so the objection goes, tend to force the conversation toward certain foregone conclusions, roughly consistent with Rorty's leftist political agenda. This is exactly the position of the religious pro-lifer: more conversation about abortion within secular terms along Rortyan lines merely promises to perpetuate what the pro-lifer sees as the wrongful death of millions of children a year. Thus, so one might contend, the particular conversation (which, as we have imagined, is being carried out along Rortyan lines) *ought* to be stopped, at least as it currently stands.

The point of stopping the conversation as it stands may be precisely to prompt a conversation of a different variety—say, for instance, one that includes discussion of the Catholic doctrine of ensoulment, etc. or one that attempts to examine the atheist's views. Thus, religion *qua* conversation-stopper may be introduced into a forum of public deliberation precisely to call into question the parameters of the discussion itself. And, unless Rorty can show that certain sorts of conversation (specifically those conversations entertained within the parameters of Rorty's secularism) ought never to be re-adjusted (which is something his pragmatism must forbid us to say), then he cannot rightfully conclude that religion should never stop a certain sort of conversation. And, if the latter cannot be established, Rorty cannot rightfully exclude religious premises from entering forums of public deliberation.

Allowing religious premises to be introduced into public debate does not necessarily entail an end to *all* sorts of conversation on a matter, though it may stop a particular conversation of a certain sort. In effect, we can simply deny premise three of Rorty's argument stated above. Introducing religious premises in public discourse does not necessarily leave us with no viable pathways for further political discussion, despite Rorty's insistence that it does. Jeffrey Stout, for instance, proposes a model of public reasoning wherein conversation operates improvisationally (2004a, 69 ff.). This view of conversation—what he calls "immanent criticism"—does not require universally accepted premises as a starting point. Rather, when a conversational impasse emerges (say, by the introduction of religious premises), an imminent critic attempts to occupy the perspective of the other interlocutor in order to determine if the view put forth by that interlocutor is consistent and coherent internal to that perspective. Stout even contends that this view of improvisational conversation is actually condoned and defended by Rorty himself in his *Philosophy and the Mirror of Nature* (1979), though he moves away from it in his later work (particularly in Rorty 1994), at least with respect to his view concerning the role religion in public deliberation (Stout 2004a, 90). I shall discuss Stout's view of immanent criticism in fuller detail in Chapter Six. The main point here is simply that Rorty is simply too hasty in holding the view that religion necessarily brings an end to all varieties of conversation. In fact, it may be the case that religious premises act to *broaden* the terms of the deliberation precisely by promoting deliberation—that is, *another conversation*—to be held about the parameters of deliberation itself. In this sense, religious premises may act to stimulate the self-reflexive mechanism of public deliberation, thereby facilitating conversational possibilities stemming from readjustments to present arrangements of political deliberation.[7]

Interestingly, Rorty's Pragmatic Argument for Separatism fails for pragmatic reasons. If we follow Rorty's advice, religion will be placed outside the domain of public deliberation from the very outset. Supposedly, this sort of religious constraint will benefit us pragmatically by preventing conversational impasses. But, Rorty does not even seem to consider the possibility that certain conversations—particularly conversations carried out in liberal terms which he would approve—ought to be stopped. Nor does he consider the possibility that other sorts of conversations are possible and even desirable at times. Or, if he does consider these possibilities, he certainly provides no argument to the effect that they should be precluded. This means that, at best, Rorty's separatist-leaning view *begs the question*. But aside from that, the sorts of constraints upon religion endorsed by Rorty *necessarily* preclude the pragmatic possibilities of conversational advancement/readjustment afforded by religious participation at the levels of imminent criticism and meta-deliberation. And, in this sense, Rorty—and not necessarily religion—acts as the conversation-stopper.[8] Not only does Rorty beg the question, he fails to be a good pragmatist. Strangely, Rorty actually advocates a plan to halt (to put a spin on Dewey's words) the conversations of men in favor of maintaining the conversation of philosophers, particularly those like him.

3.3 Cornel West's Prophetic Pragmatism

Cornel West has established himself as one of the most outspoken and powerful voices in and outside the academy. And, like Rorty, he has become one of pragmatism's most notable interpreters. Conscientiously responding to the likes of Emerson, Peirce, James, and Dewey (among others, such as W.E.B. DuBois), West has brought renewed attention to the contributions of American pragmatism, particularly calling attention to pragmatism's insight and failure in the area of race theory. In this section, I shall consider West's own self-proclaimed "prophetic pragmatism" and how it bears upon the issue concerning religion's proper role in the American public square. Unlike Rorty, West argues that religion cannot simply be overlooked when it comes to matters of public life. While Rorty (or a Rortyan) seems to view religion as a potential enemy to be kept at bay by religious reconstruction and/or privatization, West seems to be more optimistic: religion, properly reconstructed, has enormous pragmatic potential within the democratic political sphere. Such optimism leads West to articulate a pragmatism that integrates the religious with the political. I shall examine West's view by considering the prophetic pragmatic proposal expressed in his *American Evasion of Philosophy* (1989) and in his more recent *Democracy Matters* (2004). What we see in West's work is a different model of the reconstructivist strategy to negotiate the role of religion in the public square, one which is particularly aimed at getting good use out of religion in expanding democratic participation. However interesting, it is not clear that West's proposal should leave us with no reservations. I shall argue here that West's proposal fails to be a viable alternative precisely because the prophetic pragmatism underwriting his view is ethically suspect to the extent that it relies upon manipulative relationships with traditional religious believers, particularly those in African-American churches.

West is clearly troubled by the trend among contemporary intellectuals, particularly Rorty and John Rawls, "to prevent religious language in the public square, to police religious-based arguments and permit only secular ones" (2004, 160)[9]. He contends that such a trend promises to render the contributions of those intellectuals politically ineffective in light of the sociological fact that Americans are largely religious and because, both at home and abroad, "religious traditions are here to stay" (2004, 115). Explaining, West writes,

> [S]ince the Enlightenment . . . most of the progressive energies among the intelligentsia have shunned religious channels. And in these days of global religious revivals, progressive forces are reaping the whirlwind. Those of us who remain in these religious channels see clearly just how myopic such an antireligious strategy is. The severing of ties to churches, synagogues, temples, and mosques by the left intelligentsia is tantamount to political suicide; it turns the pessimism of many self-deprecating and self-pitying secular progressive intellectuals into a self-fulfilling prophecy. (1989, 234)

Seeing separatist strategies as politically impotent, West seeks to reframe the question political thinkers ask. No longer should we be asking ourselves how to keep religion out of the public square. Rather, we should be concerned with questions of "how to support prophetic voices and forge democratic identities within [religious traditions] in our day" (2004, 130). So West argues, the real problem at hand is that much of the religion in America today consists of an antidemocratic, intolerant, fundamentalist, and imperialist strand of Christianity he labels "Constantinian" (2004, 146-147). While this particular strand of Christianity has become the dominant strand in America, West maintains that there is a distinctly different strand—what he calls "prophetic Christianity"—which emerges in part from the influence of the abolitionist, women's suffrage, and civil rights movements. Not only is this prophetic strand an "ecumenical force for good," according to West, but it is also necessary that we "reassert the vital legitimacy of this prophetic Christianity in our public life" if we hope to "revitalize the democratic energies of the country" (2004, 152). Accordingly, the task for political thinkers should be aiding in the reconstruction of religious traditions and identities, especially various strands of Christianity, such that they can be rendered democratic. For, according to West, "the crisis of Christian identity in America is central to democracy matters" (2004, 159). Consequently, radically secularist and separatist approaches to thinking about democracy are simply too narrow and wooden.

West proposes his own prophetic pragmatism—one which incorporates religion into the scope of political involvement and change—as an alternative to what he sees as the politically impractical approach of secularists like Rorty. Understanding the nature of his prophetic pragmatism, then, reveals West's strategy to negotiate the proper role of religion in the public square. Given the fact that he intends his pragmatism to be fully engaged in the political sphere,[10] the role afforded to religion within his pragmatism is tantamount to the role afforded to religion within his model of the political sphere. Thus, I shall focus on fleshing out West's prophetic pragmatism in a way that emphasizes the role of religion within the scope of that pragmatism.

West characterizes his own version of pragmatism as "prophetic" inasmuch as it attempts to take up the spirit of the "Jewish and Christian tradition of prophets who brought urgent and compassionate critique to bear on the evils of their day" (1989, 233). He claims that these religious prophetic traditions are "fueled by a righteous indignation at injustice—a moral urgency to address the cries and tears of oppressed peoples" (2004, 215). Attentiveness to these traditions is crucial for the success of the democratic project insofar as it better enables us to ask the following: "how is the public interest informed and influenced by the most vulnerable in our society?" (2004, 115). Insofar as it seeks to cultivate this crucial attentiveness, according to West, his prophetic pragmatism can be fully compatible with religious involvement. "This is so," West argues, "because a prophetic pragmatist commitment to individuality and democracy, historical consciousness and systemic social analyses, and tragic action in an evil-ridden world can take place in—though usually on the margins of—a variety of [religious] traditions" (1989, 232).

Two points of interest fall out of West's pronouncement here. First, West thinks that it is possible to be a prophetic pragmatist and belong, at the same time, to any one of several different religious traditions. That is, prophetic pragmatism is not a religion-specific enterprise; it is religiously pluralistic. A prophetic pragmatist could be perhaps Muslim or Christian or Jewish or altogether unaffiliated. In any case, West does note—and this brings me to my second point—that the religious pragmatist will most likely have to stay on the *outskirts* of that tradition.

What is West getting at here? He is confessing that the prophetic pragmatist, if he is going to remain religiously affiliated, cannot swallow the entire pill of this or that particular religious tradition. Certain details of the pragmatist's chosen religion will need to be dropped or reworked. West admits that "much of [his own religious] tradition warrants rejection," and should be "stripped of static dogmas and decrepit doctrines," or should be reinterpreted through the modern lens of a democratic agenda so that it can be readied for "political engagement" (1989, 233; cf. 1988, 359).[11] Presumably, if one overlooks the metaphysical and/or theological details that separate and differentiate one tradition from the next and focuses upon how this or that tradition can help motivate the radical democratic agenda, then one will not need to jettison that tradition altogether. But, more than likely, the religious tradition chosen by the pragmatist (along with its religious claims and terminology) will need to be reworked in order to achieve compatibility with the pragmatist's meta-philosophical commitments and political agenda.

That West's pragmatism can remain religiously pluralistic means that certain differences—metaphysical and theological doctrines specific to a particular tradition—can be deemed irrelevant. What each tradition offers by way of certain narratives capable of promoting and motivating the liberal democratic agenda is of key relevance and importance. As such, the essence of religion for West is wrapped up in the motivational potential of religious narratives and beliefs within the socio-political realm, not in theology or metaphysics. At least in this respect, West's treatment of religion mimics that of his pragmatist predecessor William James. As we saw in the last chapter, the core of religion for James is to be seen in the meliorestic cash-value in the moral life of religious believers—that is, its ability to "let loose in us the strenuous mood" (WWJ, 628)—not in metaphysical or theological doctrine concerning the existence and nature of any particular God.[12] This pragmatist reconstruction of religion comes to the fore when James highlights the distinction between spiritualism, or religion, and materialism in the following way:

> Here, then, in these different emotional and practical appeals, in these adjustments of our concrete attitudes of hope and expectation, and all the delicate consequences which their differences entail, lie the real meanings of material-

ism and spiritualism—not in the hair-splitting abstraction about matter's inner essence, or about the metaphysical attributes of God. Materialism means simply the denial that the moral order is eternal, and the cutting off of ultimate hopes; spiritualism means the affirmation of an eternal moral order and the letting loose of hope. (WWJ, 398)

Of course, the worry is that religious belief, once interpreted in this pragmatic manner, becomes *merely* a means for achieving our human goals. Thus, to adopt the pragmatist's semantics with respect to religious belief is to pervert religion. Given that religion is recast in the light of human needs and purposes, it becomes narcissistic and idolatrous. West seems to recognize this concern when he writes,

I speak as a Christian—one whose commitment to democracy is very deep but whose Christian convictions are even deeper. Democracy is not my faith. And American democracy is not my idol. (2004, 171)

But, it is not clear that West can avoid this problem, given his pragmatist treatment of religion. West recommends that religious belief and tradition, and thus the obligations and commitments of religion, should be reinterpreted in light of our democratic goals. As West says,

To be a Christian—a follower of Jesus Christ—is to love wisdom, love justice, and love freedom. This is the radical love in Christian freedom and the radical freedom in Christian love that embraces Socratic questioning, prophetic witness, and tragicomic hope. (2004, 172)

But, this is precisely to subordinate religion to democratic politics, and thus to abandon the conception of, and thereby reject the authority of, the religion previously held.

By placing priority upon the practical importance of religious narratives and beliefs in achieving socio-political goals, West makes the Jamesian move to reconstruct religion in an anti-metaphysical, pragmatic fashion. Taken pragmatically, a religious belief is not interpreted as a belief *that* something exists in some literal sense, such that a religious proposition corresponds to some objective reality. Rather, a religious belief is interpreted more like a *belief in* something, or the adoption of an ideal or aspiration. Consider, for instance, West's pragmatic reinterpretation of the lynchpin Christian claim that "Jesus arose from the dead." He rejects what he calls the "salvation-history perspective" of this claim, arguing instead that this claim "should mean to us that Jesus' victory over death ushered in a new age, an age in which the almighty power of God is already fulfilled but not yet consummated, an age in which death is conquered but not yet abolished" (1980, 420). His semantic reinterpretation of this religious claim is one that emphasizes the melioristic and politically motivating nature of the resurrection story and thereby rejects any metaphysical, historical, and/or soteriological implications. Accordingly, the meaning of a religious belief is measured in terms of how it guides action and what it promises for the future, not in terms of how it corresponds to some objective reality. It is exactly this move toward a reconstructed conception of religion that allows West to advance a seemingly religiously pluralistic prophetic pragmatism. For, if metaphysical and theological differences are brushed aside as unessential, any number of religious traditions can advance politically useful narratives and beliefs for West's pragmatism. Hence, his pragmatism can seemingly include and accommodate numerous religious traditions and identities.

Interestingly, West's own version of prophetic pragmatism—though it need not be the only version, he admits—is still specifically "situated within the Christian tradition" (1989, 232). Now of course, we might ask: what motivates a Westian pragmatist to affiliate with one religious tradition over the next. Why, after all, does West choose to locate his pragmatism within the Christian tradition, as opposed to, say, the Muslim or Buddhist tradition? West gives two reasons: one is personal; the other is political. First, West explains that he finds "existential sustenance in many of the narratives in biblical scriptures as interpreted by streams in the Christian heritage," sustenance which is "indispensable *for me* to remain sane" (1989, 233). The second reason for locating his own version of prophetic pragmatism within the Christian tradition is for purposes of political expediency within the African-American community. In West's estimation, the black community has been deeply connected to the black Christian church. As such, if he is to remain an *effective* player within this community, he must maintain some affiliation with those institutions integral to that particular community and its history. West says:

> [O]n the political level, the culture of the wretched of the earth [among the most important of which includes the African-American community] is deeply religious. To be in solidarity with them requires not only an acknowledgement of what they are up against *but also an appreciation of how they cope with their situation.* (1989, 233)

The thought here is that if one severs all ties with the religious community, in particular the black Christian church, then one will be less able to have any insight into the concerns, goals, and proposed solutions articulated by the very "wretched of the earth" that one is hoping to liberate and further empower within the political domain. Maintaining community with the black Christian church requires that one be able to embrace and employ the distinctively religious vocabulary in and through which the concerns, goals, and proposed solutions of the African-American community are voiced. What this means for West is that religious vocabulary must be given space within his prophetic pragmatism in order to facilitate his political agenda of empowering black Americans. Thus, prophetic pragmatism contra Rawls and Rorty, allows religious vocabulary—particularly the religious vocabulary of the black Christian church—to enter into the scope of public deliberation and political advocacy. To exclude that vocabulary is to risk losing one's ears to hear the "wretched of the earth" and one's voice within that community.

Of course, West is quick to point out that maintaining ties with the Christian tradition and hence Christian terminology does "not entail an uncritical acceptance of religious narratives, their interpretation, or most important, their often oppressive consequences" (1989, 233). Room for pragmatic redescription and interpretation of that tradition and terminology has to be reserved. Thus, under West's view, religion can legitimately play a role in the public square as long as that religion is itself semantically reconstructed along pragmatic lines.

Let me sum up before moving on. While Rorty and other separatists view religion as a potential enemy of democracy to be kept at bay by reconstruction or privatization, West is more optimistic: religion, when properly understood, has enormous pragmatic potential within the political sphere. Such optimism leads him to articulate a strategy which seeks to avoid the shortcomings of secularists/separatists by integrating the religious with the political. He advances what we might call a pragmatic argument for a *reconstructivist strategy* to integrate the religious into the political sphere. Basically, West contends that various religious traditions offer narratives, beliefs, and vocabulary which, when sufficiently semantically reconstructed, are useful for the political purposes of achieving democracy. Incorporating such language, beliefs, and narratives into the activities of the political sphere helps particularly to accommodate the concerns, views, goals, and proposed solutions articulated by historically marginalized groups like the black community in America, thereby forcing the democracy to "take seriously the culture of the oppressed" (1984, 378; cf. 2004, 215). Thus, to the extent that religion is practically useful in accomplishing these goals, its presence within the public square is fully legitimate.

3.4 West's Suspicious Religious Fellowship

It is clear that West sees his relation to the Christian tradition as integral to his own prophetic pragmatic project.[13] Inasmuch as he needs to maintain solidarity with the African-American community, he needs to maintain religious fellowship with the black Christian church in order to be able to communicate with them about their concerns, goals, and proposed solutions. And, in West's estimation, this requires employment of and responsiveness to distinctively religious vocabulary, reasoning, and narratives—in particular Christian vocabulary, reasoning, and narratives. Despite the intuitive purchase of West's position, one wonders if there is anything unethical occurring when the prophetic pragmatist maintains religious fellowship with traditional religious believers (like those in black Christian churches)[14] by means of implementing the religious vocabulary and narratives of that group. Granted, maintaining ties with African-American churches is advantageous for West's political agenda and hence the success of his prophetic pragmatism. But, ought the Westian prophetic pragmatist maintain religious fellowship with a body of traditional religious believers like the black Christian church by means of the employment of *their* religious vocabulary? If not, then it seems that West's prophetic pragmatism cannot generate the sort of solidarity integral to the success of his political agenda; and, consequently, it fails to yield a viable strategy to negotiate a legitimate role for religion in the public square. In this section, I shall argue that prophetic pragmatists engage in deceptive behavior when they employ the religious claims of traditional religious believers for political purposes.

Recall that pragmatist theories of truth maintain that a belief can be said to be true insofar as that belief is practically advantageous in the realm of concrete experience.[15] Working with such a theory, West can say that the Christian tradition is true for him insomuch as the belief in that religious tradition causes both a personal/existential and political advantage in practical affairs. In any case, his pragmatist conception of religion as rooted in such a pragmatic theory of truth is markedly anti-metaphysical and rejects a correspondence theory of truth. But, note that this pragmatic conception of religion is at odds with the manner in which traditional religious believers understand religion. Traditional religious believers maintain a view of religion that presupposes metaphysical realism and a correspondence theory of truth. A traditional religious believer does not claim that her religious beliefs are substantiated and rendered true by means of the *consequences* of those beliefs but by the metaphysical reality of the object of those beliefs, e.g., God's actual existence or the historical event of the resurrection. What makes religion true, on traditionalist interpretation, is *not* how it makes her feel and what it causes her or others to do, but the metaphysical reality to which her religious propositions correspond. This being the case, the traditional religious believer and the pragmatic religious believer like West are getting at two very different things when it comes to how they interpret their religious belief/vocabulary. This very point motivates Bertrand Russell's objection to William James's treatment of religious belief discussed in the last chapter (2.2).

Obviously, given the nature of the pragmatist conception of religion, the traditional religious believer, from the perspective of the pragmatist, has a faulty and intellectually immature conception of religion.[16] So the pragmatist contends, to the degree that the traditionalist interprets religious narrative and belief consistent with metaphysical realism and a correspondence theory of truth, the traditionalist is committed to making claims that violate the epistemic standards of our modern, scientific community. For example, traditional Christian religious believers are committed to saying that claims about a virgin giving birth and about Jesus arising from the dead are not simply claims of emotive importance but also claims about actual historical events. Consequently, from the perspective of the pragmatist, the metaphysical claims made by the traditional religious believer ought to be semantically reinterpreted symbolically. Of course, the traditional religious believer does not interpret her religious claims in this way;

rather, much to the pragmatist's dismay, she interprets them consistent with metaphysical realism and a correspondence theory of truth.

This being the case, my concern is that, insofar as the prophetic pragmatist is aware that the traditional religious believer does not interpret her religious beliefs in the same manner as does the pragmatist, it is *manipulative*, and thus potentially humiliating, for the pragmatist to continue employing the very same religious vocabulary which traditionalists are interpreting differently. In effect, I am suggesting that it is unethical for the pragmatist to employ semantically reconstructed religious vocabulary for the purposes of maintaining religious fellowship with traditional religious believers such that he can provoke in the traditional religious believer motivation for his own political agenda.

I should make two things clear at this juncture. First, I am not arguing here that it is wrong, *per se*, for the pragmatist to recast religious belief in accordance with the pragmatist theories of meaning and truth; I am not attempting to decide if the pragmatist treatment of religion is the right one. Second, I am not suggesting necessarily that there is anything wrong with the pragmatist religious believer maintaining religious fellowship with traditional religious believers for personal, existential purposes. Religious fellowship maintained for these existential reasons seems like a sufficiently non-public matter and hence of no necessary concern to me. Rather, I am simply suggesting that if the pragmatist maintains religious fellowship with traditional religious believers for his own political purposes, and if he readily employs the vocabulary of those traditional religious believers to advance those political purposes, then there is cause for suspicion of ethical foul play.

This is true because when the pragmatist maintains religious fellowship with traditional religious believers for political purposes, the pragmatist not only sees the religious belief of the traditional believers around him to be conceived in an intellectually immature manner, but he also banks on their maintaining their intellectually immature belief structure in order to most efficiently pursue and achieve his political purposes. The motivation to pursue the political agenda of the prophetic pragmatist is fueled by *misunderstanding*—i.e., misunderstanding as measured from the perspective of the pragmatist. The pragmatist takes the traditional religious believer's interpretation of religious belief to be epistemically naïve. But, in order to achieve maximum motivation for his political agenda, the prophetic pragmatist depends upon others *not* to have a sufficiently deflated (i.e., pragmatist) interpretation of religion. That is, the prophetic pragmatist politically depends upon and exploits what he takes to be the ignorance of others.

Now, I have suggested that the prophetic pragmatist like West apparently depends upon the traditional religious believers with whom he maintains fellowship having, from the perspective of the prophetic pragmatist, intellectually immature ideas concerning religion. The prophetic pragmatist depends upon the traditional religious believers maintaining their religious belief in a manner consistent with metaphysical realism and a correspondence theory of truth. But, why is it to the advantage of the prophetic pragmatist to capitalize on the sort of belief held by traditional religious believers? The intuition here is that the prophetic pragmatist is aware of the likelihood that a body of folks who interpret their religious belief in accordance with the pragmatist theories of meaning and truth would simply not be as mobilizable and thus not as politically effective as would a body of metaphysical realists, i.e. traditional believers. At the end of the day, it is indeed difficult to imagine that religious claims can stir us as forcefully when they are interpreted metaphorically as when they are interpreted along metaphysical realist lines—that metaphorical interpretations afford the same potency as literal interpretations do. And, if it is the case that it is psychologically more difficult to be moved by a pragmatic conception of religion, then it is to the pragmatist's advantage to make sure that those with whom he maintains fellowship for political purposes *not* run up against any psychological obstacles to political efficacy. That means that it is politically advantageous for the pragmatist to maintain fellowship with traditional believers, even though he takes those believers to be wrong-headed in the manner in which they interpret their religious belief. In my estimation, what takes place in the relationship between those like West and the more traditional believers, like those within African-American churches, is a sort of religious-political placebo effect: as long as traditional believers interpret their religious belief along metaphysical realist lines, such belief will help motivate them politically, which is to the advantage of the prophetic pragmatist, if he can manage to affect the direction of political behavior. This is at best well-intended paternalism, if not just political opportunism and manipulation via equivocation. And, the risk of humiliation looms large.

Interestingly, even Rorty gestures toward the recognition that there is something problematic about the pragmatist maintaining religious fellowship with the traditional religious believer when he recognizes the risks involved in the pragmatic redescription of someone else's vocabulary. Most people, Rorty claims, "do not want to be redescribed" (1989, 89). Rather, he says:

> "[T]hey want to be taken on their own terms—taken seriously just as they are and just as they talk. The ironist tells them that the language they speak is up for grabs by her and her kind. There is something potentially very cruel about that claim. For the best way to cause people long-lasting pain is to humiliate them by making the things that seemed most important to them look futile, obsolete, and powerless . . . The redescribing ironist, by threatening one's final vocabulary, and thus one's own ability to make sense of oneself in one's own terms rather than hers, suggests that one's self and one's world are futile, obsolete, powerless. Redescription often humiliates. (1989, 89–90)

Rorty is clearly right about this threat of humiliation that comes with redescription. And, West is posing exactly that threat—the threat of what Iris Young calls "cultural imperialism" (1990, 60)—to the traditional religious believers whose vocabulary is "up for grabs" by him and his kind.

Ironically, such paternalism and manipulation is diametrically opposed to that for which the Westian prophetic pragmatist stands in theory. West's goal is to construct a pragmatism specifically aimed at liberating and empowering those who have been historically and systematically exploited. In so doing, West aims to augment democracy by increasing the space for participation in the public square. I find West's goals in this respect perfectly laudable, particularly as those goals relate to the racially and economically oppressed. But, if the actual plan to achieve this "radical democracy" practically involves the intellectual exploitation of people, then, given pragmatic standards of evaluation,[17] the end result may be radical, but it is not very democratic. For, to the extent that West's religious appeals are disingenuous and manipulative, he fails to recognize traditional religious believers as free equals, even though they are the very ones he is hoping to liberate and further empower within our political structure. It is here, I think, that West might improve his pragmatism by drawing more influence from Martin Luther King, Jr. who clearly understood that one's methodology needs to be consistent with one's democratic ends-in-sight.[18] This priority placed on mean-ends consistency is one of the main reasons, for instance, King was unable to be completely supportive of the campaigns of Malcom X.

Ultimately, West's prophetic pragmatism faces a difficult dilemma: either it maintains ethically suspicious religious fellowship with traditional religious believers, thereby bolstering its political efficacy; or it abandons such fellowship at the risk of rendering itself pragmatically and politically impotent. In the case of the former, prophetic pragmatism threatens to undermine our democratic commitments to avoid manipulation and exploitation and is thus unacceptable. In the case of the latter, West's prophetic pragmatism is ethically sound but pragmatically impotent and thus unable to yield the pragmatic justification of his reconstructivist strategy. On West's own view, it is presumably the extent to which religion is practically useful in incorporating historically oppressed groups into the political arena that justifies religion's role within the public square. Hence, in either case, West's prophetic pragmatism fails to generate a viable strategy to negotiate a legitimate role for religion in the public square. Therefore, in light of this dilemma, it appears that the neo-pragmatic reconstructivist strategy offered by West will not succeed as a strategy to negotiate the proper role of religion in the democratic public square.

3.5 West or Emerson?

It is interesting to note that West positions himself as a follower of Emerson in many respects. West holds Emerson to be at least one of the crucial fathers of the American tradition of pragmatism out of which his own prophetic pragmatism emerges. And, like Emerson, West is a reconstructivist when it comes to religion. However, there is an interesting contrast between the two figures with respect to maintaining religious fellowship with non-reconstructivist, traditional religious believers. As the discussion above indicates, West sees that it is necessary for him to maintain religious fellowship with the black Christian church in order to increase the likelihood that his prophetic pragmatism will be politically efficacious. On this point, West parts ways with his predecessor. As Emerson became convinced that the traditional religious belief of Christians in his time was bankrupt, he eventually severed the ties of fellowship with his former religious community, prompting him to step down from his position at the Second Church in 1832 (Whicher 1960, 97). Emerson's exiting of the Unitarian Church became a very public spectacle, especially in the aftermath of his theologically controversial address to the Harvard Divinity School in 1838. Moved by his conviction that his religious reconstructivism was the proper alternative to traditional religious belief interpreted consistent with metaphysical realism and a correspondence theory of truth, Emerson no longer attempted to project himself to be a participating member of that former religious community.

By contrast, West—even though he positions himself at the outskirt —still maintains religious fellowship with the African-American churches. The reason he does so is revealing. West seems to understand that, outside of religious fellowship with the black Christian church, his prophetic pragmatism is fated for political impotence. Emerson, after having exited his former church community, encountered just that. Concerning Emerson, intellectual historian Stephen Whicher writes:

> Some years later he reviewed the whole affair in an ironic allegory, his poem "Uriel," in which he made clear his unrepentant delight in the consternation his "treason" [i.e. his religious reconstructivism] had caused; "I unsettle all things," he warned in an essay. The most lasting effect of the episode, however, seems to have been to send him "into his cloud," to strengthen his natural inclination to stay above the battle and "mind thy rhyme." (1960, 98)

One wonders if West recognizes the inevitability of his being sent "into his cloud" and away from the political battleground he so often attempts to run were he to abandon religious fellowship with non-reconstructivist, traditional religious believers within African-American Christian churches. One wonders further if perhaps minding his own rhymes would be, from an ethical standpoint, the nobler route to take.

3.6 Conclusion

In this chapter, I attempted to follow the trajectory of various contemporary neo-pragmatic political appropriations of the Jamesian religious reconstructivism examined in Chapter Two in hopes of exposing more explicitly the conundrum wrapped up in the classical American pragmatist tradition concerning the role of religion in the public square.[19] Several models to negotiate the role of religion in the public square emerged in this discussion. I showed that a Rortyan Reconstructivist Allowance-strategy fails to be sufficiently inclusive of religious citizens (3.1). Moreover, I argued that Rorty's Pragmatic Argument for Separatism fails for, roughly, pragmatic reasons (3.2). Contrary to Rorty, I suggested that, in fact, religion is not a conversation-stopper. Lastly, I showed that, if we attempt to implement a reconstructivist strategy following Westian spins (3.3), we run into the problem of employing ethically suspect political methods which threaten to undermine our democratic commitments to avoid manipulation and exploitation (3.4). I conclude: the most notable neo-pragmatic attempts to negotiate the role of religion in the public square are, at best, questionable. Consequently, in the next chapter, I shall focus our attention in a different direction with the aim of trying to locate more viable strategies. In Chapter Four, I transition into the consideration of Rawlsian and post-Rawlsian political theory that attempts to deal with how we are to understand the role of religion in the American public square.

Notes

1. See, for instance, Stuhr 1997, 219 (footnote). There, Stuhr attempts to distance Rorty from those pragmatists currently working within the circles of the Society for the Advancement of American Philosophy.

2. His aspirations for pragmatic renewal culminate especially in his *Achieving Our Country* (1998a), which can be characterized as one of Rorty's most publicly accessible attempts to turn hearts and minds of leftist types toward the inspiration of Emerson, Whitman, James, Dewey and other classical pragmatic figures.

3. I refer to this reconstructivist allowance as 'Rortyan' (as opposed to Rorty's) because Rorty continues to be ambiguous as to whether he wants to actually advance or advocate such an allowance. However, as I have argued, he does provide the groundwork for such a strategy in the political sphere.

4. Cf. Simmons (2005): "pragmatic redescription [of religion] as 'social hope' amounts to a certain type of continued exclusion" (526).

5. See Carter 1993.

6. One might take Ronald Dworkin's discussion of the abortion issue as being consistent with Rorty's vision here. See Dworkin 1993. It may very well be the case that the religious citizen would want to resist that very framework for discussing the issue. Hence, the religious citizen may very well *want to stop* that kind of conversation.

7. Bohman (1996) captures this point nicely. Fore a more detail discussion of this Bohmanian argument, see Chapter 5.3.2.

8. Cf. Stout's criticism of Rorty along similar lines (2004a, 85–91).

9. It should be noted, though, that West is sympathetic to the motivations behind such separatist proposals of Rawls and Rorty. In *Democracy Matters,* West maintains that Rawls's view of public reason is driven by the desire to avoid the "divisive and dangerous" language of religion; as such, Rawls's "concern is a crucial warning" (160). Concerning Rorty, West writes: "His secular vision is motivated by a deep fear of the dogmatism and authoritarianism of the religious Right. There is much to learn from his view and

many of his fears are warranted" (161). I take up a full discussion of Rawls's separatism in the next two chapters.

10. West writes: "The political substance of the American evasion of philosophy is that what was the prerogative of philosophers, i.e., rational deliberation, is now that of the people—and the populace deliberating is creative democracy in the making. Needless to say, this view is not a license for eliminating or opposing all professional elites, but it does hold them to account. Similarly, the populace deliberating is neither mob rule nor mass prejudice. Rather, it is the citizenry in action, with its civil consciousness molded by participation in public-interest-centered and individual rights-regarding democracy.... Prophetic pragmatism *makes this political motivation and political substance of the American evasion of philosophy explicit.* Like Dewey, *it understands pragmatism as a political form* of cultural criticism and locates politics in the everyday experiences of ordinary people (1989, 213, emphasis added).

11. See West 2004, in particular chapters four and five, for his suggestions concerning how to rework contemporary Jewish, Islamic, and Christian identities and traditions such that they can be rendered compatible with democracy.

12. Consider, for instance, what James calls the "religious hypothesis" as spelled out famously in his "The Will to Believe." There James claims that "religion says essentially two things:" 1) that the "best things are the more eternal things;" and that 2) "we are better off even now if we believe her first affirmation to be true" (*The Writings of William James*, 731–732). Noticeably absent in this essentializing of religion are any metaphysical or theological claims. Rather, the focus is upon the practical human benefits of having certain beliefs.

13. In this respect, West's prophetic pragmatism agrees with, say, Martin Luther King, Jr.'s effort to advance the civil liberties of blacks. However, interestingly, King does *not* engage in the sort of semantic reconstruction which underwrites West's pragmatism. One wonders if King would have been as effective in the political sphere if he were to have interpreted religion along lines consistent with pragmatist/reconstructivists like West.

14. I am inclined to characterize the black Christian church as a body of traditionalists for good reason. See, for instance, Mitchell 2000. According to public opinion polls compiled by Mitchell, black Americans in particular are "inclined to take a stricter approach to religion," meaning, among other things, that they are likely to "view the Bible as the word of God, meant to be interpreted literally" (270). Contrast this literalist inclination with West's pragmatist reinterpretation of the Easter story cited above.

15. See, in particular, William James, "Pragmatism's Conception of Truth," in WWJ.

16. Rorty (1989) in particular characterizes the traditional religious believer in this way by considering him/her to be analogous to a "primitive culture" that gets conquered eventually by a "more advanced one" (90).

17. Specifically, I have in mind here the pragmatic theory of meaning: the way that we can know what our ideas mean is by looking at the practical cash value of those ideas. See, for instance, C. S. Peirce, "How to Make Our Ideas Clear," in *The Collected Papers of Charles S. Peirce* (Cambridge: Harvard University Press, 1931–35, 1958); see also, William James, "What Pragmatism Means," in *The Writings of William James*.

18. Consider, for instance, the emphasis King places upon self-purification (in terms of being able to squelch a spirit of violent retaliation) as an integral component of his non-violent direct action campaigns. See King, "Letter From a Birmingham Jail."

19. It would be interesting to extend this investigation into Stuhr's "no consolation view" (2003), which, in many ways, can be read as a neo-pragmatic analogue of Hook's criticism of Dewey's use of the word "God" as discussed in Chapter Two. The main point of interest here is that Stuhr contends that pragmatism, properly entertained, has no room for transcendental religion as it gets in the way of the "Herculean" efforts required by pragmatism. Stuhr, like Hook, contends that pragmatism cannot honestly incorporate religion in the sense that religious believers normally recognize. Thus, according to Stuhr, an honest pragmatism must entail a life without transcendence and religion in the usually held sense. This conclusion puts Stuhr's vision at odds with the sort of view held by other pragmatists like, for instance, Lachs (1997), who defends the notion of "transcendence in everyday life" on pragmatic grounds.

Chapter Four

Silence and Neutrality: Liberalism's Public Reason

It has been said concerning those writing in the area of political theory that one must either respond to Rawls's work, or at least explain why not (Nozick 1974, 183). This statement, though perhaps a bit overstated, contains something worthy of our attention. It goes without saying that, since the publication of *A Theory of Justice* in 1971, Rawls has been one of the most, if not *the* most, influential political theorists of the Twentieth and Twenty-first Centuries.[1] And, insofar as the Rawlsian vocabulary is currently the dominant vocabulary in political theory,[2] it is crucial for my investigation to make itself privy to the conversations and debates taking place both within and about this Rawlsian language concerning the role of religion in public life. This chapter shifts from the discussion of explicit treatments of pragmatism, both classical and contemporary, into the debate concerning religion's role in the public square currently taking place in more analytic-leaning American political theory.

This move should not be interpreted as a disjointed leap from one conversation to another. Rather, it should be recognized that, in fact, contemporary Rawlsian and post-Rawlsian political theory attempts to resolve the very same issues we saw emerging from the writings of those working within the classical American and neo-pragmatic schools examined in preceding chapters. And, like the pragmatists and neo-pragmatists, Rawls is attempting to resolve an issue that gripped many of the founding fathers. At least to this extent, both Rawls and the pragmatists are doing much for American public philosophy: they are both within the trajectory of American intellectual attempts to resolve a problem which lies at the heart of the American democratic project. In the last chapter, I explored various contemporary appropriations of the classical American pragmatist tradition. Both the neo-pragmatism of Rorty and the prophetic pragmatism of West fail to yield a viable strategy to negotiate the role of religion in the public square. Given this failure, I now turn our attention toward an altogether different strategy found within more mainstream analytic political theory. In doing so, I consider the recent work of John Rawls and other leading liberals like Thomas Nagel, Stephen Holmes, Bruce Ackerman, Robert Audi, Joshua Cohen, and Charles Larmore. While there are significant and important differences between these individual liberal theorists—only some of which I attempt to uncover—it is fair to say that Rawls more or less captures and systematizes the essence of the various liberal strategies concerning the relationship between religion and the public square. Consequently, the focus of this chapter falls largely upon Rawls. Whereas the pragmatists generally provide the groundwork for some variation of what I called a *reconstructivist strategy* when thinking about the issue of religion in public life, Rawlsian liberals tend to propose what I call a *separatist strategy*.

Although Rawls is not a "pragmatist" *per se* (i.e., in title) in the sense of responding *explicitly* to the writings of the classical American pragmatist tradition, his later work, especially his *Political Liberalism* (1996), certainly has its pragmatist overtones and can therefore be read as continuous with the discussions in Chapters Two and Three in a second important sense. Rorty is among the first to point out these pragmatist tendencies in Rawls (1988). He contends that Rawls follows up on the work of John Dewey and, in so doing, "shows us how liberal democracy can get along without [the] philosophical presuppositions" found in theology, theories of the self, or transcendental deductions (Rorty 1988, 179). According to Rorty, Rawls is like Dewey and the other classical pragmatists insofar as he seeks to put politics ahead of philosophy and allow philosophical apology to trace, as opposed to define, the trajectory of politics. Rawls moves away from the comprehensive liberal theoretical aspirations of his earlier work (e.g., in *A Theory of Justice*) and attempts to stay "on the surface, philosophically speaking," he exemplifies a very pragmatic urge: to begin where we find ourselves and to avoid getting tangled in "philosophy's longstanding problems" which involve seemingly useless and interminable metaphysical questions (Rawls 1985, 395).[3] This characterization of Rawls (as expressing pragmatist proclivities) seems like a fairly accurate one and has been highlighted by several scholars commenting on Rawls (Habermas 1995; Dombrowski 2001; Talisse 2001).[4] And, given that even Rawls himself sees his later pragmatic-leaning work as an attempt to meet some of the objections brought against his earlier work,[5] this chapter will focus attention primarily upon that later work, namely his *Political Liberalism*. My chief objective here is not to articulate a systematic reading of Rawls's political theory or to engage very deeply in Rawlsian scholarship. Rather, the aim is to get clear on how Rawls (and fellow Rawlsian liberals) understands the proper role of religion in the public square. In particular, this issue comes to the fore in Rawls as it relates to the deliberation of public policy and voting. Consequently, this chapter will consider Rawlsian "public reason" and the consequences on religion that this idea entails.

4.1 The Fact of Reasonable Pluralism

Before zeroing in on Rawls's idea of public reason, it is important to take note, at least in passing, of a few distinctions found in Rawls and to understand what Rawls considers the "important differences" that underlie the shift from his *A Theory of Justice* to his later political liberalism (1996, xvii). Rawls says that the initial formulation of his preferred version of liberalism, i.e. justice as fairness,[6] was rooted in what he calls a "comprehensive philosophical doctrine" (1996, xviii). He recognizes that this poses serious problems for the justificatory structure of that view precisely because there is a wide range of reasonable comprehensive moral, religious, and philosophical doctrines held by citizens. And, as there is a plurality of reasonable comprehensive doctrines held by citizens, no one particular doctrine can provide the justificatory structure of his liberalism. He writes,

> A modern democratic society is characterized not simply by a pluralism of comprehensive religious, philosophical, and moral doctrines but by a pluralism of incompatible yet reasonable comprehensive doctrines. No one of these doctrines is affirmed by citizens generally. Nor should one expect that in the foreseeable future one of them, or some other reasonable doctrine, will ever be affirmed by all, or nearly all, citizens . . . The fact of a plurality of reasonable but incompatible comprehensive doctrine—the fact of reasonable pluralism—shows that, as used in *Theory,* the idea of a well-ordered society of justice as fairness is unrealistic. This is because it is inconsistent with realizing its own principles under the best of foreseeable conditions. (1996, xviii)

Given this tension present within the justificatory structure of *Theory,* according to Rawls, we must start where we find ourselves and not assume some *a priori* agreement upon any one comprehensive doctrine—even a liberal one—upon which to build justification for liberalism.[7] And, if we abandon such universalist, comprehensive theoretical aspirations, where we find ourselves is standing before what Rawls terms the "fact of reasonable pluralism" (1996, 4). This is where we must begin.

It is important to note the distinction between the simple fact of pluralism as such, and the fact of reasonable pluralism as understood by Rawls. On the one hand, pluralism as such, or sociological pluralism, simply says that there is a multiplicity of comprehensive moral, religious, and philosophical doctrines adhered to by citizens. On the other hand, reasonable pluralism is the existence of a plurality of *reasonable* comprehensive moral, religious, and philosophical doctrines. Whereas the former implies merely that there are a number of doctrines held—including perhaps "unreasonable, and irrational, and even mad" ones—the latter implies that there are a number of reasonable doctrines held by citizens (1996, xvii–xix), stemming from what Rawls sees as the "long-run outcome of the work of human reason under enduring free institutions" (1996, 129).[8] Such reasonable pluralism is not a mere historical contingency likely to soon fade away; "it is a permanent feature of the public culture of democracy" (1996, 36). Rawls continues:

> Under the political and social conditions secured by the basic rights and liberties of free institutions, a diversity of conflicting and irreconcilable—and what's more, reasonable—comprehensive doctrines will come about and persist if such diversity does not already obtain. (1996, 36)

This claim lies at the heart of Rawls's later work[9] and is significant insofar as it differs from the Enlightenment assumption that disagreement over comprehensive doctrines was the result of a malfunction or suppression of reason. We might think of Rawls's view as post-Enlightenment at least in this respect. Gerald Gaus (2003) argues that the Enlightenment view of reason (found particularly in the work of Kant and Mill) is such that when reason is freely and properly employed, there would be convergence upon truth.[10] By contrast, Rawls maintains that the free operation of reason, in fact, does not lead to convergence upon a unified truth, but rather to a plurality of diverse, reasonably held comprehensive doctrines.

But, why is it that the "work of human reason" leads us to this fact of reasonable pluralism? According to Rawls, human reason even when properly employed is, for better or worse, weighted down by what he calls "burdens of judgment" (1996, 55). These are the "many hazards involved in the correct (and conscientious) exercise of our powers of reason and judgment in the ordinary course of political life." (1996, 56). Paraphrasing Rawls, we can summarize these burdens of judgment as follows:

1. the evidence is often conflicting and difficult to evaluate;
2. even when we agree on the relevant considerations, we often weigh them differently;
3. because our concepts are vague, we must rely on interpretations that are often controversial;
4. the manner in which we evaluate evidence and rank considerations seems to some extent the function of our total life experiences, which of course differ;
5. because different sides of an issue rely on different types of normative considerations, it is often hard to assess their relative merits;
6. in conflicts between values, there often seems to be no uniquely correct answer. (Gaus 2003, 14)[11]

Insofar as this fact of reasonable pluralism obtains as a result of free human reason weighted down by these burdens of judgment above, the implication is that an absence of such pluralism in a political regime is the result of oppression. Rawls refers to this as the "fact of oppression":

> [A] continuing shared understanding on one comprehensive religious, philosophical, or moral doctrine can be maintained only by the oppressive use of state power. (1996, 37)

The significance of the fact of reasonable pluralism and the fact of oppression is that, taken together, there will be a number of reasonable comprehensive doctrines among the citizenry unless that citizenry is otherwise oppressed. This means that Rawls must abandon the justificatory structure of his liberalism as articulated in *Theory* precisely because it was rooted in one of many reasonable comprehensive doctrines, which entails the fact of oppression, and hence an illiberal regime. Thus, Rawls concludes, any regime that is rooted in a particular comprehensive doctrine—even one that affirms justice as fairness—"would not be liberal," that is, "if justice as fairness were not expressly designed to gain the reasoned support of citizens who affirm reasonable although conflicting comprehensive doctrines" (1996, 143). So, surrendering the ambitions of the Enlightenment liberal project to find a comprehensive doctrine in which to situate liberal theory, Rawls moves to articulate a noncomprehensive—that is, *political*—liberalism, concluding that "the question the dominant tradition has tried to answer has no answer: no comprehensive doctrine is appropriate as a political conception for a constitutional regime" (1996, 135).

4.2 From Pluralism to Public Reason

What we see in the later Rawls is an earnest attempt to take seriously the problem of pluralism. As Rawls says, "Political liberalism starts by taking to heart the absolute depth of that irreconcilable latent conflict" (1996, xxviii). Among other things, this means that Rawls attempts to grapple with the importance of religious pluralism deeply embedded in our democratic society when considering the justificatory structure of his liberalism. Not only do we see religious pluralism as such, but also assuming Rawls is correct about reasonable pluralism, we see the fact of reasonable *religious* pluralism. Not only are there a number of comprehensive religious doctrines at play in American society, but there are a plurality of reasonably held ones.

Now, recall my aim is to try to understand the Rawlsian view concerning the role of religion in public life. Instead of focusing attention upon the way in which the fact of reasonable pluralism prompts Rawls to argue for an "overlapping consensus" in order to provide the justificatory structure to his political liberalism, I shall below specifically hone in on the manner in which fully acknowledging the fact of reasonable pluralism yields practical statements about the role of religion in the public square for Rawls.

Coming to terms with the fact of reasonable pluralism poses questions not only for the justificatory structure of society but also serious questions about how deliberation of public policy is to take place. The question for Rawls is roughly this: Given the fact of reasonable pluralism, how are we as a political society to deliberate concerning matters of public policy? This is a question about the manner in which a body politic goes about "formulating its plans, of putting its ends in an order of priority and of making its decisions accordingly"

(1996, 212). The answer Rawls gives to the above question is this: through reason. Of course, the answer becomes a bit more complex. A political society is to deliberate by means of what Rawls calls "public reason."

The question about the shape of public deliberation is an important one for Rawls because the deliberation of public policy by its very nature deals with the wielding of political power over that public. For, it is through deliberation that "equal citizens who, as a collective body, exercise final political and coercive power over one another in enacting laws and in amending their constitution" (1996, 214). And, insofar as all political power is seen by Rawls as "always coercive power backed by the government's use of sanctions," the question becomes this: when is coercive power ever appropriate (1996, 136)? Rawls answers in following way:

> [O]ur exercise of political power is fully proper only when it is exercised in accordance with a constitution the essentials of which all citizens as free and equal may reasonably be expected to endorse in the light of principles and ideals acceptable to their common human reason. This is the liberal principle of legitimacy. . . . Only a political conception of justice that all citizens might be reasonably expected to endorse can serve as a basis of public reason and justification. (1996, 137)

According to Rawls, it is only when this liberal principle of legitimacy is met that coercive power is appropriate (cf. Nagel 1987, 218). And, the only way to achieve this legitimacy is through the use of public reason. As Rawls says, "Our exercise of political power is proper only when we sincerely believe that the reasons we offer for our political action may reasonably be accepted by other citizens as a justification of those actions" (1996, xlvi). That is, political power is only justified by public reasons—those reasons "guided by a political conception the principles and values of which all citizens can endorse" (1996, 10).

But, what exactly makes this public reason, in fact, *public*? Rawls enumerates three defining features. First, it is the reason of persons *qua* citizens. Second, the subject matter of public reason is "the good of the public and matters of fundamental justice" (1996, 213). And, third, the nature and content of public reason is itself public, "being given by the ideals and principles expressed by society's conceptions of political justice, and conducted open to view on that basis" (1996, 213).

We can understand this first feature in terms of *status*.[12] The reasons of persons used during deliberation are to be those that are reasons held by persons *qua* citizens, as opposed to, say, reasons of persons *qua* Christians or of persons *qua* members of a particular association or group. When engaged in public matters, one should identify as a citizen of the body politic, and one should reason and deliberate according to that status/identity as citizen.

The second feature of public reason can be thought of in terms of *scope* or *subject matter*. The subjects of public reason are specifically those matters which pertain to a special portion of the political sphere. This is an important feature, as Rawls insists that the limits of public reason do not apply across the board, but "only to those [political matters] involving what we may call 'constitutional essentials' and questions of basic justice" (1996, 214).[13] These matters are those relevant to the basic structure of society, including such "fundamental questions" as "who has the right to vote, what religions are to be tolerated, who is to be assured fair equality or opportunity, or to hold property" (1996, 214). Only these and similar sorts of questions require that deliberation remain within the parameters of public reason. So the limits of public reason, on Rawls's view, do not apply to such political issues as, say, environmental regulation or tax legislation. However, Rawls does contend that when individual citizens engage in public deliberation and political advocacy and *even voting*—at least when matters of fundamental questions are at stake—individuals should proceed in accordance with the limits of public reason. But, the limits of public reason do not apply to matters of "personal deliberation and reflections about political questions, or to the reasoning about them by members of associations such as churches and universities" (1996, 215). For, the reasoning of such non-public associations (like churches, civil societies, scientific societies, and professional groups) proceed according to "how the nature (the aim and point) of each association is understood and the conditions under which it pursues its ends" (1996, 221). Their reasoning is, to be sure, *social* (and in that sense not private), but it is not public in the relevant sense (1996, 220, fn.7).

But, what are these *limits* of public reason to which Rawls refers—sometimes applying, sometimes not applying? Answering this question brings us to the third feature of public reason mentioned above, which we can think of in terms of *source*. Stated roughly, the limits of public reason, when applicable, mark the parameters around the pool of reasons from which one can appropriately draw in public deliberation and when voting about fundamental questions. Only those reasons drawn from this pool are appropriately public; hence, the *limits* of public reason. The implication, of course, is that not just any old set of reasons will properly get to count as reasons when fundamental questions are at stake. Rather, one must employ (and, in turn, be moved by) public reasons, which are those reasons one can reasonably expect others to endorse as reasons. That is, one must employ (and likewise respond to, e.g. when voting) reasons which one expects others will likewise see to be reasons. The content of this public reason is "formulated by what [Rawls] call[s] a 'political conception of justice'" (1996, 223). That political conception is "elaborated in terms of fundamental ideas viewed as implicit in the public political culture of a democratic society"[14]—ideas that are "embedded in our society's main institutions and the public traditions of their interpretation" and can be "regarded as implicitly shared" (Mulhall and Swift 1996, 173). Moreover, this political conception of justice is freestanding and can be understood as independent of any particular comprehensive doctrine. In short, the political conception contains the principles and values which all citizens can endorse; and therefore, it provides the source of public reason (Rawls 1996, 10). Only by deliberating in accordance with public reason (drawn from the political conception of justice), can the relevant public policies and basic structure of society be justifiable to *all* citizens within the body politic, thereby meeting the demands of the liberal principle of political legitimacy (1996, 224). Rawls explains that public deliberation, when under the limits of public reason, should, given this justificatory obligation, "appeal only to presently accepted general beliefs and forms of reasoning found in common sense, and the methods and conclusions of science when these are not controversial" (1996, 224). That is, public deliberation should "rest on the plain truths now widely accepted, or available, to citizens generally" (1996, 225).

We can now start to see the ramifications of Rawls's view of public reason as it pertains to the employment of comprehensive doctrines in the public square. Insofar as public deliberation (and voting) on fundamental matters should be justified according to those reasons and ways of reasoning which are common and shared, then reasons drawn from a particular religious doctrine are at least initially suspect. This is because those particular comprehensive doctrines are not themselves an element of the political conception of justice, i.e. the common pool of reasons implicit in our shared public culture with which one can appropriately meet the demands of the liberal principle of legitimacy. Inasmuch as there are a number of reasonable and incompatible comprehensive doctrines (among which include religious doctrines), one cannot expect reasons drawn from one's own comprehensive doctrine to be common and thus acceptable (as reasons) to someone subscribing to a different comprehensive doctrine. Hence, these non-public reasons cannot accomplish the tasks of justification in the public square.

An example may help clarify this point. Let us say that Adam is advocating a public policy *P* (which touches on a fundamental question) to Betty. According to Rawls, Adam should only advocate *P* with reasons which are acceptable as reasons to Betty in order to justify *P* in such a way that meets the liberal principle of legitimacy. Now, let us assume that Adam is a Christian and Betty is an atheist. According to Rawls's ideal of public reason, Adam should not argue for *P* using reasons drawn from his own comprehensive doctrine like, say, an appeal to Christian scripture. Such an appeal to scripture will not be endorsable as a reason to Betty inasmuch as she already rejects the necessary condition for the possibility of understanding such a religious appeal as a reason, namely she rejects the existence of a god altogether. Rather, according to Rawls's view of public reason, Adam ought to employ reasons which are drawn from the political conception of justice

What emerges from Rawls is what we might call the *doctrine of neutrality*, which simply states that in public deliberation, when matters of basic justice or constitutional essentials are at stake, citizens should employ only those reasons which are neutral to one's comprehensive doctrine and are drawn rather from the political conception. Thus, following the doctrine of neutrality, we must try to give and entertain reasons that do not depend upon one's acceptance of a particular comprehensive doctrine, whether that be Catholicism, utilitarianism, deontology, or some other such doctrine. Of course, it should be noted here that Rawls (1996 and 1997) attempts to amend his view above—and hence soften the doctrine of neutrality—to say that citizens may *also* properly employ reasoning drawn from a comprehensive doctrine as long as they eventually offer neutral public reasons as justification for their political positions. For reasons articulated in the next section (4.3), Rawls's amendment proves unsuccessful in altering the essence of this position. We can see that it is in fact Rawls's attempt to attend to the implications of the fact of reasonable pluralism that motivates this doctrine of neutrality.[15] Because there is a diversity of comprehensive doctrines at play among citizens, public deliberation must remain neutral among those conflicting comprehensive doctrines, or otherwise it is not properly public. Rawls's ideal of public reason is therefore conceptually married to this doctrine of neutrality.

Now, it is important to point out at least part of what this ideal of public reason provides for Rawls. In short, this ideal of public reason projects an image of what it means to be the ideal democratic citizen. Ideal citizenship is marked by its "moral, not a legal, duty—the duty of civility" to be able to provide reasons to others for the policies, campaigns, and votes that one advocates (1996, 217). As Rawls says, "Understanding how to conduct oneself as a democratic citizen includes understanding an ideal of public reason" (1996, 218)

4.3 Rawlsian Separatism

What we have seen is that Rawls's view of public reason restricts the role that comprehensive doctrines can play when fundamental questions of constitutional essentials and matters of basic justice are at stake. Insofar as religion is a type of comprehensive doctrine, we can easily draw out the consequences of his view of public reason as it pertains to religion in the public square. According to Rawls, religion ought to be bracketed before citizens enter the public square insofar as any religion is one of several competing comprehensive doctrines, the whole class of which is inadequate to the tasks of political justification. This implied restriction on religion constitutes Rawls's separatism: religion should remain a non-public matter to be kept separate from matters of the public square.[16] Though the implications of Rawls's separatist proposal should be clear from the previous section, we can now explicitly state two important implications of Rawls's separatist proposal:

1. Religious reasons should not be introduced into public deliberation and political advocacy when fundamental matters are at stake;
2. Religious reasons should not determine how citizens vote when fundamental questions are at stake.

Employment of religious reasons belongs only within the non-public domain, where churches, civil societies, etc. help determine what Rawls calls the "background culture" (1996, 211, n. 42). Consequently, if a citizen employs only religious reasons in the public square, that citizen violates the duties of democratic citizenship and acts irresponsibly.

Chapter Four

There may be some question as to whether (or, at least, to what extent) Rawls's view entails the separatism I attribute to him above. While it is clear that Rawls's view of public reason (as I have discussed it so far) does, indeed, commit him to saying that citizens should not rely *exclusively* upon religious reasons in public deliberation, his view does not necessarily rule out submitting both religious *and* public reasons during the course of public deliberation and political advocacy (Reidy 2000, 51). And, while Rawls's initial articulation of his ideal of public reason in the first edition of his *Political Liberalism* (1993) seems to be unclear on this point, he does eventually clarify his position in the second edition (1996). In revisions upon his initial view of public reason, Rawls explicitly allows for non-public reasons drawn from one's comprehensive doctrines (including religious reasons) to be submitted in the course of public deliberation, "provided that in due course public reasons, given by a reasonable political conception, are presented sufficient to support whatever the comprehensive doctrines are introduced to support" (1996, li–lii; cf. 1997, 591).[17] This proviso identifies what Rawls calls his "wide view of public reason" (1996, lii; cf. 1997, 591, ff.). Given this wide view, religious reasons are not necessarily kept at bay during public deliberation. Rather, they are permitted as long as neutral public reasons are offered as a justification for the political position in question. In this sense, the wide view of public reason allows for a sort of IOU submission of religious reasons.

The significance of Rawls's wide view of public reason is that it *seems* to dilute the extent to which we can accredit to him a robustly separatist proposal concerning the role of religion in the public square. For, if religious reasons can be submitted in the course of public deliberation—albeit attached to some sort of promissory note—religion is not wholly separated from the public domain. Thus, we might conclude that Rawls's wide view of public reason commits him to what we might call a *mild separatism*.

But, this sort of concession to religious reasoning by Rawls is problematic. While the wide view of public reason seems to move in the direction of diluting his separatism, upon closer examination we can see this is not the case in any significant sense. Consider an example.[18] Let us say that Abigail proposes P to Bob (where P touches on a fundamental political issue), supporting her proposal with religious reasons. Abigail has in mind that she can (and will) eventually come around with a neutral, public reason as well, in such a way as to meet the requirements of Rawls's proviso. On the surface, of course, everything appears to be acceptable given the milder requirements of Rawls's wide view of public reason. Yet, the question remains: if Abigail knows that she can meet the requirements of the proviso when she submits her religious reasons, why does she not just go ahead and offer that neutral public reason (which would meet the proviso) in the first place? As Gaus says,

> Why give an argument that will not appeal to reasonable others when one has an argument that will? If, on the other hand, [Abigail] does not know that the proviso is met because she does not know of the argument for [P] on the basis

of [neutral public reasons], then it seems she has no business advancing [religious reasons]. The only case in which the proviso makes (some sort of) sense is when a person knows that there is a good public argument for [*P*] but does not know what it is, so instead she advances an argument based on her comprehensive doctrine, which she knows does not provide public reason. But it really is hard to see how one can be confident that there is a good public argument without knowing what it is, and why, faced with that knowledge, one's response is to provide an argument that one knows is *not* a good public argument. (2003, 200)

The fact of the matter is that, for Rawls, the actual justificatory work is done by neutral public reasons given during the course of public deliberation. Of course, it seems that religious *language* may be to some degree permissible in some cases. But, that language is not what takes the cake at the end of the day. Instead, neutral public reasons, and neutral public reasons alone—either given now or in due course—are precisely what carry force in public deliberation *insofar as they alone do the justificatory work.* So, while permissive of religious language, Rawls's wide view of public reason cannot accommodate those citizens who take their actual justificatory reasons to be, in the end, religious. So, even his IOU-view makes no significant alterations on his initial view of public reason. Religious *reasons* are still kept in the closet, so to speak, with respect to justification of public policy. And, hence, Rawls's separatism is not significantly diluted in any important sense.

Now, of course, there is also an interesting question as to the *range* within which Rawls's separatist proposal functions. In other words, it is not utterly unambiguous as to when the limits of public reason are to be observed and thus the restrictions on religion upheld. Rawls asserts that the limits of public reason (and thus his separatist proposal) are not necessarily applicable in most situations. Recall that the limits of public reason are only *necessarily* applicable when fundamental questions involving constitutional essentials and questions of basic justice are at stake. But, according to Rawls:

> Many if not most political questions do not concern those fundamental matters, for example, most tax legislation and many laws regulating property; statutes protecting the environment and controlling pollution; establishing national parks and preserving wilderness area and animal and plant species; and laying aside funds for museums and the arts. (1996, 214)

If we take Rawls at his word here, we can see that his separatist proposal, while still separatist in the manner described, has a limited range within which it takes effect. We might call this Rawls's Limited Range Separatist Proposal: separatism obtains, but only when certain sorts of questions are before us.

Of course, Rawls sees the red flag coming. Why not just say that the limits of public reason apply to all questions involving the use of political power? (Recall the demands of the liberal principle of justification). "Why would it ever be admissible to go outside its range of political values?" Rawls asks (1996, 215).

He answers his own question by suggesting, roughly, that we should take first things first. Clearly, along Rawlsian lines, if the limits of public reason should not be applicable to fundamental questions about constitutional essentials and matters of basic justice, then they ought not to be applied to other matters. "Should they hold here [on fundamental questions], we can then proceed to other cases" (1996, 215). So, given his preoccupation with fundamentals first, Rawls does not contend that the limits of public reason should necessarily apply across the board; this is an open question of sorts. And, while he does think that all political questions are better off if settled when the limits of public reason are applied, Rawls does admit that "this may not always be so" (1996, 215)

But, there remains some ambiguity about this question concerning the range of Rawls's public reason.[19] *What gets to count* as touching on a fundamental question about constitutional essentials or questions of basic justice such that the limits of public reason and (hence his separatism) come into full effect? Unfortunately, Rawls does not (and perhaps cannot) provide criteria for making this judgment. While he excludes certain non-fundamental questions (like tax issues or environmental issues) from the range of applicability of public reason, we may be right to ask with L. E. Goodman if this exclusion actually works. Goodman argues,

> In a telling, but soft-pedaled admission, [Rawls] acknowledges that such concerns "sometimes do involve fundamental matters."[20] In a money economy like ours, where revenues are fungible, or in a litigious society like that of ancient Athens, or any society where rights matter or precedence counts—in any human society, then—it is both easy and natural to trace claims to fundamental principles. That's what lawyers do when they press a matter in a higher court. Christmas trees in the mall, flag burning, lap dancing, the pledge of allegiance, blood transfusions, exorcisms, health care—all have been claimed as matters of basic rights. It is not just free choice about abortion that has been made a constitutional matter. So has the "taking" of property by regulatory agencies and "unfunded mandates." These affect seatbelt design, toys, ladders, scaffolding, automobiles, food labels and drug and cosmetic testing. The more detailed the regulation, the more ardent and conceptual the protest. . . . Can the environment be protected, or public security maintained, without the prospect of encroaching on what someone will deem a basic right? Can any legislation be drafted or funds spent without raising fundamental questions about the aims and goals of those who will live under the resultant laws or foot the resultant bills? (Goodman, Forthcoming)

What Goodman seems to be getting at here—and I think that he is right—is that it is not always clear how exactly to distinguish those political questions that involve fundamental matters from those that do not. And, any attempt to draw a *principled* distinction will require that Rawls draw upon some kind of comprehensive doctrine, which of course he wants to avoid doing.

Of course, Rawls might want to respond in the following sort of way: while perhaps there are cases where it is *claimed* that fundamental questions are involved, the mere fact that such a claim is made does not entail that fundamental questions are *actually* involved. Clearly, Rawls might say, there is a distinct difference between political matters like zoning laws and questions about who gets to vote. The former is simply not a fundamental matter while the latter is. Constitutional essentials, Rawls explains, fall into the following two categories:

   a. fundamental principles that specify the general structure of government and the political process: the powers of the legislature, executive and the judiciary; the scope of majority rule; and
   b. equal basic rights and liberties of citizenship that legislative majorities are to respect: such as the right to vote and to participate in politics, liberty of conscience, freedom of thought and of association, as well as the protections of the rule of law. (1996, 227)

So, if a political question does not touch down into one of these categories, then, according to Rawls, it does not involve fundamental matters and, as such, deliberation about that non-fundamental matter does not require the limits of public reason.

Fair enough. But, it is not clear that this sort of Rawlsian rejoinder is going to be entirely satisfactory, especially against the sort of objection raised by Goodman. Rawls may want to claim that a certain issue does not involve fundamental matters; however, if Goodman is right, we can easily find reasonable arguments to the effect that it does. Such is the case even with, say, zoning laws. Rawls assumes that it is rather clear when political issues involve fundamental matters, as if there were no contestation about that. But, given the reality of exactly this sort of contestation, we are left asking for criteria which could be used to settle that contestation. And, without any such criteria, it is indeed "hard to find an area where claims are not treated as matters of fundamental rights" (Goodman, Forthcoming). And, as Goodman continues, any attempt to provide these criteria *a priori* would result in an illegitimate appeal to some comprehensive doctrine. The real problem for Rawls here is this: there is as much reasonable disagreement about what a constitution is and about what gets to count as a matter of basic justice, as there is concerning comprehensive doctrines. Rawls, however, assumes that the political level (where questions about whether an issue is fundamental arise) is insulated from the sort of disagreement he recognizes at the level of comprehensive doctrines. But, this seems strange, to say the least. For, we *do* disagree about justice (Sandel 1998a, 204). And, this means that we also disagree about when a particular issue actually involves a question of basic justice.

Thus, it appears that accrediting the Limited Range Separatist Proposal to Rawls seems problematic. If it is the case that political questions touch on fundamentals more often than Rawls suspects (or at least admits), then—even if we take his first-things-first approach—the limits of public reason would have to come into effect on most every political question. As such, the range of the applicability of the limits of public reason is much broader than our initial reading suggests. Consequently, it seems fair to accredit Rawls with what we might call Rawls's Broad Range Separatist proposal: separatism obtains in nearly all political matters.

4.4 Other Leading Liberals

This chapter has thus far focused primarily upon Rawls and his view of public reason and the separatism that it entails. This is for a good reason. Once again, it seems that Rawls sets the agenda—or at least comes to catalogue and articulate that agenda—for much of contemporary analytic political theory. While a good many liberal theorists are writing specifically about the role of religion in public life, it seems fair to say that most of that writing has in some way or another dialectically responded to the problematic that has come to be defined by Rawls. It is clear that Rawls has been heavily influenced by the input of several of the most important liberal thinkers in the formulation (and reformulation) of his political liberalism and his ideal of public reason.[21] And, perhaps it is precisely because of these influences that Rawls presents the view of public reason that most seems to capture what is at the heart of mainstream contemporary liberalism concerning the role of religion in the public domain. Of course, this is not to say that there are not variations among liberals writing on this issue. However, it seems that Rawls captures the essence of those views, presenting what may be thought of as the paradigmatic liberal view concerning the role of religion in public life.

For instance, the manner in which Rawls's ideal of public reason restricts the degree to which comprehensive doctrines can come into play during public deliberation captures what Thomas Nagel refers to in his own his writing as "epistemological restraint" (Nagel 1987, 229).[22] Nagel argues that one has a moral duty to withhold from making "appeals to the truth" (as dictated, say, by one's religious belief) in public deliberation (1987, 227). But, why should one not be able to appeal to the truth, perhaps as derivative of one's religious belief, in public deliberation? This restraint, according to Nagel, is not mandatory because of some skeptical consideration concerning the source of that appeal to the truth. Rather, "the distinction between what is needed to justify belief [for instance, in one's religion] and what is needed to justify the employment of political power depends on a higher standard of objectivity, which is ethically based" (1987, 229). Nagel writes,

> The idea is that when we look at certain of our convictions from outside, however justified they may be from within, the appeal to their truth must be seen merely as an appeal to our beliefs, and should be treated as such unless those beliefs can be shown to be justifiable from a more impersonal standpoint. If not, they have to remain, for the purpose of a certain kind of moral argument, features of a personal perspective—to be respected as such but no more than that. (1987, 230)

Thus, according to Nagel, in order to meet the demands of political justification from this more impersonal standpoint—where others can accept the reasons given in public deliberation as, in fact, reasons for justification of a given proposal—one must be prepared to submit reasons to others so that "they have what you have, and can arrive at a judgment on the same basis" (1987, 232). This precludes, according to Nagel, appeals to one's personal faith or revelation of the truth (i.e. appeals to one's religion) precisely because that faith or revelation is not something that "they have"—*it is not shared*. Consequently, one should only employ reasons which are neutral with respect to one's religion so that those reasons can be impersonal, objective, and, in short, be reasons that "they have." Similarly, Joshua Cohen argues that we should "restrict ourselves in political argument to the subset of moral considerations that others who have reasonable views accept as well" (1993, 283; cf. 1996a, 74). We thereby "restrict ourselves to common ground in the face of the fact of diversity" (1993, 284). By doing so, we refrain from imposing our moral views upon those with whom we disagree but who are nonetheless reasonable in holding the views that they hold.

Clearly, Rawls's view of public reason attempts to incorporate both Nagel's and Cohen's view. That one should rely upon reasons that are "common ground" and upon reasons that "they have" is captured by Rawls's insistence that public deliberation be carried out in terms consistent with the pool of reasons given by the political conception, which is, by its very nature neutral with respect to competing comprehensive doctrines. Likewise, Rawls's argument for the limits of public reason does not rely upon skepticism about the truth of comprehensive doctrines and religion. Rawls's political liberalism attempts to avoid the question of "which moral questions are true"—such is not a matter for political liberalism (1996, xxii). Rather, Rawls tells us, "we are to recognize the practical impossibility of reaching reasonable and workable political agreement in judgment on the truth of comprehensive doctrines, especially an agreement that might serve the political purpose, say of achieving peace and concord in a society characterized by religious and philosophical difference" (1996, 63).[23] Rawls's reliance upon the political conception in order to meet the demands of the liberal principle of legitimacy (as implied by the fact of reasonable pluralism), then, acts as an analogue to Nagel's insistence that public deliberation be carried out in terms such that "they have what you have" and to Cohen's insistence that we restrict ourselves to "common ground in the face of diversity."

Similarly, Rawls's idea of public reason captures the basic argument given by Bruce Ackerman for what he calls "conversational restraints" (1989, 16). According to Ackerman, conversational restraint is that restraint which seeks to avoid getting tangled up in moral arguments which hold little promise of getting resolved due to a lack of common ground. This restraint should be practiced in order to avoid what Alasdair MacIntyre aptly describes as "a civil war carried out by other means" (MacIntyre 1984, 253). Stephen Holmes, another leading liberal, advocates what he calls "gag rules" or the "politics of omission"—a sort of self-imposed conversational restraint—that can act to "profitably shift attention away from areas of discord and toward areas of concord" (1995, 203). He gives several historical examples of how self-imposed gag rules have acted to advance the possibility of strengthening the cause of peace and social stability by focusing the political agenda upon matters where some agreement is, at the time, possible. In their respective discussions, Ackerman and Holmes imply the same point: religious reasons are to be sidelined in the public square for practical reasons (Ackerman 1989, 19; Holmes 1995, 222). As Ackerman explains:

> When you and I learn that we disagree about one or another dimension of the moral truth, we should not search for some common value that will trump this disagreement; nor should we try to translate it into some putatively neutral framework;[24] nor should we seek to transcend it by talking about how some unearthly creature might resolve it. We should simply say *nothing at all* about this disagreement and put the moral ideal that divides us off the conversational agenda of the liberal state. In restraining ourselves in this way, we need not lose the chance to talk to one another about our deepest moral disagreements in countless other, more private contexts. We simply recognize that, while these ongoing debates continue, we will gain nothing of value by falsely asserting that the political community is of one mind on deeply contested matters. (1989, 19)

Again, the basic idea is simply that, by employing some limit on the types of reasons to which we can appeal and to the types of issues to be considered in public deliberation, there is at least some hope of deliberating matters with reasons that are neutral with respect to one's comprehensive doctrines. Hence, the pragmatic potential of conversational restraints and gag rules. Rawls's insistence that deliberators voice public reasons drawn from the political conception aims precisely at this pragmatic potential of evading "the most decisive issues, serious contention about which must undermine the basis of social cooperation" (Rawls 1996, 157). Consequently, like Ackerman and Holmes, Rawls insists that religious questions and religious reasons be relegated to non-public realms.

Robert Audi (1997) makes an interesting contribution to the debate among liberal theorists concerning the role of religion in the public square. Audi argues, contra Rawls's *initial* view of public reason, that religious reasons can appropriately be introduced into public deliberation within a liberal democracy. However, according to Audi, it is important that when one offers religious reasons in public deliberation, one should also offer secular reasons to support one's proposals. Audi offers two principles for clarification. First, he offers the "principle of secular rationale" which states:

> [O]ne has a *prima facie* obligation not to advocate or support any law or policy that restricts human conduct, unless one has, and is willing to offer, adequate secular reason for this advocacy or support (say for one's vote). (1997, 25)

Second, he offers the "principle of secular motivation." This principle "simply adds to the rationale principle a motivational condition" (1997, 28).

> It says that one has a (*prima facie*) obligation to abstain from advocacy or support of a law or public policy that restricts human conduct, unless one is sufficiently *motivated* by (normatively) adequate secular reason, where sufficiency of motivation here implies that some set of secular reasons is motivationally sufficient, roughly in the sense that (a) this set of reasons explains one's action and (b) one would act on it even if, other things remaining equal, one's other reasons were eliminated. (1997, 28)

What is significant about Audi's view is that it allows for overdetermination in public deliberation. That is, religious reasons are permissible to the degree that secular reasons are the determining factor in deliberation. Having sufficient secular reasons in place during public deliberation makes any additional religious reasons play the role of overdetermining considerations. In any case, religious reasons are not, *per se*, required to sit out entirely. However, some questions remain as to whether such allowable religious "reasons" are rightly to be considered *reasons*, in any important sense, to the degree that they carry no determining justificatory force within public deliberation. While Audi's view can be read as a criticism of Rawls's initial view of public reason, as discussed above, Rawls does amend his view with the proviso.[25] That proviso, while perhaps not catching the motivational condition of Audi's second principle, does capture the thrust of Audi's first and more significant principle. Consequently, we see that Rawls's wide view of public reason accommodates the thrust of Audi's contribution, and, as such, still stands as the paradigmatic liberal view concerning religion in the public square.[26]

Another separatist view concerning the role of religion in the public square is articulated primarily from the angle of the religious. This view, as a number of scholars have pointed out, maintains essentially that religion should be sidelined in political matters primarily in order to protect religion itself (Audi 1997; Sandel 1996; cf. Rorty 1994). According to this line of thought—what we might call the Separatism for Purity of Religion Argument—religion runs the risk of being too entangled in political matters. Summarizing this view, Audi writes:

> [I]f a government prefers the religious over the non-religious, it will tend, through the pronouncements and social policies that express that preference, to influence churches, and in deciding what to promote in the religious sphere, to begin to set criteria for what counts as being religious in the sense that qualifies institutions for preference. Once there are benefits to be had, there will be stretching to meet the criteria for getting them. (1997, 8)[27]

This is an interesting view primarily because of *why* it supports liberal separatism. Mainly, this view is motivated by the interest in protecting the enterprise of religion from too much "outsider" influence, namely the influence that the government may have over the understanding and practice of one's religion. The driving worry, it seems, is that the government may have too much say over religious matters if that door is opened. So, things are best if that door is kept shut.

Despite this interesting twist, it seems that Rawls's separatist view can accommodate this variety of separatist argument. Recall that the driving motivation behind Rawls's view of public reason, and his political liberalism more generally, is to remain sensitive to the fact of reasonable (religious) pluralism. In doing so, his liberalism aims to remain "impartial between the points of view of reasonable comprehensive doctrines" (1996, xxi). This means, among other things, that his liberalism "does not attack or criticize any reasonable view" (1996, xxi). It strives to remain hands-off as to the content of those reasonable comprehensive views. "As part of this," Rawls explains, "it does not criticize, much less reject, any particular theory of the truth of moral judgments" (1996, xxi–xxii). And while Rawls's chief concern in *Political Liberalism* may be to achieve social stability within a pluralistic democracy, clearly a consequence of this goal is to protect, at least on some level, the sanctity of each comprehensive doctrine that resides within that pluralism. Again, it appears that Rawls's separatism stands as the paradigmatic liberal view.

Of course, it would be nearly impossible for me to canvas all of the different liberal views concerning the role of religion in the public square. Clearly, liberals are still thinking about this issue and adaptations on the liberal view are still in the making. For instance, Charles Larmore defends the Rawlsian view of public reason as that practice which makes the vision of "mutual recognition" a reality (2003, 391). However, Larmore argues that Rawls weakens his view of public reason by amending it with the proviso. Such permissiveness toward comprehensive doctrine has a rightful place in what Larmore calls "open discussions" (cf. Rawl's "background culture"). According to Larmore, "In the forum where citizens officially decide the basic principles of their political association and where the canons of public reason therefore apply, appeals to comprehensive doctrines cannot but be out of place—at least in a well-ordered society" (2003, 387). In any case, Larmore clearly continues to work within the field defined by Rawls. And, while I readily acknowledge the possibility that some important nuances may have been glossed over, the main point in this section has been to show that there is good reason to suppose that the views espoused by many leading liberal theorists are, indeed, Rawlsian in type. A defining point of commonality can be seen in each of the liberal views: each affirms, to some degree or another, what I have called the doctrine of neutrality with respect to the public domain. That is, like Rawls, leading liberals tend to argue that public deliberation should be carried out in neutral terms. It is the civic duty of deliberators to try to give reasons drawn from a "common ground"—Rawls's political conception—thereby not submitting reasons drawn from one's comprehensive doctrine or religion. In order to achieve this, liberals recommend limits upon the type of reasons that can be given, whether those be labeled as "epistemological restraints," "conversational restraints," or "gag rules." Despite varying description, the point is the same: religious reasons ought not to be brought to the table during public deliberation. In this respect, the liberal view toward the role of religion in public deliberation tends to be separatist. As I discussed in Section 4.3, there may be different ranges and degrees in which and to which this separatism obtains; however, the basic tendency is the same.

4.5 Conclusion

We are now in a position to see what distinguishes separatist views from the reconstructivist views examined in the previous two chapters of this book. What renders separatism (even in its varying degrees and ranges) distinct from reconstructivism is the *kind* of constraint upon religion that is advocated. On the one hand, *quantitative constraints* are those which limit *how much* religion can come into play. On the other hand, *qualitative constraints* are those which limit *what sort of* religion can come into play. Whereas pragmatic and neo-pragmatic (reconstructivist) proposals tend toward the latter; as we have seen, Rawlsian separatist proposals tend toward the former. I use the language of "tendency" here for good reason. Clearly, in Rawls's initial and narrower view of public reason we see a straight ahead quantitative constraint: when deliberation is taking place, all religion (thereby answering the question, how much religion?) is to be excluded except in rare cases. This labeling may not hold to the same degree when considering Rawls's revisions to his view of public reason. Recall, his wide view allows for religious reasons to be included in public deliberation as long as neutral reasons can be given in due course. One may want to say that this proviso does away with quantitative constraints in Rawls's view. *How much* religion is no longer the issue at hand. Rather, the issue becomes whether religious "reasons" are reduced, on his wide view, to mere religious rhetoric that can, at best, play the role of overdetermination, as Audi suggests. Thus, one might say, Rawls imposes instead a qualitative constraint: the issue is now what sort of religion (i.e. what sort of religious expression) is allowable in public deliberation. Perhaps this is true. But, I maintain that Rawls imposes a quantitative constraint across the board insofar as, even if he does allow religious rhetoric into deliberation, he still excludes what many citizens take to be their actual reasons (i.e. religious reasons) from deliberation to the extent that those religious reasons carry no justificatory force. The basic point is this: Rawls still keeps religion (where religion is understood as a potent, determining source of reasons) outside of the public domain. Reconstructivists, by contrast (at least in theory), characteristically aim to alter the meaning of religion itself (and thus religious language and reasons). As such, they impose a qualitative constraint: only religion *of a certain sort* (i.e. religion that has undergone sufficient semantic alteration) can enter into the public domain. Interestingly, though, as the investigation in Chapter Three implies, such qualitative constraints advocated by pragmatists/reconstructivists are, ultimately, tantamount to the quantitative constraints imposed by liberals.

What I considered in this chapter is the manner in which Rawls's attunement to the fact of reasonable pluralism prompts his view of public reason (4.1). I then examined this view of public reason and argued that it is undergirded by the doctrine of neutrality (4.2). Moreover, this view of public reason entails Rawls's separatist proposal (4.3). I considered this separatist view in Rawls alongside other leading liberal analytic political theorists, arguing that Rawls's view of public reason can accommodate the high points of those theorists, thereby establishing his view of public reason as the paradigmatic liberal statement concerning the role of religion within public deliberation (4.4). These Rawlsian liberal proposals can be seen as an attempt in contemporary analytic political theory to face the issue that the sociological reality of religious pluralism is a problem to be dealt with when trying to imagine what public life and democratic citizenship ought to look like. The *ex ante* conversational restraints of neutralist liberalisms are intended to provide a way of conceptualizing a public life that properly respects the fact of religious pluralism while providing for a stable society.[28]

In the next chapter, I examine the doctrine of neutrality, which undergirds the separatism of liberal proposals concerning the role of religion in public life. One wonders whether the cornerstone of the liberal separatist view can withstand the pressure of critical scrutiny.

Notes

1. Nagel quoted in Alterman 2002.
2. For instance, Ronald Dworkin has commented that his "present view is opposed to his in some ways, but only from within a field *defined by him*" (Alterman 2002, my emphasis); cf. Mulhall and Swift: "Rawls simply *did* define the agenda and continues to do so" (1996, 1).
3. Cf. to the pragmatist response to Cartesianism, as discussed in Chapter 2. West, for instance, characterizes this move as the "American evasion of philosophy" (1989).
4. For a contrasting view, see Mulhall and Swift 1996. They contend that Rawls's "turn to the political culture is not driven by pragmatism. It is rather that he attaches great importance to the public justifiability of a political theory." (1996, 193). Even if Rawls's *motivation* is not *per se* pragmatic, his political liberalism clearly involves several pragmatist inclinations as discussed above.
5. For instance, it seems that the shift to political liberalism away from the comprehensive liberalism in *A Theory of Justice* can be read as a concession of sorts to critics like Sandel 1982; MacIntyre 1984 and 1988; Taylor 1994, 1999; and to some extent Walzer 1983. For commentary on this concession of sorts, see Talisse 2001 for a helpful discussion.
6. It is assumed that the reader is at least roughly familiar with Rawls's justice as fairness. Gaus (2003) summarizes this liberalism in the following way: "This theory . . . argued that parties to an original contract, situated without knowledge that might bias them, would accept two principles of justice to regulate the basic structure of society: 1) Each person is to have an equal right to the most extensive system of equal basic liberties

compatible with a similar system of liberty for all. 2) Social and economic inequalities are to be arranged so that they are both (a) to the benefit of the least advantaged. . . . (b) attached to offices and positions open to all under conditions of fair equality of opportunity" (177–178). For more on justice as fairness, see Rawls 1971. For summary and commentary see Mulhall and Swift 1996; Gaus 2003, chapter six; Talisse 2001.

7. For a more detailed discussion on this tension that Rawls attempts to resolves in his later work, see Mulhall and Swift 1996; Talisse 2001; Gaus 2003.

8. For more on the distinction between the simple fact of pluralism and the fact of reasonable pluralism, see Cohen 1993. Apparently Cohen urges the importance of this distinction (Rawls 1996, xxxiii).

9. Rawls says explicitly, for instance: "It is the fact of reasonable pluralism that leads . . . to the idea of a political conception of justice and so to the idea of political liberalism" (1996, xlvii).

10. See Gaus 2003, particularly his Chapter 1, for this discussion.

11. I use Gaus's paraphrasing of Rawls's list of the burdens of judgment for the sake of clarity and brevity. For Rawls's own list, see Rawls 1996, 56–57.

12. Here and in the two subsequent paragraphs, I draw upon Mulhall and Swift's way of discussing the respects in which the political conception of justice is political, as opposed to comprehensive (1996, 172–173). Though slightly different, the three features of public reason are analogous to the manner in which Rawls understands his conception of justice to be political.

13. Rawls writes, "Constitutional essentials concern questions about what political rights and liberties, say, may reasonably be included in a written constitution, when assuming the constitution may be interpreted by a supreme court, or some similar body. Matters of basic justice relate to the basic structure of society and so would concern questions of basic economic and social justice and other things not covered by a constitution" (1996, l, fn. 23).

14. Rawls quoted in Mulhall and Swift 1996, 173

15. The connection between neutrality and negative liberty should be acknowledged. See Berlin 1969.

16. It should be noted that Rawls's "non-public" realm does not entail its being a *private* realm, in the sense that, say, Rorty discusses. See Rawls 1996, 220, n. 7 for that full discussion. See my Chapter Three for a discussion of the private in Rorty.

17. This revision first came in Rawls's Introduction to the Paperback Edition of *Political Liberalism* (1996). Other revisions to his view of public reason came in "The Idea of Public Reason Revisited," in Rawls 1997, later reprinted in Rawls 1999.

18. In the following discussion, I follow Gaus's example used to criticize Rawls's wide view of public reason (2003, 200).

19. By "range" here, I do not mean what Rawls goes on to discuss as a wider and more inclusive view of public reason. Range, which I describe in terms of "limited" or "broad," should not be confused with the adjectives "wide" or "narrow" as Rawls uses them. Range of public reason is a question of *when* public reason is to take effect Wider and/or narrow views of public reason is a question of what gets to count as a public reason. The former is a question of scope. The latter is a question of content and source.

20. Rawls 1996, 214.

21. See Rawls's rather long list of acknowledgements, including names like Scanlon, Dworkin, Nagel, Cohen, Shklar, Thompson, Audi, etc. (1996, xxxii–xxxvi).

22. The connection between Rawls and other neutralist liberals, like Nagel, is discussed in part by Raz 1990.

23. Cf. to what West characterizes as the characteristically pragmatic evasion of epistemology-oriented philosophy. See Chapter 2 for a discussion of the attempt by James to evade the legacy of Descartes' skepticism.

24. Cf. reconstructivist strategies advocated by pragmatists

25. Rawls does acknowledge Audi as one of the main contributors to his thinking about the adjustments to this view of public reason.

26. I should note that I still have some questions as to where to locate Audi in this investigation. On the one hand, given his view of "theo-ethical equilibrium," he seems to fall into the reconstructivist camp. However, clearly, he has very separatist aspects to his proposal, especially given his advocacy of ecclesiastical and clerical neutrality. In many respects, Audi's view is very similar to Rawls's wide view of public reason. It may just be the case that Audi's view is simply difficult to categorize given the way that I have organized the issue. On the other hand, it may be the case that Audi's view shows the connection between reconstructivist proposals and separatist proposals: the former collapses into the latter.

27. Consider the move in 2004 by the office of Texas Comptroller attempting to refuse to categorize the Unitarian Church as a religion (for the purposes of the 501(c) 3 tax exemption status) on the grounds that said church has no identifiable conception of a god. See Dyer 2004 for this discussion.

28. It should be noted that there is a distinction between neutralist liberalisms found in Rawls 1971 and 1996; Dworkin 1985; Nagel 1987; Holmes 1995; Cohen 1993, 1996a and 1996b; Ackerman 1989 and the non-neutralist liberalisms found in the likes of Raz 1968; Sher 1997; Taylor 1994 (here, though there is some controversy in calling Taylor a liberal, he refers to his own view as a "non-procedural" liberal view); Gutmann 1987; Gutmann and Thompson 1996; and Macedo 1990. As I cannot hope to address all "liberal" proposals, my concern in the book is with explicitly neutralist-leaning liberal proposals. It should be noted, however, that these non-neutralist liberalisms are outside the mainstream of liberal theory. And, insofar as these non-neutralist liberalisms shift away from the right-over-the-good brand of liberalism, they are themselves questionably liberal, at least from the perspective of more pure breed liberal theorists like Rawls and Dworkin. (Here, I draw upon Sandel's characterization of liberalism (1998a) as maintaining the primacy of the right-over-the-good.)

Chapter Five

Liberalism's Hidden Garments: A Multidimensional Response to the Naked Public Square[1]

In the previous chapter, I explored the Rawlsian liberal paradigm of public discourse and the religious-political separatism that it entails. At the heart of this separatism is the doctrine of neutrality: that citizens and governmental officials deliberating public policy should remain neutral among comprehensive doctrines, and thus religions. Public policy and legislation should be justified by public reasons, according to Rawls and other liberal separatists. The aim of this chapter is to develop a multilayered response to the sort of parameters and constraints placed by neutralist liberals on religious participation in the public square. I shall pose several questions that need to be answered. Does the public square ever achieve the sort of neutrality required by the Rawlsian proposal? Is the sort of neutrality required by liberals even possible? In any case, would that neutrality requirement be a desirable regulative ideal governing political justification? I think there is good reason to suppose that the answer to each of these questions is, in fact, "no." Although these questions are obviously interrelated, I shall investigate each of these questions independently. In doing so, I shall consider what I take to be some of the most important arguments currently afloat in portions of the so-called liberal-communitarian/civic republicanism debate[2] and in other areas of contemporary democratic political theory. While I seek to provide a careful and detailed critique of dominant liberal treatments of the religious participation in politics, it is not my intention to advance any wholly novel or distinct lines of criticism of the liberal position. Rather, my aim is to catalogue what I take to be the already well-articulated and most heavy-hitting critiques of the separatist position. That being said, the manner in which these criticisms are organized and presented here no doubt constitutes an extension of the criticism of the separatist position insofar that it offers a multidimensional response to both the practical and the theoretical implications of the Rawlsian view of public discourse. In this sense alone, my critique is more nuanced and more thoroughgoing than, say, just one line of criticism offered by any one particular critic of the liberal separatist position.

5.1 The Practical Improbability of Neutrality

Michael Sandel has been widely recognized as one of the most decisive critics of Rawls (Mulhall and Swift 1996; Talisse 2001; Beiner 1998; Kymlicka 1990 and 1998; Buchanan 1989; Walzer 1990). And, his criticism of Rawls's earlier work (Sandel 1982) has been instrumental in the instigation of many of the reformulations advanced by Rawls in his later work (Talisse 2001; cf. Rawls 1996, 27, fn. 29). Since then, Sandel's more recent work, especially his *Democracy's Discontent* (1996), can easily be read as a continued criticism of Rawls's political liberalism, what Sandel calls "minimalist liberalism" (Sandel 1996, 18). As such, I will focus my attention upon that more recent work of Sandel in which he criticizes the increasingly prevalent Rawlsian proposals concerning public life and democratic citizenship.

Sandel attempts to examine the public philosophy of what he calls the "procedural republic" (1996, 4). This procedural republic in which we live, Sandel claims, is one guided by "a certain version of liberal political theory," where the "central idea is that government should be neutral toward the moral and religious views its citizens espouse" (1996, 4).

> Since people disagree about the best way to live, government should not affirm in law any particular vision of the good life. Instead it should provide a framework of rights that respects persons as free and independent selves, capable of choosing their own values and ends. Since this liberalism asserts the priority of fair procedures over particular ends, the public life it informs might be called the procedural republic. (1996, 4)

Much of Sandel's effort is geared toward understanding the derivation of the public philosophy of this procedural republic by examining the varied strands of constitutional interpretation in American history. What Sandel clearly shows is that there has been a consistent trend toward understanding the public square in such a way as to render it compatible with Rawls's separatist, liberal vision as discussed in the previous chapter. That is, especially over roughly the last fifty years, American public philosophy has increasingly, particularly by means of liberal constitutional interpretation, moved toward affirming the idea that the state can (and should) remain neutral concerning questions of the good (and thus comprehensive moral doctrines, including religions) by giving pride of place to the right over the good (Sandel 1998a, 216). With this trend comes the increased insistence that we should bracket moral and religious doctrines during the course of public deliberation, legislation, and interpretation of public policy. Crudely put, Sandel shows that there is a trend toward attempting to realize Rawls's ideal of public reason.

While Sandel presents an interesting alternative to this so-called procedural republic—one I think well worth more consideration[3]—I mean to bring focus simply on the critical aspects of Sandel's investigation. And, we need not adopt his positive proposals to see the force of his critique of the Rawlsisan liberal separatist position. In fact, we may be better served to uncouple the two, and certainly the latter does not imply the former. What Sandel aptly points out in his criticism of the liberal position is the practical failure of the procedural republic in realizing its own goals. With an eye toward Sandel, then, I shall answer the first question: Does the public square ever achieve the sort of neutrality required by the Rawlsian proposal? Sandel presents us with numerous empirical examples that indicate the improbability of the actualization of this neutrality. Below, I briefly highlight three.

Consider, for example, recent developments in family law, particularly as it involves divorce. In keeping with the trends toward achieving the Rawlsian vision, the "no-fault" divorce law enacted by California in the 1970s has now spread across the nation such that, by 1985, "every state in the nation had adopted some version of no-fault divorce" (Sandel 1996, 110). The significance of this move toward no-fault divorce can be found in its attempt to "bracket the moral considerations that had traditionally governed the law of divorce" (1996, 109). Under the no-fault divorce law, either party can unilaterally decide to obtain a divorce without arguing that the other party is guilty of any moral wrongdoing, as determined, say, by one's comprehensive doctrine of the good or by one's religion. Such reference to moral wrongdoing is replaced by citations to "irreconcilable differences." Likewise, the new divorce law "brackets marital roles as well," such that it remains gender neutral when considering financial support and child-rearing responsibilities. In general, the new divorce law, in keeping with the Rawlsian ideal of public reason, attempts to bracket all considerations that might be drawn from one's comprehensive doctrine (including one's religion) about which, given the fact of reasonable pluralism, there might be contention. Consequently, as guilt is increasingly eliminated in divorce proceedings and considerations of traditional gender roles are bracketed, alimony, child-support, and custody rights are assigned without the backdrop of "desert-based considerations" (1996, 110).

But, while the new divorce and family law may represent to some a laudable stride toward sexual equality, as Sandel points out, it has also "brought about economic hardship for women and children that its proponents did not foresee" (1996, 111). Statistics show that, since the enactment of these new divorce laws, divorce "brings [men] a 42 percent increase in standard of living, while divorced women and their children suffer a 73 percent decline" (1996,

111). Permanent alimony settlements have all but dwindled out of existence, and child support obligations increasingly are largely unenforced (1996, 110). Of course, a more conceptual problem hides beneath the surface. And, as Sandel points out, the problem is this: while these laws are designed to be neutral among competing comprehensive doctrines of the good, they are in fact not neutral at all.

But, in what respect are these new divorce laws not neutral? The problem is not simply that these laws have a non-neutral outcome by affecting certain people differently. That much is clear enough, though any law, regardless of its design, will likely have this effect. The problem is that these laws are not neutral in their *justification* insofar as they presuppose a morally non-neutral conception of the self. According to Sandel, underwriting these new divorce and family laws is a distinctively modern, liberal conception of the self. He says,

> [T]he provision for divorce as a unilateral decision without mutual consent, the rejection of marital roles tied to lifelong obligations, and the emphasis on self-sufficiency after divorce all reflect the liberal conception of persons as unencumbered selves independent of their roles and unbounded by moral ties they choose to reject. (1996, 112)

Written in such a way, these new family and divorce laws systematically rule out of consideration and, in turn, disadvantage those whose identities are constituted by their roles and obligations, i.e. those more traditional, situated, and "encumbered" selves. What this then means is that the new divorce laws are not, in fact, neutral with respect to comprehensive doctrines insomuch as they implicitly presuppose (and, in turn, privilege) a conception of the self as unencumbered. Rewards are attached to those selves that are consistent with this presupposed conception, and penalties are attached to those selves that are not. States Sandel:

> [T]he clear message of divorce settlements is that "women had better not forgo any of their own education, training, and career development to devote themselves fully or even partially to their families. The law assures that they will not be rewarded for their devotion, either in court or in the job market, and they will suffer greatly if their marriage dissolves." (1996, 114–115)[4]

The point in Sandel's investigation is simple: while projected as neutral among competing comprehensive doctrines, marriage and family law is neutral neither in outcome nor in justification. It is rooted in a particular comprehensive doctrine—albeit a decidedly liberal one. As Sandel suggests, the institution of marriage is itself "recast . . . in the image of the unencumbered self" (1996, 115). Meanwhile, other comprehensive doctrines, including religious doctrines, are excluded from the deliberation, legislation, and interpretation of family and divorce law. What looks like neutrality at some level amounts to systematic bias against other comprehensive doctrines.

Another interesting case in which neutrality pans out as a practically improbable goal is in the case of anti-obscenity/pornography laws. Again, in keeping with the Rawlsian vision of neutrality among comprehensive doctrines of the good, we are increasingly told by the courts that anti-obscenity/pornography laws which, are justified on moral grounds, are in violation of the First Amendment and thus unconstitutional. Interestingly, the courts continue to uphold those restrictions on obscenity and pornography; however, the justification for upholding the restrictions is supposedly fundamentally altered in such a way to meet the Rawlsian requirement of neutrality.

> In *Roth [v. United States]*, the Court based its decision on traditional moral grounds; obscenity was "utterly without redeeming social importance," and so wholly outside constitutional protection. In the 1970s, by contrast, the Court began to examine the state interest underlying obscenity laws. It upheld most of the laws, but only after attributing to them a purpose that did not involve moral judgment against obscenity as such. (1996, 76)

No longer were the laws seen as justified by appeal to some comprehensive doctrine of morality or religion according to which obscenity/pornography would be labeled morally wrong or sinful. Rather, the laws were justified by appeal to such things as "quality of life," "community environment," "tone of commerce," and public safety [as in *Paris Adult Theatre I v. Slaton* (1973)]; "preserving the character of its neighborhoods" [as in *Young v. American Mini Theaters, Inc.* (1976)]; and, so-called secondary effects related to quality of life [as in *City of Renton v. Playtime Theaters, Inc.* (1986)]. In each case, the justification for the restrictions was seen to be consistent with the demands of neutrality.

Of course, as Sandel rightly suggests, these justifications *do* involve some moral judgment which draws upon a comprehensive doctrine. As one dissenting justice claimed in the *Renton* case, "the Court allowed the city of Renton 'to conceal its illicit motives'" when it upheld anti-obscenity/pornography laws on the basis of secondary effects (1996, 78). The recognition here is that, in fact, the claim to moral neutrality was nothing short of a farcical cover-up.

The abortion debate presents us with perhaps the most interesting and contentious of issues about which the question of neutrality emerges. Political or minimalist liberals like Rawls require neutral proposals which bracket religion or other comprehensive doctrines in the public deliberation, legislation, and interpretation of laws concerning abortion. Presumably, this bracketing is for the purpose of "securing social cooperation in the face of disagreement about ends" as opposed to, say, upholding comprehensive liberal ideals such as "autonomy or individuality" (Sandel 1996, 100). However, the suspicion is that debate over this important moral question is *prima facie* skewed in a certain way, precluding certain non-liberal viewpoints. According to this line of thought, the "neutrality" claimed by liberalism starts to look more like loaded dice.

Consider *Roe v. Wade*. The Texas law prohibiting abortion was rooted in the understanding that life begins at conception. According to the Court, such justification was illegitimate inasmuch as it assumed a particular, and hence non-neutral, theory of when life begins. In the Court's estimation, this non-neutral theory was highly contentious, given the "wide divergence of thinking on this most sensitive and difficult question."[5] Consequently, compelled to seek neutrality concerning theories of when life begins, the Court struck down the Texas law as being illegitimately non-neutral. But, as Sandel points out, what the Court did was replace one theory of when life begins with another non-neutral theory of when life begins when it argued that the protection of the fetus should come at the point of viability.[6] As such, the move to bracket moral and religious considerations in the name of neutrality resulted in a non-neutral justification of the Court's ruling insofar as "the Court's decision presupposed a particular answer to the question it claimed to bracket" (1996, 101). And, such a move "den[ies] minimalist liberalism its minimalism," thereby implicating "its putatively political conception of justice in moral and philosophical commitments it seeks to avoid" (1996, 103).[7]

We should be careful at this point to understand the ramifications of Sandel's investigation. What he gives us are three poignant examples of how the claim to neutrality falls on its face. In fact, in each case, neutrality was achieved neither in the outcome of the law nor, more importantly, in the *justification* of the law. This poses serious questions to the proponents of neutrality. Neutrality is required, according to the Rawlsian proposal. But, following Sandel, it seems that we have good reasons to challenge Rawlsians to show us an example of when neutrality is ever achieved. And, following Sandel, we have reason to suppose that this is at least a difficult challenge for Rawlsians to meet.

5.2 Is Neutrality Possible?

While Sandel gives us generous reasons to be doubtful concerning the probability of neutrality—i.e. that the policies of the "procedural republic" actually are neutral concerning comprehensive doctrines—there is still a deeper concern on the table. My suspicion is that perhaps Sandel does not go far enough through the door he opens. What he shows us, definitively, is that neutrality is indeed difficult to achieve, perhaps improbable, in the most important and interesting cases in currency. But, that does not answer our second question that we asked at the outset of this chapter: Is neutrality as Rawls understands it *ever* possible? When pushed on the issue, it seems that Sandel seems to want to avoid making the claim that neutrality is *impossible*. And maybe this is for good reason. He seems to be mainly concerned with practical cases, leaving questions of possibility open. But, I want to push Sandel on this point a bit and see if we can extend his criticism of Rawlsian neutrality. Is there a flaw in the way in which Rawls understands the conditions for the possibility of neutrality? If so, then it seems that Rawls starts to lose much of the force with which he denies religion (among other comprehensive doctrines) entrance into the public square. In this section, I shall answer this second question by considering whether neutrality is itself an internally problematic doctrine—that is, whether neutrality is actually *not only improbable* in our current practice, but *impossible* as Rawls understands it.

In a 2004 public lecture,[8] Sandel argued—I think unsuccessfully—that neutrality may be possible in some cases. He gave the example of Michael Kinsley's argument that, in order for the state to remain neutral concerning matters of the good (thereby remaining neutral among competing comprehensive doctrines) in the same-sex marriage issue, the state should relegate matters of marriage to non-state institutions such as one's church or group organization (Kinsley 2003, A23). That is, according to Kinsley, the state should simply get out of the business of officially recognizing any marriage, gay or straight. While not necessarily endorsing this view, Sandel seemingly agrees that this proposal is properly neutral (and hence, liberal), insofar as the state officially brackets moral questions over marriage. Presumably, this arrangement could act as a model for properly liberal proposals and thoroughgoing neutrality of the sort that would meet the demands of the Rawlsian ideal of public reason.

Note that Kinsley's proposal is simply to remove the question of gay marriage from the public agenda and make the issue a matter for non-public civil societies. The state simply abandons the institution of marriage. In this respect, Kinsley's proposal is reminiscent of Ackerman's argument for conversational restraint: take contentious moral questions off the table for practical purposes of social cooperation (See 4.4). But is this sort of evasive proposal really neutral? Kinsley's proposal here is supposedly neutral to the extent that it makes no explicit moral claims about the nature of either gay or straight marriage. But, this claim to neutrality seems problematic. William James is helpful here. In his "Will to Believe" essay, James suggests that the moral choice concerning whether to believe or disbelieve the religious hypothesis is not one that can simply be altogether evaded. "Indeed we may wait if we will," for evidence which confirms that belief; "but if we do so, we do so at our peril as much as if we believed" (WWJ, 734). He continues, "In either case *we act*, taking our life in our hands" (WWJ, 734, emphasis added). The point we can extract from James here is this: making the decision to not even make a decision is, in fact, still a *moral* decision itself. What this means then is that, if we decide not to make any moral claims about gay marriage by simply relegating all marriages to the non-public domain, then we in fact do make a moral claim in the matter, though implicitly. The implication is that gay marriage is, *de facto*, morally equivalent to straight marriage. But, clearly, this is a contentious matter about which there is disagreement. To make such a claim—albeit an implicit claim—would be to appeal to some moral doctrine for justification. For, there is no morally neutral way of drawing a distinction between those issues that are moral questions (such that they must be pushed to the non-public domain) and those that are not. Thus, the liberal doctrine of neutrality is violated.

So, it seems that there is good reason to want to push Sandel about matters of impossibility. What he gestures to as a potentially paradigmatic case-example of possible neutrality seems problematic. However, perhaps we cannot rightly draw the conclusion that neutrality is altogether impossible by simply problematizing individual cases. A separate argument for the impossibility of the sort of neutrality required by Rawls's ideal of public reason would need to be advanced at a higher level of abstraction. Let me turn our attention in this direction.

Recall that, for Rawls, public deliberators, legislators, judges, etc. can remain neutral to the extent that they employ public reasons drawn from the political conception of justice, which is itself "freestanding" with respect to comprehensive doctrines and religions (Rawls 1996, 10). This political conception is a neutral, independent source of reasons to the extent that it is comprised of values and principles the likes of which all citizens can be expected to endorse insofar as they are drawn from a shared political culture. In this respect, the existence and availability of the political conception understood in this way is the condition for the possibility of neutrality.

The job of the political theorist, so Rawls implies, is to analyze the political culture "into its constituent ideas, and then elaborate those ideas into principles specifying the fair terms of social cooperation between citizens regarded as free and equal" (Wolterstorff 1997, 93). Once this is done properly, we will have a source of public reasons which is neutral among comprehensive doctrines. And, moreover, these public reasons can act to meet the demands of the liberal principle of legitimacy (See 3.2).

But, there is an assumption operative in Rawls's understanding of the shared political culture and, hence, in his understanding of his political conception. And, a fair amount hinges on this political conception for Rawls. As Nicholas Wolterstorff rightly points out, Rawls assumes that our shared political culture is some *ideal* type of liberal democracy (1997, 97). That is, Rawls assumes that our shared political culture is like a Platonic form of liberal democracy. What this assumption overlooks, according to Wolterstorff, is that this ideal is "nowhere fully exemplified; exemplification of the type in any particular society is never anything more than approximate" (1997, 70). Consequently, we can only say that our society, like any other, is nothing more than "*more or less* a liberal democracy" (1997, 70). Wolterstorff explains that our political culture in the United States is a "mélange of conflicting ideas," only some of which go into the composition of the ideal form of liberal democracy (1997, 97). "But, those are far from universally embraced" (1997, 97).[9] And, this seems like a point about which Wolterstorff and Sandel actually agree. As Sandel suggests, Rawls "must assume not only that the exercise of human reason under conditions of freedom will produce disagreements about the good life [i.e. concerning comprehensive doctrines] but also that the exercise of human reason under conditions of freedom will *not* produce disagreements about justice" (1998a, 204). And, clearly, the subtext to Sandel's *Democracy's Discontent* is precisely that our American political culture, at least as far as constitutional interpretation is concerned, is not (and has not been all along) some ideal form of liberal democracy. Rather there are at least two dominant yet opposing traditions of constitutional interpretation present in our actual shared political culture and history, one of which is mainly liberal, the other of which is definitively *not liberal* but civic republican. This confirms Wolterstorff's view that there is disagreement at the level of the shared political culture, which implies that the "prospect of extracting, from that political culture, principles of justice that are both *shared* and *appropriate to a liberal democracy*, is, hopeless" (1997, 97); hence the need for Rawls's illicit assumption. And, while Wolterstorff's line of criticism here is indeed positioned within the context of both his reformed epistemology and his "consocial" political philosophy (1997, 115), we need not commit ourselves to those controversial views to make use of his critique of Rawls. And, thusly, we can do without the conceptual baggage and travel more lightly.

The ramifications of this assumption on the part of Rawls are telling. If it is the case that our shared political culture is struck through with disagreement (as Wolterstorff argues and Sandel shows), then it seems that that political culture cannot yield any principles and values which *all* reasonable citizens can be expected to endorse. Recall, the political conception is identified as containing those values and principles which *all* citizens can endorse (1996, 10). But, if the shared political culture does not yield agreement (as an *ideal* liberal democracy would), then the idea of a political conception such as Rawls understands it is doomed. Because there is disagreement at the level of the shared political culture, there will likewise be disagreement at the level of the political conception, which is parasitic upon that political culture. This means that the fact of reasonable pluralism haunts even the political conception.[10] And, this further implies that there is no single source of neutral reasons from which deliberators can draw. Without identifying this source of neutrality, the conditions for the possibility of the neutrality demanded by Rawls's view of public reason are not in place. As such, it seems that an answer to our second question asked at the outset of this chapter emerges. Until the conditions for the possibility of neutrality are shown to be in place, we can suppose that neutrality, as Rawls needs it, is not possible.

5.3 Some Problems with Neutrality as a Regulative Ideal

I think, following Sandel, we have good reasons to think that neutrality is not practically probable. And, following Wolterstorff, there are good reasons to want to strengthen that claim and think that neutrality, as Rawls understands it, is not possible. Now, this might all be the case and one might still want to claim that Rawlsian neutrality ought to act as a regulative ideal in policy matters and public life in general. In fact, some interpreters of Rawls are tempted to read his requirement of neutrality in this way. Wolterstorff suggests that a charitable reading of Rawlsian public reason will lead us in this direction:

> It turns out that the idea of public reason is an ideal . . . and may never be anything more. We debate with each other with the goal in mind of discovering principles of justice that are faithful to the liberal principle of legitimacy and that we can reasonably expect all our reasonable and rational fellow citizens to endorse. We may never find them. That is acceptable. We can live with the fact that the independent source that we have identified does not, and may never, actually yield principles of the sort we thought we needed. It may be that at most what it does is eliminate certain principles. (1997, 101)

Even if this is the claim that we are left with—that neutrality is a regulative ideal which eliminates certain principles—there remain several problems with upholding neutrality in this normative light. In the remaining portion of this chapter, I shed light on three concerns: 1) that neutrality even in this sense is overly exclusive; 2) that it cripples deliberation; 3) that it is politically/pragmatically dangerous. In the following subsections, I examine these three concerns. While I do not suggest that the following represents an exhaustive list of the problems with neutrality (understood as a regulative ideal), my hope is that, by highlighting these three concerns, we can come closer to providing some answer to the third and final question asked at the outset of this chapter: Is the doctrine of neutrality desirable as a regulative ideal for the democratic public square?

5.3.1. Neutrality and the Problem of Exclusivity

In order to meet the demands of neutrality, liberal public discourse requires that deliberation be carried out in terms that are not drawn from one's comprehensive doctrine. Thus, when one enters into the public square, so to speak, one must leave at home the comprehensive doctrine to which one subscribes. This means, for the most part, that one's comprehensive doctrine is to be relegated to the non-public realm. Individuals have, according to this arrangement, two identities operative: one is private or non-public; the other is public. The non-public identity revolves around the comprehensive doctrine to which one subscribes. The public identity is formulated in such a way that brackets the scope of that comprehensive doctrine. An interesting question emerges: Is there motivation (that does not beg the question against the liberal) for citizens to participate in such potentially schizophrenic arrangements? I am not sure there is, other than the fear that if they do not, they will not be invited to the party of neutralist liberals—i.e. they will not get to fully participate in the procedural republic. To ask a person to bracket her religious considerations (or considerations drawn from one's comprehensive doctrine) on a public matter may very well be to ask a person to undo her identity as it is rooted in a comprehensive doctrine (Elshtain 2000, 20). For, there are certain types of identity (both voluntarily and involuntarily acquired) that prevent a person from maintaining separate private and public identities. (Consider, for instance, the manner in which one's religious identity requires her to take a public stance on certain public matters). Thus, to require the public/private split (which neutrality depends upon) is tantamount to excluding those with certain identities.

In order to get clear on this issue, we should back up for just a moment to investigate Rawls's notion of reasonableness. Recall that Rawls contends that the demands of legitimacy do not require the consent of unreasonable citizens—legitimacy only requires the consent of reasonable citizens. So, for instance, the consent of mad or irrational citizens is not required for legitimacy. But, what makes a citizen reasonable? According to Rawls, the root of reasonableness is the acknowledgement of the fact of reasonable pluralism. That is, a reasonable citizen understands that there are multiple comprehensive doctrines which are reasonable. As such, a citizen understands that there are other citizens with whom she disagrees concerning comprehensive doctrine who nevertheless come to hold those opposing comprehensive doctrines for good reasons. Reasonable citizens are those "ready to propose principles and standards as fair terms of cooperation and to abide by them willingly, given the assurance that others will likewise do so" (Rawls 1996, 49). What this means, then, is that reasonable citizens, pursuing such "fair terms of cooperation," will employ only those reasons which are neutral among comprehensive doctrines (since they know that reasonable citizens disagree about those); and they will "reasonably think that those citizens to whom such [reasons] are offered might also reasonably accept them" (1996, xliv). One is unreasonable, accordingly, when one demands that the terms of cooperation be drawn from one's own comprehensive doctrine. This implies, then, that it is "unreasonable . . . to want to use the sanctions of state power to correct, or to punish, those who disagree with us" (1996, 138).

Notice the odd conclusion that can be drawn from this discussion. Citizens are reasonable only when they seek to actualize Rawls's ideal of public reason. That is, reasonable citizens are those that seek to employ only neutral reasons in the course of public deliberation. But, as Robert Talisse rightly argues "this is to say that reasonable persons are necessarily political liberals. Stronger still, it is to say that *only* political liberals are reasonable persons, and that the consent of political liberals is sufficient for political legitimacy" (2005a, 59).

Let us consider an example to flesh out this point.[11] Consider a devout Christian who maintains that something or other is just only to the extent that it is decided by reference to, say, the "what would Jesus do?" principle (hereafter, WWJD).[12] What renders a state action legitimate in this person's view is the degree to which it follows the above principle. Now, if state actions are decided on any other basis than WWJD, the devout Christian will object that the state's action is unjust and thus illegitimate.

Of course, the liberal response to this fellow is fairly predictable. It is reasonable for this Christian to abide by the dictates of his comprehensive doctrine in his own personal life, that is, within the non-public domain of his own church or civil society; however, when this citizen expects state action to be dictated in accordance with his own comprehensive doctrine, he goes too far and acts unreasonably (Rawls 1996, 138). The obvious question at this point is this: is it possible for this Christian citizen to hold that it is true that justice is dictated by WWJD and yet not demand that the state should make decisions by reference to the same principle? Rawls insists that it is (1996, 138). As Rawls suggests, this Christian can affirm the truth of his comprehensive doctrine; but, if he is to be reasonable, he "must accept the proposed distinction between the political and non-political domains and must additionally subordinate the specific values associated with [his Christianity] to the 'political' values associated with the political domain" (Talisse 2005a, 60).[13]

But, Rawls's move here seems unsatisfactory. And, here's why. Our devout Christian above holds that (1) something or other is just only if it is in accordance with WWJD. Yet, he is reasonable if and only if he adopts the view (2) that the state has no obligation to pursue the WWJD principle. Thus, according to Rawls, this Christian, if he is to be reasonable, should maintain that (3) state actions can be legitimate even though they are not guided by the pursuit of justice. Talisse explains the problem in this way:

> Part of what makes [Christianity, or any other comprehensive doctrine] a comprehensive [religious] view is that it proposes *its own* conception of political justice and *its own* distinction between the political and the non-political. So whereas it is possible for someone to believe both (1) and (2), it is not possible for a [Christian] to do so. If he accepts (2) he ceases to be a [Christian]. As Rawls maintains that rejecting (2) would render the [Christian] unreasonable, it follows that, according to Rawls, [Christians] are unreasonable. (2005a, 60)

The basic point is that in order for the Christian in our example to become reasonable, in Rawls's view, he must necessarily limit the scope of the WWJD principle which is constitutive of his identity as a Christian. Of course, this alteration might not be that big of a deal for some. But, the point remains the same: to make those changes in scope is to become what we might call (following Talisse's cue) a "compromised" Christian (2005a, 60). That is, the comprehensive doctrine once held to is altered in order to meet the demands of Rawls's concept of reasonableness. Of course, we are right to ask what reasons Rawls can give this Christian for making this alteration. Reasons which do not beg the question, indeed, do not seem forthcoming.

Now, we might say that Rawls can offer a sort of *ad baculum* reason for such compromise (Talisse 2005a, 61). That reason is essentially this: alter your comprehensive doctrine or find yourself excluded from that group of reasonable citizens whose consent is necessary for political legitimacy. Let's call this Rawls's *compromise-your-comprehensive-doctrine-invitation,* or CYCDI for short. The basic point here is that if citizens wish to participate in what Marilyn Friedman calls the "legitimation pool" (2000, 16), then those citizens must make the necessary accommodations to their respective comprehensive doctrines.

Otherwise, being among the unreasonable, those citizens with uncompromised comprehensive doctrines may be *contained* so that "they do not undermine the unity and justice of society" (Rawls 1996, xvi–xvii).

Fair enough, one might say—if you want to play ball, you have to abide by the rules of the game. But, the problem runs a bit deeper for Rawls's political liberalism. To see this, it is important to understand Rawls's distinction between what he calls an "overlapping consensus" and a *"modus vivendi"* (1996, 145). A *modus vivendi* can be thought of as a truce of sorts. Neither party gets exactly what they want, so they agree to terms that each can live with, so long as the balance of power remains the way it is. So, while one may want the public square to be defined in terms completely consistent with one's own comprehensive doctrine, recognizing the difficultly of achieving this might lead one to agree to liberalism as a digestible compromise. But, this sort of *modus vivendi* agreement is not sufficient to uphold political liberalism, according to Rawls, for "social unity is only apparent, as its stability is contingent on circumstances remaining such as not to upset the fortunate convergence of interests" (1996, 145).[14] The stability of a *modus vivendi* depends in part upon "happenstance and a balance of relative forces" (1996, 148). This consideration leads Rawls to argue that his political liberalism must be the focus of an overlapping consensus, in order to attain "stability for the right reasons" (1996, xliii). This sort of consensus is where "all those who affirm the political conception start from within their own comprehensive view" (1996, 147) and eventually come to "support the political conception for its own sake, or on its own merits" (1996, 148).

That Rawls requires this overlapping consensus reveals the reason why it is problematic to offer his CYCDI. If one heeds this CYCDI in order to join the legitimation pool, then one has not started from within the perspective of one's own comprehensive doctrine. Thus, even though one may come to affirm the political conception in heeding this CYCDI invitation, one has not done it in a way that would give Rawls the overlapping consensus he desires. At best then, this leaves Rawls with a mere *modus vivendi* agreement concerning his political conception (and hence his liberalism), which, *on his own terms*, just will not do, for it is "political in the wrong way" (1996, 142). At this point, the specter of instability looms large.

Recognizing this problem concerning the operation of the public/non-public split required by Rawls's notion of reasonableness reveals the elitism latent within a theory of democracy that would seek to impose neutrality requirements, as does Rawls's separatist view of public reason. While the former is a conceptual problem internal to Rawls's own theory, the latter is a sociological one concerning the way in which a theory such as Rawls operates in our society. It is a well-established, sociological fact that Americans are largely religious. However, our forums of deliberation—from our schools and universities to our town hall meetings to the Supreme Court (as Sandel shows)—are increasingly fashioned according to the Rawlsian vision. What does this say about the model of deliberation handed down to us from neutralist liberals? For one, it tells us that, in fact, ideas do have consequences. As Richard John Neuhaus (1984) rightly suggests, we are told by neutralist liberals that when we *really* look at it, we can see that our shared political culture is a secular and neutral territory from which can derive the political conception which is to be the source of our neutral reasons to be used in public deliberation.[15] Guided by this myopic view of the political culture, liberal intellectuals construct theories of democracy upon a doctrine of neutrality sensitive to this narrow vision of the shared political culture. This, of course, overlooks the sociological reality of our American landscape. This convenient disregard results in the elitism of neutralist liberal theories. Many of those to whom a democratic government should be legitimized (i.e. many within the *whole* citizenry) are summarily overlooked. Rather, according to Rawlsian theories, public policy and the actions of the state do not need to be seen as legitimate to the whole citizenry, but only to a select elite of the citizenry—the "reasonable" according to the Rawlsian definition, i.e. political liberals. But, as we have seen, this definition of "reasonable" tends to exclude a great number of religious Americans. So, we are told, either those citizens (i.e. those holding to certain comprehensive doctrines) must change something fundamental to their identities, or be left out of the legitimation pool. At this point a crucial question emerges: how is this sort of elitist view compatible with an inclusive and participatory democracy?

5.3.2. Neutrality and the Crippling of Deliberation

The doctrine of neutrality required by the Rawlsian view of public reason effectively limits the sort of reasons that can be introduced into and the sort of issues that can be discussed in the course of public deliberation. This may be good for public deliberation, according to the Rawlsian theorist, as it allows for less heat on seemingly endless and interminable matters of deep disagreement.[16] But this too is wrong. The truth is: we do not know until we give it a shot.[17] It may very well be the case that liberal *ex ante* conversational restraints prevent us from considering a wide range of reasons on a wide variety of topics. Consequently, such restraints on deliberation may act to cripple the forum of deliberation itself. In this section, I shall consider two threats posed to public deliberation by the *ex ante* conversational restraints required by the doctrine of neutrality. First, there is the concern that such restraints will render deliberation impotent and inconclusive on a number of fundamental matters. The second concern is that such restraints will calcify public deliberation itself, thereby precluding the democratizing capacity of the self-reflexive mechanism of more inclusive models of deliberation.

5.3.2.1. The Problem of Indeterminacy
Rawls admits that the neutralist restraints of his public reason may not always leave citizens able to determinately and conclusively decide a number of political questions (1996, 215). Yet he does insist that, when fundamental matters (i.e.

constitutional essential and questions of basic justice) are at stake, public deliberation entertained under the neutralist terms of his public reason will be able to yield determinate and conclusive results. David Reidy argues forcefully that Rawls fails to "show what his account of public reason requires him to show, namely that the content of public reason will prove rich enough to enable the majority of citizens to reach a determinate and reasoned resolution of such [fundamental] issues without appeal to non-public reasons" (2000, 64, fn. 17). In many cases, Reidy contends, the political values of public reason—i.e. those supposedly neutral reasons drawn only from the political conception of justice—stand in competition. When deliberating issues like affirmative action, human cloning, prostitution, pornography, or euthanasia, the liberal political values like "individual liberty, happiness, political equality, equality of opportunity, distributive justice, social stability, the orderly reproduction of political society, fraternity, openness and honesty in government, economic prosperity, social diversity, liberal democratic citizenship, the common defense, the general welfare and cultural vibrancy often conflict and compete with one another" (2000, 65). This means, of course, that public reason is unable to yield the sort of conclusions it needs, unless those values can be prioritized by deliberators according to some "criteria found within liberal public reason itself" (2000, 65). This may not be as possible as Rawls would have us believe, according to Reidy. This is because many citizens will find no way to order these competing political values precisely because "no such criterion or criteria may be extracted from common sense modes of reasons, non-controversial facts of science and the like" (2000, 65). This leaves only two options. Deliberators and officials can order competing values by appeal either to some non-public comprehensive doctrine or to "some special and well-developed faculty of moral intuition or judgment" (2000, 66). Thus, either the neutrality of public reason generates indeterminacy and inconclusiveness, or public reason itself must be altered (so as to allow for some appeal to non-public reasons) in such a way as to violate the liberal doctrine of neutrality. Hence it turns out that, according to Reidy, Rawlsian public reason is "heteronomous and incomplete" (2000, 63).

Reidy further contends that there are a number of other issues about which Rawlsian public reason, again guided by the doctrine of neutrality, will prove indeterminate. These issues cannot be resolved by public reason not because they require the ordering of competing political values, but because they require the resolution of "a crucial preliminary or background issue with respect to which public reason is silent or inconclusive" (2000, 69). Instead, the resolution of this background issue requires the use of non-public, and hence non-neutral, sorts of reasons. For example, whether humans have property rights with respect to animals hinges upon "how animals are viewed in moral and political terms in the wild" (2000, 69). But, again, public reason proves inconclusive when these sorts of questions are being asked. Reidy argues,

> While many citizens view animals in the wild as something like the common property of humans who have collective dominion over them, this view cannot

be justified without appeal to non-public reasons. It is true, of course, that there are good and sufficient reasons within liberal public reason for prohibiting animal cruelty. And there may even be good and sufficient reasons for prohibiting the capture of higher primates and perhaps some other species for the sole purpose of display in zoos for the pleasure of humans. But what about the capture or ownership of higher primates of other species for the purposes of medical research? Here, it seems, there is no avoiding the deepest aspects of the moral status question with respect to such animals. But liberal public reason by itself cannot resolve it, since it is indeterminate or incomplete in the matter. (2000, 69)

What Reidy shows us is that public reason, when guided by the liberal doctrine of neutrality, proves itself incapable of producing the sorts of results it was designed to produce. Rawlsian public reason, because it prohibits the employment of comprehensive doctrines within the forum of political deliberation, is unable to come to any determinate conclusions on a great number of fundamental matters as well as many background issues relevant for deciding certain other political issues. Public deliberation then, if limited by the conversational restraints of neutralist liberals, is rendered impotent and, for the most part, useless.

5.3.2.2. The Self-Reflexive Problem

A second sort of problem emerges for the deliberation of public policy when limited by the restraints of the doctrine of neutrality. Roughly stated, the problem is that public deliberation will be unable to revise itself in any meaningful way precisely because the conditions for the possibility of deliberation about the nature of deliberation itself are not in place within the Rawlsian, neutralist view of public reason. Recall that the doctrine of neutrality prohibits citizens from drawing upon their respective comprehensive doctrines when entering the public square. In an attempt to approximate Rawls's regulative ideal of public reason, deliberators are expected to restrict themselves to the employment of those reasons and values (drawn from the political conception) which are shared and hence public. Effectively, the *ex ante* conversational restraints imposed by the doctrine of neutrality establishes *from the outset* the parameters within which deliberation can take place. These parameters rule certain sorts of reasons and conversational topics out of bounds. But, notice that such a pre-setting of the parameters of public deliberation undermines the possibility of public deliberation concerning how public deliberation should itself look. For, any such second-order public deliberation, under the Rawlsian view, would have to be carried out within the boundaries of neutralist restraints. As such, any second-order type of public deliberation would merely re-confirm and reflect the pre-established boundaries of public deliberation at the first-order. This means that the possibility of deliberatively revising the parameters of public deliberation is effectively precluded altogether. Because of the formal *ex ante* neutralist restraints, Rawls's view of public reason is incapable of self-reflexive alteration.

Insofar as Rawlsian public reason defines the nature of the game at the outset, it prohibits any robust challenge to the rules already established.

A number of thinkers have pointed out this problem with the Rawlsian view of public reason (Benhabib 1992 and 1996; Mouffe 2000; Rautenfield 2004). James Bohman, for instance, argues that, given the absence of this self-reflexive mechanism in the neutralist liberal conception of pubic deliberation, such a forum of public deliberation is not poised to address the reality of cultural minorities and social inequalities present within a pluralistic society (1996, 82). This is in large part due to the fact that the *ex ante* conversational restraints prevent the full participation of those critical of the manner in which deliberation currently takes place by "restrict[ing] the scope of opinion" (1996, 203). Bohman continues,

> Not only existing rules and procedures, but also many of the biases and blind spots of current forms of deliberation favor the most effective and advantaged members of the public. If the public is to see such biases and limitations and undertake to correct them, critics and other actors must convince them that their public reasons are in fact non-public and thus not answerable to others. (1996, 203)

Critics, then, must be able to pose a "reflexive challenge to the normative framework for deliberation" (Bohman 2003, 771). In order to do so, critics must be able to step outside the restraints of neutrality and "unblock dialogue by changing the conditions of communication" (Bohman 1996, 203). Otherwise, the concern is that the problems relevant to and the solutions proposed by certain marginalized groups will not be able to enter into the public discussion, as they are deemed out of bounds from the outset. This sort of challenge leveled by the critic "asks citizens to rethink the very nature of the democracy in which they live" (Bohman 2003, 771). Rethinking the nature of forums of deliberation—and hence the democracy itself—is vital to "self-correction and continual self-transformation." And, without such an openness to revision, our forums of public deliberation—and our democracy itself—run the risk of not being very democratic.

Bohman points out an example of how this self-reflexive mechanism promotes and strengthens democracy.

> Racism has historically been a direct manifestation of power. American Constitutional law abounds with statements about political equality, yet these statements were for decades interpreted as consistent with both slavery and the restricted political status of women. Abolitionists ultimately succeeded in bringing new interpretations into public debate, often by insisting that religious and philosophical doctrines invoked in the Constitution did not sanction slavery. By mobilizing themselves into a public movement, abolitionists challenged the prevailing interpretative framework sufficiently to bring new moral intuitions into the public debate; the public reinterpretation of norms brought into play the dialogical mechanism of reflective equilibrium. Such a hermeneutic

process of retrieving aspects of America's political traditions and democratic culture eventually became even deeper as other excluded groups entered the public sphere and advanced their own interpretations of shared moral intuitions. (1996, 117)

Notice that, in this telling example, the self-reflexive mechanism of public deliberation was activated by the appeal to religious doctrine. Such an appeal acted to call the forum of public deliberation into question, thereby opening up the space for further broadened pubic deliberation. Under the Rawlsian view of public reason, however, such an appeal to comprehensive doctrine would be prohibited from the outset.[18] As such, the doctrine of neutrality would have prevented the challenge leveled by Abolitionists and the subsequent democratization that followed from that challenge.

Both Reidy and Bohman show us that the doctrine of neutrality, when implemented within public deliberation, threatens to incapacitate public deliberation itself. As Reidy shows, the doctrine of neutrality likely yields indeterminacy in public deliberation. That is, public deliberation, entertained under neutralist terms, cannot produce the sorts of results it is designed to produce. Effectively, this means that the forum in which citizens are to deliberate on how best to govern themselves is impotent; the central tool of democracy is blunted. Similarly, Bohman shows us that the doctrine of neutrality threatens to shut down the self-reflexive mechanism by which the very nature of the democracy is revised and expanded. Both show us that the doctrine of neutrality puts the Rawlsian view of public reason at odds with vital participatory democracy.

5.3.3. Neutrality and the Problem of Polarization

There is a third problem that haunts the Rawlsian doctrine of neutrality upheld as a regulative ideal. This problem stems from the fact that the doctrine of neutrality as required by the Rawlsian view of public reason (which would exclude certain religions from the public domain) poses the threat of group polarization, particularly among religious groups. In a nutshell, the contention is that, if citizens are not allowed to discuss what they want to discuss and *in their own voice*, they will, if trends persist, find their own enclave audience. And, this usually leads to polarization. Such polarization poses very practical threats to political stability.

With an eye toward the relevant social-scientific research, Cass Sunstein (1993; 2001; 2002; 2003) has done much to draw attention to the reality of group polarization. He describes group polarization in the following way: "group polarization means that members of a deliberating group predictably move toward a more extreme point in the direction indicated by the members' predeliberation tendencies" (2002, 176). According to Sunstein, this sort of polarization is driven chiefly by two factors. First, members of a particular deliberating group, driven by a desire to socially identify with the group, tend to want to be viewed favorably by the other members of the group. As such, the tendency is for individuals to adapt one's view such that it is consistent with the general position espoused by the deliberating group at large. The result is twofold: individuals tend toward the view generally held by the group; and, the view of the group, as a consequence, tends to become more extreme (2002, 179). Second, given that the group deliberation is a sort of "enclave deliberation," where only members identifying with the group at large participate in the deliberation, "argument pools" tend to be limited in size (2002, 176–177). This has the effect of limiting the sorts of arguments heard and entertained during the course of deliberation. As such, according to Sunstein:

> Because a group whose members are already inclined in a certain direction will have a disproportionate number of arguments supporting that same direction, the result of discussion will be to move individuals further in the direction of their initial inclinations. The key is the existence of a limited argument pool, one that is skewed . . . in a particular direction. (2002, 180)

By contrast, according to Sunstein, groups will tend in the opposite direction—that is, toward depolarization—when deliberation includes "equally opposed subgroups" such that the argument pools are enlarged (2002, 180). Guided by the recognition of this trend, Sunstein argues for the inclusion of dissenting voices within forums of deliberation, such that a "culture of free speech" can be realized (2003, 112).

Talisse (2005b) has drawn out many of the interesting implications of Sunstein's findings concerning group polarization as they relate to Rawls's view of public reason. According to the Rawlsian model of public deliberation, reasons drawn from, and matters of, comprehensive doctrines are relegated to the nonpublic realm in order to abide by the doctrine of neutrality. In this respect, Rawlsian public reason generates deliberative enclaves. This is because "public reason *cannot* countenance a public deliberative space in which these fundamental issues can be reasonably engaged" (Talisse 2005b, 114). Such reasons and matters of comprehensive doctrine are to belong to non-public domains. So, for instance, the religious believer who opposes abortion on religious grounds is told that such reasoning is only appropriate within the "background culture" of one's church or civil society. Talisse argues:

> Believing, correctly, that there is no point in raising their arguments in public, they will likely form small groups devoted to the advancement of their position; these groups will meet regularly to discuss the group's views and devise strategies for disseminating their message. Conditions will be ripe for polarization. As the groups polarize, individuals will not only come to hold more extreme versions of their initial position, but will come to see themselves as excluded, victimized, and oppressed; naturally, they will also grow increasingly dismissive of opposing views, and will regard those that affirm them as either evil or benighted. (Talisse 2005b, 114)

The ramifications of both Sunstein's and Talisse's investigation are as clear as they are important in trying to determine whether the doctrine of neutrality, understood as a regulative ideal, is desirable. What both Sunstein and Talisse show is that there are significant reasons to suppose that, if trends persists, group polarization will ensue if public deliberation is carried out under the terms of Rawlsian public reason, which is guided by the regulative ideal of the doctrine of neutrality. This may potentially result in the encouragement of religious or other forms of fanaticism extremism. And, this threatens "precisely the kind of instability Rawls sought to avoid" in articulating the need for an overlapping consensus as opposed to a *modus vivendi* (Talisse 2005b, 114). Moreover, this kind of extremism may lead to the kind of instability "associated with hatred and violence" (Talisse 2005b, 114; cf. Sunstein 2003, 12).

5.4 Conclusion

What I attempted to show in this chapter is that the doctrine of neutrality is bankrupt, both as a descriptive and as a normative proposition.[19] And, because this is the case, strategies to conceptualize a relationship between religion and the public square guided by the doctrine of neutrality are highly problematized. What this means is that the separatist proposals of neutralist liberals fail insofar as they rely upon a theoretically and practically problematic neutralist politics. Separatists, like Rawls and other neutralist liberals, explicitly require a neutral public reason. And, although I geared my criticism of neutrality primarily against liberal neutrality, it may very well be the case that acknowledging the failure of neutrality *as such* also indicts reconstructivist proposals as well to the degree that those proposals depend upon a neutral way of semantically reconstructing religion such that it can be integrated into public life. Ultimately, I hope to have provided in this chapter a useful moment in which to step back and note a main point of departure with the Rawlsian paradigm of public reason underwritten by the doctrine of neutrality. Doing so is a necessary move in the direction of my own positive thesis. I asked three questions at the outset of this chapter: Is neutrality ever achieved (5.1)? Is it possible as Rawlsian liberals conceive it (5.2)? Is it desirable as a regulative ideal for political justification (5.3)? I have shown how the critical insights of a variety of thinkers—from civic republicans and communitarians to reformed epistemologists to contemporary deliberative democrats—can be uncoupled from their accompanying positive commitments, organized and recombined in a multidimensional manner that illustrates the flaws to the mainstream liberal treatments of religious participation in the political domain.

Notes

1. I lift the term "naked public square" from Neuhaus 1984.
2. I should note that the "liberal-communitarian" label is not altogether an unproblematic label for this debate. Sandel (1998b), for instance, expresses some queasiness about this label with respect to his own project.
3. See the essays contained in Allen and Regan, eds., 1998 for debate over much of Sandel's own positive public philosophy.
4. Here Sandel is quoting sociologist Lenore Weitzman.
5. *Roe v. Wade* Court cited in Sandel 1996, 101. See Wertheimer 1974 concerning the divergence in our conceptions of the fetus.
6. Sandel quotes the Court: "With respect to the State's important and legitimate interest in potential life, the 'compelling' point is at viability. This is so because the fetus then presumably has the capability of meaningful life outside the mother's womb. State regulation protective of fetal life after viability thus has both logical and biological justifications" (1996, 101).
7. Cf. to Reidy: "While [Rawls] is certainly correct that liberal political values bear on abortion issues, some of these cannot be decided without taking a stand on the moral status of the fetus. But public reason is inconclusive here. Rawls seems to suggest that, like the Court in *Roe v. Wade*, citizens and officials should undertake to resolve abortion issues within public reason without fully determining the moral status of the fetus: but it cannot be avoided. To proceed as Rawls suggests is just indirectly, covertly and without public justification to adopt a particular resolution of this question" (2000, 70).
8. "Rawls, Liberalism, and Justice" presented at Vanderbilt University on January 26, 2004, as a part of the Legacy of John Rawls Public Lecture Series. The discussion below draws on the question and answer session following the lecture.
9. Wolterstorff: "Current controversies about the rights of practice homosexuals and about the propriety and legitimacy of prayers in the public schools are illustrative examples. On these particular issues, the Idea of liberal democracy yield clear conclusions: homosexuals should enjoy equal freedom under law to live their lives as they see fit, and state sponsored schools should not include prayers as an official part of the school program. Yet large numbers of Americans see otherwise" (1997, 97).
10. Recall that Rawls says that reason will lead free and equal citizens to affirm some liberal conception of justice. However, this does not mean that all will embrace his own preferred version, i.e. justice as fairness. This indicates, according to Gaus (2003), that Rawls must admit that reasonable pluralism resides at the level of even political conceptions. "At only the most abstract level—the level of the very concept of a liberal order—does Rawls indicate that the exercise of the powers of human reason produces agreement. At a more specific level—and by 'specific' here, I mean something as abstract as justice as fairness—our use of reason leads to reasonable disagreement" (Gaus 2003, 192).
11. The following discussion draws heavily from Talisse 2005a, 60, though with alterations to fit the concern of this book.
12. One needs only to note the recent popularity of the "WWJD?"—what would Jesus do?—bracelets to see that this is not an entirely farcical example. Notice that I am describing the WWJD principle here as a decision-rule as opposed to describing it as a standard which must be satisfied. For, it may be the case that a policy proposed by a utilitarian is consistent with what Jesus would do but is not decided by reference to a consid-

eration of what Jesus would do but rather by reference to the maximum happiness principle.

13. Wolfe (1995) presents sociological research which suggests that middle-class religious Americans increasingly understand their religion as a mainly personal matter. Commenting on Wolfe's research, Elshtain writes, "They seem to have struck a tacit bargain with themselves that goes like this: If I am quiet about what I believe and everybody else is quiet about what he or she believes, then nobody will interfere with the rights of anybody else. But this is precisely what real believers, whether political or religious or both, cannot do: keep quiet" (2000, 19). While it may be true that many religious citizens are increasing viewing their religion as a private matter, the question is whether doing so has made an alteration on the content of the religion that has been privatized.

14. For more discussion on the instability of *modus vivendi* agreement, see Gaus 2003, esp. chapter three.

15. See Neuhaus 1984, particularly chapter thirteen, for this point.

16. Cf. Dombrowski: "Politics and religion are, as a recent president of the American Philosophical Association has put it, a dangerous mixture; combining them, even in an academic context, is likely to generate more heat than light" (2001, 1).

17. Cf. to Sandel: "Whether it is possible to reason our way to agreement on any given moral or political controversy is not something we can know until we try" (1998a, 210-211).

18. Rawls, then, violates C.S. Peirce's recommendation to not block the road to further inquiry. Cf. to the discussion in Chapter Three, where I argue that Rorty's proposal acts as a conversation-stopper.

19. It may be the case that non-neutralist liberal proposals such as Raz 1968; Sher 1997; Taylor 1994; Gutmann 1987; and Macedo 1990 might be able to get past some of the issues that have been identified.

Chapter Six

Public Deliberation After Rawls: Stout's Contribution and Instructive Shortcoming[1]

In the last chapter, I showed that the doctrine of neutrality is thoroughly problematic both as a descriptive and normative proposition and, as such, cannot yield a viable strategy to conceptualize the proper relationship between religion and the democratic public square. Hence, the Rawlsian view of public reason and the separatism entailed by that view will not suffice. Given the failure of the Rawlsian project, I turn our attention in this chapter toward a very recent and increasingly important contribution to the debate concerning the relationship between religion and democracy found in the work of Jeffrey Stout. His *Democracy and Tradition* (2004a) is an interesting attempt in political theology—one that draws considerable influence from the classical American pragmatist tradition—to be thinking *after* Rawls, so to speak, and it has been the focus of considerable attention since its publication.[2] He recognizes many of the problems facing the mainstream neutralist liberal view, prompting him to propose an "alternative understanding of public reasoning" (2004a, 10). Like Rawls, Stout correctly understands that one of the most important questions for contemporary political thinkers is roughly this: What should public deliberation in a pluralist society such as ours look like? And although he is still working within the Rawlsian problematic, Stout attempts to approach this question differently than does Rawls. Whereas the Rawlsian strategy, as we have seen, is animated by the doctrine of neutrality, Stout's project surrenders such a framework and is driven instead by a genealogical account of the secularization of public discourse. By making this conceptual shift, Stout presents us with a much different view of public deliberation—and hence a different strategy to conceptualize the proper relationship between religion and the democratic public square—than is given to us by neutralist Rawlsian liberals. In this chapter, I examine Stout's proposed alternative to the Rawlsian view—what I call "Stout's New View of Public Reason"—highlighting along the way what Stout takes to be the main improvements he is making on the Rawlsian model he means to be moving beyond. While he laudably makes certain moves in the right direction, I contend that there remains a fundamental tension in Stout's view which prevents it from making as much progress as he would wish. Identifying his shortcoming, then, will be instructive as doing so will help reveal not only what Stout contributes to this discourse, but also what moves need to be taken in the future when attempting to conceptualize the proper relationship between religion and democratic citizenship.

6.1 Stout's New View of Public Reason

Stout contends that the Rawlsian view of public reason—even allowing for the proviso—is simply too restrictive upon the kinds of reasons that can be admitted into public deliberation. Agreeing with Wolterstorff, such Rawlsian restrictions upon religion seem incompatible with the spirit of liberal democracy, where citizens enjoy equal protection under law to express themselves freely (2004a, 68). Consequently, Stout contends, "we ought to reframe the question of religion's role in political discussion in quite different terms" (2004a, 70). A better and more properly liberal view of public reason is less restrictive upon religion. "All democratic citizens should feel free," Stout writes, "to express whatever premises actually serve as reasons for their claims" (2004a, 10). If an element of a citizen's religion actually serves as his reason for supporting a particular public policy or candidate, then that religious reason should be admitted into the forum of public deliberation. When it comes to how religion should factor into public deliberation, Stout advises us: "say what you please" (2004a, 85). And, on the face of it, this permissiveness toward religion puts Stout's new view at stark contrast with Rawlsian separatist view.

Predictably, this permissiveness sounds quite dangerous to Rawlsian liberals. For, admitting religious reasons into public deliberation seems to introduce terms which are not acceptable to all parties included, given the fact of reasonable pluralism. So the Rawlsian story goes, admitting religious reasons results in a style of deliberating which does not respect all parties as free and equal participants, as some citizens do not recognize the religious reasons employed as, in fact, *reasons*. And, under such arrangements the demands of the liberal principle of legitimacy cannot be met. This leaves Rawlsians wondering how we are to avoid all out religious war if such permissiveness is allowed. Does such permissiveness not leave us with nothing less than what MacIntyre labels a "civil war carried on by other means"? (MacIntyre 1984, 253). As Rawls asks, if we do not impose such restrictions upon religion in public deliberation, "what's the alternative?" (Rawls 1998, 620).[3]

Stout believes that he can answer Rawls's question by presenting a viable alternative. He argues that Rawls mistakenly sees the employment of religious reasons as a form of disrespect. This is because, according to Stout, Rawls's conception of respect is inadequate and flawed. According to Rawls, a citizen shows respect for her interlocutors by employing reasons which they too will endorse as reasons. But, the problem with this Rawlsian conception of respect, according to Stout, is that it "neglects the ways in which one can show respect for another person in his or her particularity" (2004a, 72). Rather than view respect as a function of one's attempt to draw reasons from some neutral political conception, Stout recommends (following Wolterstorff)[4] that we adopt a conception of respect which is constituted by an attempt to understand, to take seriously, and to engage "the distinctive point of view *each* other occupies" (2004a, 73). Respect in this sense is a respect for individuality and difference inherent to the perspective of each deliberator. Stout contends that the "respect for others that civility requires is most fully displayed in the kind of exchange where each person's deepest commitments can be recognized for what they are and assessed accordingly" (2004a, 10). However, what respect does not require under Stout's view is for a citizen to bracket what she takes to be her actual reasons in public deliberation. As such, no moral injunctions against religious reasoning are required.

Of course, the objection to this permissiveness and the related conception of respect comes from those who wonder how deliberation can move forward if, in fact, there is not firm reliance upon common or shared reasons drawn, say, from some shared political conception (as Rawls has in mind) or some such neutral source.[5] Stout thinks that the idea that conversation (and hence public deliberation) *always* requires the employment of neutral reasons is misguided. Such a view underestimates the important role that *immanent criticism* can play in moving conversation forward. On Stout's view, immanent criticism takes place when deliberators "either try to show that their opponents' views are incoherent, or they try to argue positively from their opponents' religious premises to the conclusion that the proposal [in question] is acceptable" (2004a, 69). What is important about this idea of immanent criticism is that the deliberator, guided by Stout's conception of respect, attempts to hear the opposing interlocutor out and engage that interlocutor on his own terms. By adopting the perspective of her interlocutor for the purposes of discussion, the immanent critic can hope to criticize her interlocutor's proposals from within his own view. This form of conversation differs from the form of deliberation implied by Rawls's view of public reason insofar as immanent critics are not attempting to "argue from a purportedly common basis or reasons in Rawls's sense" (Stout 2004a, 69). As such, immanent criticism provides a model of conversation which is not animated by the doctrine of neutrality implicit in the Rawlsian paradigm.

The significance of immanent criticism for Stout is that it affords us a viable way of advancing the conversation when faced with certain dialogical impasses.

We know that in a pluralistic society such as ours, citizens have different perspectives when it comes to matters of religion. So, we might wonder what should happen when a certain policy is proposed by a group of religious citizens and other deliberators ask for reasons why such a policy should be adopted. Commenting on his view of immanent criticism, Stout says:

> Suppose their [the group of religious citizens] actual motivating reasons are religious ones not widely shared among their fellow citizens, and it is clear that some citizens, employing their own reasonably held collateral commitments as premises, would be entitled to reject them. In that case, there appear to be three options: (1) to remain silent; (2) to give justifying arguments based strictly on principles already commonly accepted; and (3) to express their actual (religious) reasons for supporting the policy they favor while also engaging in immanent criticism. (2004a, 88)

According to Stout, option (1) and (2) may, in fact, not be open to us. For, it may be the case the severity of the situation at hand precludes option (1). And, it may well be the case that option (2) is either too "difficult or impossible to pursue" precisely because those principles already commonly accepted "when conjoined with factual information accessible to the citizenry as a whole, do not entail a resolution of the issue" (2004a, 88).[6] Faced with the threat of either ignoring a real problem or leaving it unresolved pushes (3) to the surface as the best option, at least in some circumstances. For, according to Stout, the "political discourse of a pluralistic democracy, as it turns out, needs to be a mixture" of what he calls "normal conversation" which proceeds from premises and principles already commonly accepted combined with the sort of "conversational improvisation" implied by immanent criticism.

Stout's New View of Public Reason also seeks to recognize the importance of what we might think of as conversational virtues. These virtues are those habits and dispositions which act to guide citizens "through the process of discursive exchange and political decision making (2004a, 85). A list of such virtues includes things like "civility;" the willingness and "ability to listen with an open mind" to others; the "will to pursue justice where it leads;" the "temperance to avoid taking and causing offense needlessly;" "practical wisdom to discern the subtleties of a discursive situation;" and the "courage to speak candidly" among others (2004a, 85). These virtues are important insofar as they ought to guide those participating in public deliberation, particularly those offering religious reasons.

Let us sum up before moving forward: Stout's New View of Public Reason contains at least three main components.

1) Permissiveness toward the employment of religious reasons in public deliberation
2) The advocacy of immanent criticism as a style of deliberation
3) The recognition of the importance of conversational virtues

6.2 Secularization and Prudential Constraint

Initially, it appears as though Stout gives us a strikingly new view of public reason. And, indeed, much of Stout's energy is geared toward diagnosing and rectifying the problems facing Rawls's view of public reason, especially with respect to the relationship between religion and public deliberation. For reasons explained in the previous chapters of this book, I find Stout's aims perfectly laudable, and I am largely sympathetic both to his critique of Rawlsian neutrality and to the direction his wishes to push the debate. But, upon closer examination, it is not clear that Stout's attempt to move beyond Rawls's view of public reason is altogether successful. For, what Stout presents as his new view of public reason actually stands in conflict with other things that he has to say about his own view, namely his take on the secularization of public discourse. Exposing this conflict in Stout's view of public reason leaves us with the suspicion that his view is ultimately susceptible to many of the very same problems facing the Rawlsian view. In order to see this line of criticism, we should first consider how Stout's account of secularization and resentment factors into his view of public reason.

In part, Stout attempts to present a view of public reason that religious citizens can come to embrace without resentment. Central to his view of the proper role of religion in public deliberation is his historically informed genealogy of the development of secularized public ethical discourse. On Stout's account, we are mistaken when we suppose that secularized public ethical discourse is (as some critics of liberalism suppose) the result of anti-religious, liberal impositions. He claims that, "Secularization was not primarily brought about by the triumph of secularist ideology, 'first constructed,' as [John] Milbank puts it, 'in the discourses of liberalism'" (2004a, 102). Rather, the secularized public forum developed *among* religious thinkers who saw that they were "not in a position to take for granted that their [religious] interlocutors are making the same religious assumptions they are" (2004a, 97). Hence, the impetus for secularization was not to undermine or do away with religion, but "the increasing need to cope with religious plurality discursively on a daily basis under circumstances where improved transportation and communication were changing the political and economic landscape" (2004a, 102). So, for instance, even among those early modern religious thinkers who viewed the Christian Bible as an authoritative text with respect to political matters, there remained among them disagreement as to what that Bible says, what it implies, who gets to interpret it, whether it is the only source of normative insight, and who gets to "resolve apparent conflicts between it and other putative sources of normative insight" (2004a, 93). Because of these points of disagreement, religious thinkers involved in political discussion increasingly shunned appeals to biblical authority as a way of resolving ethical and political matters. "The reason was simple," Stout tells us—"the appeal did not work" (2004a, 94).

Thus, Stout claims, the secularized forum of contemporary public deliberation is neither necessarily foreign to religious thinkers (given that it developed *among* them) nor is it necessarily hostile to them. "Secularization in this sense is not a reflection of commitment to *secularism*" (2004a, 93). And given this, Stout argues, it is worrisome that some of the most important religious thinkers like Richard John Neuhaus, John Milbank, Alasdair MacIntyre, and Stanley Hauerwas either express lamentation concerning the secular public square or, even worse, advocate the refusal of the secular. These thinkers, according to Stout, manifest a sort of distasteful resentment toward secularized public discourse. But, Stout asks, "if theological premises . . . receive little discursive attention for this perfectly understandable reason [i.e. they do not work], why would anyone have just cause for resentment of the resulting type of secularized discourse?" (2004a, 99). The resulting resentment of secularized public deliberation, Stout explains, is effectively "resentment of religious diversity" (2004a, 99).

Clearly Stout means to be distancing himself from these theologians of resentment. Stout seems to suppose, not unlike Rawls, that religious pluralism is not only a sociological fact at present, but that it is some sort of permanent fixture of reality.[7] Therefore, it is simply fruitless to resist this inevitable element of reality in adopting an orientation of resentment. Of course, we can imagine the retort that the theologians of resentment might have: granted, we now have religious plurality, but given enough time, energy, and resources, who is to say that one of those religions will not prove itself to be the most reasonable? It is conceivable, in other words, that the *vera religione* will, in fact, prove triumphant. Hence, so the theologians of resentment might claim, the problem with Stout's view is that religious pluralism is taken to be some sacrosanct fixture of permanence that is both inevitable and silly to resent.

Let us for the moment simply grant Stout's account of secularization and that religious diversity is a near-permanent fixture in our pluralistic society. Still, it is not exactly clear why religious citizens should be motivated to accept secularized public discourse *without resentment*. Granted, religious diversity may be here to stay. But, why should religious citizens *not* resent the secularization of public discourse (that stems from religious diversity) and simply continue—albeit resentfully—to say what they please in public discourse? Stout's answer seems to be pragmatic: such resentment simply gets us nowhere. He writes, "[T]here is no point in trying to wish the social reality of religious diversity away, or in resenting this diversity as long as it lasts" (2004a, 100). Resentment will simply lead to further frustration. If a citizen resentfully employs religious reasons in secularized public discourse, she will be faced with the frustrating reality that her religious reasons simply will not work to convince her interlocutors in the public square. In a society such as ours, Stout claims, there tends to be inevitable and irresolvable disagreement concerning religious matters. And, it is for this reason, according to Stout, that religious appeals carry little weight in public deliberation. He writes,

And this consequence of theological plurality has an enormous impact on what our ethical discourse is like. It means, for example, that in most contexts it will simply be *imprudent*, rhetorically speaking, to introduce explicitly theological premises into an argument intended to persuade a religiously diverse public audience. If one cannot expect such premises to be accepted or interpreted in a uniform way, it will not necessarily advance one's rhetorical purposes to assert them. (2004a, 98–99, my emphasis)

What Stout seems to be implying here is that if citizens desire to be persuasive or convincing in the context of public deliberation which is marked by the permanence of religious pluralism, then they should employ secular reasons, thereby abandoning any resentment of the secularized public square that stems from that religious pluralism. Presumably, the very *practice* of public deliberation will prompt religious citizens to adopt a more prudent, secularized mode of discourse and, in doing so, prompt them to embrace religious diversity in a non-resentful manner. Otherwise, religious citizens who continue to employ religious reasons will find themselves frustrated and their political goals largely unfulfilled.

Notice, though, that the abandonment of resentment advocated by Stout is tantamount in practice to saying that religious citizens should employ a certain sort of conversational constraint. Moreover, notice that this sort of conversational constraint stands in tension with Stout's "say what you please" view. And, of course, this starts to sound a lot like Rawls. What distinguishes Stout's view from Rawls's, however, seems to be that the sort of constraints implicitly advocated by Stout are not formal *ex ante* constraints like those recommended by Rawls. That is, Stout does not explicitly say that religion ought to be excluded from the public domain *from the beginning*; he does not advocate those constraints that are externally placed upon religious citizens. But, while moving away from explicitly formal *ex ante* conversational constraints which would prevent religion from playing a role in public deliberation altogether, Stout implicitly advocates a set of *prudential constraints* upon religion in the public square. These constraints operate in the following way: if a citizen wants to convince others successfully in the public forum, she should avoid using religious reasons. Moreover, the nature of these prudential constraints is such that they are self-imposed by the religious citizen (as their derivation stems from the secularization that took place *among* religious thinkers) and are not thrust upon the religious citizen from some external source like, say, the "discourses of liberalism," as Milbank claims, or the formal *ex ante* constraints of the Rawlsian view of public reason. Under such self-imposed prudential constraints, religious citizens should employ only those sorts of reasons which are useful in convincing their interlocutors in public deliberation. In theory, this does not *necessarily* exclude the employment of religious reasons. For, as long as those reasons are useful in convincing interlocutors, religious reasons can be employed in a non-resentful and thus proper manner. Of course, on Stout's view, given the secularization of public discourse due to religious diversity, citizens will be mostly unsuccessful and thus imprudent when employing religious reasons in public discourse.

6.3 More Than Convincing

It is not difficult to imagine that religious citizens will wish to be successful in achieving their political objectives in forums of public deliberation. And, this will at times require the employment of reasons which will be convincing to others in public discourse, *but not always*. When the goal is to convince others, citizens are of course well advised to discuss the matter in those terms which are uncontroversial from the perspective of their interlocutors. Stout thinks— and we may, for the sake of discussion, grant—that this will usually lead citizens to employ secularized sorts of reasons in public deliberation. But, sometimes the goal of participation in a forum of public discourse is not necessarily to convince others. Stout's view of public reason as informed by his desire to move beyond resentment of the secularized public discourse assumes a limited understanding of the goal of conversation and thus overlooks this fact. For Stout, the only legitimate and ultimate purpose of conversation in the public forum is to convince others to accept a particular position. Hence, the constraints implied by his view limit the role of religion in the public forum to the degree that religion is *prudential in convincing others*. But, understanding conversation, and thus prudence, exclusively in terms of convincing is myopic and overlooks other functions that conversation can play within a democracy. Sometimes conversation is aimed at confronting, converting, contesting, complicating, and warning.

Consider, for instance, the role that conversation might play for the religious prophet: the duty of the prophet is to warn and *not* to convince.[8] Conversation might then be used by the religious prophet as a vehicle for publicly posing to her interlocutor(s), say, a warning from God. As such, religion then might be prudential in another sense within public discourse—i.e., prudential in prophetically warning others that something about the *status quo* needs to change (e.g. topics of discussion, the terms of discussion, the values assumed, etc.). Effectively, religious reasons advanced as a warning may be used as a way of triggering the self-reflexive mechanism of public deliberation in hopes of prompting a higher-order deliberation about deliberation at the first-order. Still, this employment of religious speech may prove inefficient in *convincing* others to adopt a particular policy position within the current framework of public discussion. Yet, we can see that the religious speech act *qua* prophetic warning is not aimed at convincing but at jogging a forum of public deliberation such that it can itself be restructured so as to incorporate the voices, values, topics, and concerns which, prior to such a jogging, are prevented from entering into conversation. In this sense, the religious speech act, while imprudent in convincing, may prove quite prudent for other goals. Religious speech acts may be prudent in achieving such meta-deliberative goals as calling into question the prevailing way an issue is framed, challenging standing assumptions, calling attention to different points of agenda, or even resisting the dominant framework altogether. As such, the unconvincing religious speech act introduced into public deliberation may prove to be analogous to the challenge posed by political activism—from sit-ins to street demonstrations to boycotts to picketing and so forth—*outside* a forum of public deliberation like, for instance, the protests outside the World Trade Organization meetings in Seattle in 1999.[9]

In any case, this kind of discursive activity (challenging, contesting, confronting, warning, interfering, interrupting, resisting, etc) belongs as much to the nature of democratic participation as does cooperative dialogue.[10] As Seyla Benhabib points out,

> All struggles against oppression in the modern world begin by redefining what had previously been considered private, non-public, and nonpolitical issues as matters of public concern, issues of justice, and sites of power that need discursive legitimation. (1992, 84)

The discursive acts advanced by abolitionists and civil rights leaders might provide good historical examples for Benhabib's point here.[11] Interestingly though, these sorts of discursive acts which cause self-reflexive deliberation must occur *outside* the scope of the terms and assumptions of normal public discourse, which on Stout's account, is largely secular in nature. Thus, such discursive acts aim not at convincing others (in terms acceptable within the given framework of deliberation) but at Socratically confounding them.

A case example may be helpful here. Consider the issue surrounding Jehovah's Witnesses (hereafter, JWs) and blood transfusions.[12] A tenet of the JW faith is that it is wrong to receive blood transfusions. However uncomfortable this religious belief makes non-JWs, we are probably mostly willing to allow mentally competent adult JWs to refuse blood transfusions if they so choose, even if doing so results in death. However, the issue is complicated considerably when children are involved. Should JW parents be allowed to refuse blood transfusions for their child even if doing so resulted in the child's death? If we try to answer this question by deliberating exclusively within "normal" secular terms, we would clearly come to the conclusion that the health of the child should outweigh all other considerations at play and that the transfusion should be allowed. Given that the child is not old enough to make a competent, autonomous decision to refuse treatment, his health should be protected, even against the wishes of the parents.

But imagine how the child's parents might respond. They might claim that to give the child a blood transfusion, while protecting his *bodily* health, seriously endangers the health of his *soul*, which is more important. Of course, introducing such explicitly religious terms into this discourse will probably *not* convince many non-JWs. However, those religious terms might prompt a reconsideration of what the term "health" should mean—does "health" mean bodily health, or spiritual health? Effectively, the JWs' religious speech act, while unconvincing, challenges and thereby forces the disambiguated explication of standing assumptions and interpretations implicit within the present forum of deliberation—namely those concerning the nature of health as a strictly physiological category in this case. And, this challenge might prompt further inquiry as to the appropriateness of those implicit assumptions, which may be useful in deciding how the deliberation of the issue at hand should proceed.

Stout's view of public reason frowns upon this form of religious speech, given that it is *imprudent* in convincing others. This form of religious speech manifests a distasteful resentment—a resentment that Stout would have us abandon—toward the manner in which public discourse is most often entertained. But, understanding the purpose and goal of conversation exclusively in terms of convincing others commits Stout to a rather narrow view of prudence and hence to a narrow view of what religious claims are permissible in the public square. Recognizing this, we are now in a position to see the problem with Stout's view of public reason. While it initially appears as though Stout's prudential constraints on religion are not *ex ante* constraints—that is, religion is not formally banished from public deliberation altogether—if religion is prudentially limited to terms of convincing as Stout implies, then religion is already limited in all the ways that the Rawlsian view requires, given the present reality of religious pluralism and secularized public discourse (on Stout's account). As such, Stout's prudential constraints on religion are, *in practice*, tantamount to the *ex ante* neutralist constraints imposed by Rawls in theory. So, while Stout seems to want to move away from the formal separatism of Rawls, he eventually comes to embrace it, though not in the name of moral duty, but in the name of prudence.

But, to attribute to Stout a separatist view seems to fly in the face of what he says earlier when he advises us to "say what you please" in the course of public deliberation. How is this say-whatever advice consistent with the prudential constraints implied by his view? Recall that Stout's view of public reason initially committed him to three things:

1) Permissiveness toward the employment of religious reasons in public deliberation.
2) The advocacy of immanent criticism as a style of deliberation.
3) The recognition of the importance of conversational virtues.

It now seems that we can amend this list with a fourth element:

4) The advocacy of prudential constraints upon religious reasons in public deliberation such that religious citizens can move beyond resentment.

Of course, this seems strange. Notice that (1) and (4) stand in direct tension with one another. On the one hand, Stout's "say what you please" view seems to suggest that the virtues of democratic citizenship are not violated when citizens introduce religious reasons into public deliberation. On the other hand, it seems that Stout is committed to saying that citizens act resentfully and thus viciously if they imprudently (read: unconvincingly) introduce religious reasons within public deliberation. And, even on Stout's own account, religious reasons will most always prove imprudent given the secularization of the public square. But difficult questions remain for Stout's view. How is a citizen ever to voice his religious reasons in a way that, in Stout's view, is not imprudent and hence resentful given the secularization of public discourse? How is a citizen going to say what he pleases, even though he knows—albeit resentfully—that what he wants to say has little chance of convincing any of his interlocutors? Perhaps convincing is not his goal after all. Should he avoid resentment or saying what he pleases? Clearly, this is a case where (1) puts a participant in public deliberation at odds with (4). Hence the tension implicit in Stout's New View of Public Reason.

6.4 Stout's Reply to My Objection

In response to my line criticism above, Stout (2004b) argues that I misinterpret the function of his account of secularization within his overall view of public reasoning. He claims that he does not intend for his account of secularization to be used as a point with which "to counsel religious believers to avoid expressing their religious beliefs in public settings" (2004b, 376). Rather, Stout says, "I explicitly encourage them to express whatever reasons they wish to express, including religious ones" (2004b, 376). Of course, the real issue of concern is whether his view can both encourage religious citizens to express whatever reasons they may have *and* motivate them to avoid resentment of religious diversity and secularized discourse in the process. Admittedly, I think that Stout sincerely wishes to carve out some space in the democratic public square for religious citizens who wish to voice religious reasons in the course of public deliberation. But, I do not see how a citizen can at once voice her religious reasons in a generally secularized forum of public discourse without resenting the fact that her religious reasons are likely going to be rhetorically imprudent, i.e. unconvincing. In light of the fact that her reasons fail to convince interlocutors within a secularized public discourse, how is she to avoid resentment of the secularized forum which, on Stout's view, emerges from the facts of religious diversity? Stout responds:

> How do I try to supply religious people with reason for non-resentful democratic engagement? By engaging them democratically in a spirit that is charitable, respectful, and free from both resentment and manipulation; by encouraging them to express their actual reasons for favoring one set of policies over another, and then subjecting those reasons to criticism on their own terms. (Stout 2004b, 377)

Presumably, this is to say that religious citizens can employ religious reasons while avoiding resentment, as long as they are willing to participate in immanent criticism with fellow citizens.

Accordingly, when citizens engage in respectful immanent criticism with one another, they are not attempting to convince their interlocutors in the sense of providing non-controversial and previously agreed upon reasons. And, insofar as the goal is not necessarily to convince interlocutors in this sense, religious citizens need not find themselves resentful over the fact that their objectives have been unaccomplished. Stout takes this to mean that he, too, well understands other non-convincing roles that speech acts can play within the democratic public deliberation. Thus, when it is argued that the Socratic aim of confounding belongs as much to democratic speech as does convincing reasons, Stout replies:

> What, I wonder, did they think I had in mind when I criticized Rawls . . . for drastically underestimating the significance of "immanent criticism"? What do they take me to be doing at the beginning of chapter seven, where I emphasize that "I am not encouraging [Hauerwas] to be less vehement or less theological in denouncing evil and vice" (162)? I am encouraging him to go on confounding while living up to his own highest standards. (Stout 2004b, 378)

The problem with Stout's reply here is two-fold. First, to critique an interlocutor's position from within his own perspective is not exactly the same as Socratically confounding one's interlocutors. Recall that my objection to Stout was that his view precludes the sorts of non-convincing religious speech acts aimed at jogging the current framework of discussion by prompting a second-order deliberation about how deliberation should be entertained at the first order. In this sense, to Socratically confound is to bring interlocutors to a critical state of *aporia*, or perplexity, in the hopes of challenging any implicit assumptions in the current conversation. Admittedly, immanent criticism may not be aimed at convincing interlocutors on the basis of neutral, previously agreed upon reasons. Yet, clearly immanent criticism is aimed at convincing one's interlocutor that his position is wrong or misguided, even if that is determined exclusively from within his own perspective. And, while I am also optimistic about some of the potential uses of immanent criticism for democratic deliberation, it is not entirely clear how an assessment of an interlocutor's views from within his perspective alone acts to promote the self-reflexive mechanism of public deliberation at the first order. And that is precisely the non-convincing function of religious speech acts that motivates my objection to Stout's prudential constraints upon religious reasons.

Second, it is crucial to see that Stout's attempt to resolve the tension implicit within his view of public reasoning (between his say-what-you-please view and his desire for religious citizens to avoid resentment) by means of an appeal to immanent criticism effectively acts to relocate the problem of concern, not solve it. It is not difficult to imagine that some religious citizens will simply refuse to engage in respectful immanent criticism with interlocutors because they do not recognize their interlocutors—either non-religious or of a different religious tradition—as properly qualified to assess their views from within their own religious perspective. And, if immanent criticism is going to do any work for democratic deliberation, all involved parties must be willing to participate. That is, citizens being immanently criticized must be willing to be have their deepest commitments engaged by someone who does not already share those commitments. And this means that would-be participants in immanent criticism conceive of each other as deliberative equals, i.e. as a fellow democratic citizens. But, notice that Stout appeals to immanent criticism as a way of providing citizens with a way of employing religious reasons while avoiding resentment in the face of religious diversity. Yet, immanent criticism itself requires participants not to resent the facts of religious diversity, at least to the extent that they can consent to being immanently criticized by someone of a different religious persuasion. Interestingly, Stout admits the difficulties of motivating what he calls "high-profile, die-hard traditionalists" to be willing to overcome resentment by way of opening themselves up to immanent criticism (2004b, 381). And for that very reason, Stout claims, he addressed the arguments of *Democracy and Tradition* "especially to young people in the process of deciding what causes they are going to make their own" (2004b, 381). But, one wonders: is this not just to admit that he ultimately cannot say why committed religious citizens should not resentfully refuse to participate in immanent criticism? And, if that is the case, it appears that we are right back where we began: How can Stout's view of public reasoning countenance permissiveness of religious reasons *and* an avoidance of resentment in the face of religious diversity?

6.5 Several Rawlsian Problems Revisited

Insofar as Stout's account of public reason avoids the language of neutrality, it does evade some of the difficulties examined in the previous chapter concerning the practicality and possibility of neutrality. But, notice that Stout's view of public reason does invite several of the most important problems that we saw facing the Rawlsian view, particularly those problems affiliated with upholding neutrality as a regulative ideal. While he seeks to be more permissive of religious voices in the public square, Stout's desire to avoid resentment entails in practice the very same restrictions and constraints Rawls seeks to impose. As such, Stout's view hangs on to some of the same problems we saw haunting the Rawlsian view as a consequence.

In Chapter Five, we saw that Rawls was unable to motivate anything other than an unstable *modus vivendi* type of agreement upon his liberalism (5.3.1). Citizens are required by Rawls to bracket their religious convictions and relegate them to the non-public realm in order to participate properly in the activities of the democratic public square. But, precisely insofar as citizens have to compromise their comprehensive doctrines in order to gain admittance into the public square, Rawls cannot achieve the overlapping consensus he desires; he merely gets a sort of second-best compromise. Similar to the manner in which Rawls desires an overlapping consensus, Stout wants to be able to give an account of public reason which can be endorsed by all citizens, including religious citizens, without resentment. That is, Stout wants something more than a mere second-best compromise. But, at the end of the day, it appears that Stout cannot fully motivate the abandonment of this resentment while at the same time allowing a citizen to participate in the public square in her own voice. So, just as Rawls fails to achieve an overlapping consensus, Stout fails to move the religious citizen beyond the resentment of the secularized public domain.

As we have seen, Stout's prudential constraints are tantamount in practice to the sorts of *ex ante* constraints imposed by Rawls's view of public reason. Just as those constraints prevent Rawls's view from benefiting from the democratizing potential of self-reflexive deliberation, Stout's prudential constraints effectively prevent those speech acts—albeit resentful religious speech acts—which may prove useful for promoting the flexibility of public deliberation to call itself into question and to transform. And, recall that Rawls's view of public reason invites the problems affiliated with deliberative polarization (5.3.3). Similar to Rawls, given his implicit prudential constraints, Stout effectively suggests to citizens that their most deeply held convictions have no rightful place in the public square, given that they are unconvincing and/or resentful. In the face of Stout's implicit prudential constraints, religious citizens will likely seek out some enclave forum of deliberation, which, as Sunstein definitively shows, poses the threat of polarization. And this is something which Stout himself clearly wants to avoid (2004b, 376).

6.6 Conclusion

The problems facing Rawls are serious ones, and Stout falls short of overcoming them all to the extent that he wishes. Yet, his shortcoming in this respect is both interesting and instructive. In this chapter, we saw that Stout correctly challenges the notion that all constructive political conversation requires participants to "argue from a purportedly common basis or reasons in Rawls's sense" (2004a, 69). We saw that Stout's conception of immanent criticism carves out an interesting, alternative conversational space (6.1). In doing so, Stout shows that "normal conversation" in the Rawlsian sense is not all there is and can be—a demonstration which will be helpful as we continue to try to conceptualize the proper relationship between religion and the democratic public square. Unfortunately, though, Stout's project falls prey to the same sort of move he makes against Rawls. That is, Stout's conception of conversation (and prudence) remains itself too restrictive in that he conceives of conversation (and prudence) largely in terms of convincing (6.2–6.3). Hence, to constrain religious reasons on the grounds that they are not prudential in convincing overlooks other important democratic functions that religious reasoning can bring to the table of public discourse.

We now know more clearly what difficulties need to be addressed and what tools are available to us in light of Stout's important contribution to this discourse. Our task now is to pick up where Stout leaves off by being particularly attentive to the various and potentially beneficial democratic aims of religious speech acts that forego or suspend temporarily the goal of convincing interlocutors within public deliberation.

Notes

1. A significantly adapted version of this chapter appears in Talisse and Clanton 2004.

2. See, for instance, Allen 2004; Bromwich 2004; Dunn 2004; Reidy 2004; Talisse and Clanton 2004; Reutzel 2004; Reynolds 2004; West 2004.

3. Rawls quoted in Stout 2004a, 72.

4. See Wolterstorff 1997, 109–111.

5. This sort of objection is, for instance, voiced by Rorty (1994), who views religion as a conversation-stopper. See Chapter 3.2 for the discussion of this view.

6. Stout points out that Greenawalt (1988) has argued forcefully that there are a number of important issues—issues like welfare assistance, punishment, military policy, abortion, euthanasia, and environmental policy—that fall into this category. For a similar line of argument, see Greenawalt 1995; Wolterstorff 1997; Reidy 2000; Goodman, Forthcoming.

7. Cf. Rawls: "Thus, although historical doctrines are not, of course, the work of free reason alone, the fact of reasonable pluralism is not an unfortunate condition of human life. In framing the political conception so that it can, at the second stage, gain the support of reasonable comprehensive doctrines, we are not so much adjusting that conception to brute forces of the world but to the *inevitable* outcome of free human reason" (1996, 37, my emphasis).

8. Consider the so-called watchman passage of Ezekiel 33: 2–6 (NIV): "Son of man, speak to your countrymen and say to them: 'when I bring the sword against a land, and the people of the land choose one of their men and make him their watchman, and he sees the sword coming against the land and blows the trumpet to warn the people, then if anyone hears the trumpet but does not take warning and the sword comes and takes his life, his blood will be on his own head. Since he heard the sound of the trumpet but did not take warning, his blood will be on his own head. If he had taken warning, he would have saved himself. But if the watchman sees the sword coming and does not blow the trumpet to warn the people and the sword comes and takes the life of one of them, that man will be taken away because of his sin, but I will hold the watchman accountable for his blood."

9. For an interesting discussion of activist challenges to forums of deliberation, see Young 2001. For a response to and extension of Young's argument, see Talisse 2005c.

10. See my discussion of Bohman in Chapter 5.3.2.

11. Rawls disagrees. He claims that in the case of abolitionists and civil rights leaders, "the proviso was fulfilled in their cases, however much they emphasized the religious roots of their doctrine, because these doctrines supported basic constitutional values—as they themselves asserted—and so supported reasonable conceptions" (1997, 593). I think Rawls is simply wrong here to suppose that those religious reasons were later supported by neutral reasons drawn from the political conception. If anything, the political conception was redefined by the religious reasons advanced by these revolutionary moral thinkers. Of course, abolitionist religious doctrine supported the values of equal rights of all men as guaranteed by the letter of the Constitution. However, the abolitionist interpretation of those values differed significantly from the prevalent interpretation: they saw those values as applicable to all men (and women), white and black. See Bohman 1996, 117.

12. The discussion below draws influence, in part, from a case involving Delores Henton, a Jehovah's Witness who, despite refusing, was ultimately administered blood transfusions by her physicians after the courts appointed a guardian who consented. See *JFK Memorial Hospital v. Heston* (in Arthur, ed. 2002, 377ff.).

Chapter Seven

Speculations on an Open Socratic-Peircean Public Square

The preceding chapters of this book have examined several attempts within the American tradition of public philosophy to deal with the problem of religion in the public square. We have seen that none of the examined views succeed in articulating a viable strategy to conceptualize the proper relationship between religion and democratic citizenship. What shall we then say about religion's role in the public domain? Can the apparent tensions between religion and democratic citizenship be resolved? In this final chapter, I take up these questions by first assessing our predicament with respect to the issue at hand, briefly reviewing what we have examined. Given the failures outlined in the previous chapters, I shall draw on the influence of Socrates and C.S. Peirce to conceptualize a model of deliberative democracy aimed at accommodating religious reasoning and participation within the activities of the public square. While some (perhaps many) religious persons will inevitably be excluded from my proposed normative model of the public square to the degree that they do not meet the minimal criteria for democratic participation, my model, unlike most in currency, is designed so as not to exclude any democratically predisposed citizens, religious or non-religious.

7.1 Beyond the Politics of Omission

The Rawlsian liberal principle of legitimacy maintains that the wielding of coercive political power "is only proper when we sincerely believe that the reasons we offer for our political action may reasonably be accepted by other citizens as a justification of those actions" (Rawls 1996, xlvi). This principle establishes a burden of responsibility upon those seeking to exercise political power over others, whether that be in the course of deliberation of public policy, political advocacy, campaigning, or voting. Accordingly, citizens have a responsibility to give reasons for that exercise of power in terms which are acceptable to all parties involved, including those citizens over whom the power is to be exercised. All exercise of power must be, on this liberal view, justified to "every last individual" (Waldron 1993, 37). In order for citizens to be able to meet the demands of this responsibility, Rawlsians argue that citizens must participate in the activities of the public square in such a way that leaves their deepest comprehensive doctrinal commitments at home—i.e. in the non-public realm. Only by doing so, can citizens expect to voice public reasons which, by virtue of being neutral with respect to those comprehensive doctrines which divide us, are acceptable to all others in a pluralistic society. And, only by employing these sorts of reasons—neutral public reasons—can citizens express respect for fellow citizens as being free and equal, thereby fulfilling the obligations entailed by the liberal principle of legitimacy.

But, interestingly, neutralist Rawlsian liberalism does not itself meet the demands it makes of others. Religious citizens are handed down certain gag rules by neutralist liberalism, presumably in an effort to force religious citizens to abide by the liberal principle of legitimacy. Yet, if the liberal principle of legitimacy applies across the board, should liberalism not be required by its own standard to provide reasons to those religious citizens for that exercise of power (i.e., in establishing gag rules)—and not just reasons but reasons which are acceptable to those religious citizens as reasons? This is a burden of responsibility both defined and skirted by liberals. For, as I argued in Chapter Five, the reasons offered to religious citizens for these gag rules, as it turns out, are merely those reasons which would be acceptable as reasons to Rawlsian political liberals. At the end of the day, it may very well be the case that religious citizens ought not bring their religious views and reasons into the public domain. But, the burden of responsibility is upon liberals to explain why not; it is *not* the *prima facie* responsibility of religious citizens to explain why they can.

With respect to the *ex ante* gag rules and conversational restraints imposed upon religious citizens, the separatist strategy of Rawlsian liberalism proves itself to be a politics of hypocrisy. That is, Rawlsian liberalism says one thing and does another, particularly with respect to its requirement of neutrality. Rawlsian liberalism is underwritten by a view of public reason which expects religious citizens (and citizens in general) to employ only those reasons drawn from the political conception, which is presumably a "shared fund" of commonly held neutral reasons (Rawls 1996, 8). But, as we have seen, distinctively *liberal* values and principles end up defining the parameters of this supposedly "neutral" political conception whence those neutral reasons are to be drawn. And, this is just to say that there is no source of neutrality as Rawlsian liberals claim. Thus, when Rawlsian liberals tell religious citizens that they have a responsibility to abide by the doctrine of neutrality, religious citizens are right not only to wonder where the source of neutral reasons is supposed to be found, but also to point out that Rawlsian liberals cannot make good on the same responsibility they seek to impose upon others.

Other separatists like Rorty advocate the muzzling of religion in public deliberation for roughly pragmatic reasons. So we are told, religion just does not work. It stops the conversation. Religion tends to be unconvincing. Of course, as with all pragmatist proposals, we must be sure to ask the following: What are our goals? Who gets to constitute this "we" that peppers your pragmatism? As we have seen, "our" goals are not always to convince interlocutors within the current framework of public deliberation. Perhaps the goal is to interrupt the current conversation in hopes of prompting a new or second-order public inquiry. Unfortunately, pragmatist-separatists tend to overlook this other democratic function of public speech acts. And, as such, they tend to overlook important pragmatic benefits which might be drawn from the very religion they seek to silence or otherwise prudentially constrain in the public square. In short, their pragmatisms fail to be viable strategies for precisely pragmatic reasons.

Reconstructivist strategies to negotiate the role of religion in the public square prove hypocritical in a manner not unlike the Rawlsian strategy. As we have seen in Chapters Two and Three, reconstructivist strategies implicitly claim to be inclusive of religion within the public domain. However, given the semantic reworking of religion demanded as a prerequisite for admission into the public square, reconstructivist strategies effectively exclude the religion they supposedly include, i.e. the traditionalist religion normally held by religious citizens. So, in practice, reconstructivist strategies require the very exclusions that they mean to overcome in theory. The qualitative constraints imposed by reconstructivists are tantamount to the quantitative constraints expressed by separatist gag rules.

In all cases, the restrictions and constraints imposed upon religion translate not only into the politics of omission but also into the politics of oppression. In all cases, religious citizens are told that their deepest commitments and convictions simply have no proper place in the public square. Yet, no adequate justification for that coercive prohibition is successfully advanced. And, as we have seen, this poses serious practical threats to the public square. Not only are our forums of public deliberation potentially calcified such that they cannot undergo critical reevaluation and transformation (5.3.2), but the threat of polarization looms large as enclave deliberation potentially takes the place of robust public engagement of the deep convictions held by citizens (5.3.3).

With good reason, then, we can conclude the following: the restrictions imposed on religious participation advocated by both the separatist and reconstructivist strategies that we have examined are not going to work. I should be careful here, of course, to spell out exactly what this means. Note that the burden of responsibility is on the side of those who wish to exclude religion to show us why such a prohibition should be put in place. I have argued thus far that several outstanding attempts to do so have failed. Of course, this alone does not necessarily entail that religion has a proper place in the public domain, but simply that the arguments against religious participation I have examined are not going to yield a viable strategy for settling this issue. At this point, then, it makes sense for us to step back and readdress the issue in light of the failures we have examined in this book. In what follows, I attempt to imagine what a good democratic public square might look like if the prohibitions upon religion are suspended.

7.2 Risking Deliberative Defeat

What might a public square which is open to religious reasoning look like? Given that there are no *ex ante* conversational restraints imposed, my view of the democratic public square says that religious citizens are free to employ whatever reasons they see fit to advance in the course of public deliberation. Likewise, the secularist is free to do the same. Of course, simply because the religious citizen is free to advance religious arguments as informed by religious reasons does not mean that her argument will win (i.e., prove to be the best argument) in the course of deliberation. In fact, her religious argument may be defeated. In the course of the deliberation, it might be shown, for instance, that the religious argument advanced is internally incoherent or contradictory; that it commits the religious citizen to other things to which she is unwilling to commit; that it does not present adequate evidence for the conclusion or one of the premises; that the conclusion does not follow from the premises; or that the consequences entailed by the conclusion are themselves undesirable or in conflict with one another. In any case, the religious citizen when employing religious reasons in the course of public deliberation implicitly takes a certain risk: her religious line of reasoning may actually be defeated. For example, a religious citizen employing religious reasons with respect to some particular matter, M, may be engaged, as Stout aptly explains, in immanent criticism by one of her secularist interlocutors.[1] The secularist immanent critic might then point out to the religious citizen that her view is inconsistent from within the perspective her religious doctrine. And, this may cause the religious citizen to abandon or refine her previous line of reasoning concerning M. Of course, it might very well be the religious citizen who engages the secularist in immanent criticism. The risk of defeat, then, cuts both ways: it may be the secularist's line of reasoning that gets defeated in the course of deliberation. And, prior to deliberation there is no way of knowing for sure which side will win out over the other; hence the *risk* implicit in the participation in public deliberation.

Admittedly, it is no easy task to determine when, in fact, an argument or line of reasoning in the course of public deliberation has been definitively defeated, i.e. when *deliberative defeat* has occurred. This is a point to which I shall return (7.6). For the moment, though, let us simply ask: what happens if and when, in the course of deliberation concerning M, a particular religious argument/line of reasoning, R, is defeated? If it is the case that a religious citizen's R

is defeated in public deliberation, that citizen has basically two options. First, she might pursue some variation of an *ex post* separatist strategy. One variation of this *ex post* separatist strategy available to the religious citizen is simply to abandon the particular element of her religious system of belief which pertains to the expression of R, meanwhile leaving other elements of her religious system of belief intact. Another type of *ex post* separatist strategy available to the religious citizen is to adopt what Rorty calls "Jefferson's compromise" (1994, 169) and merely "privatize" that particular element of her religious system of belief pertaining to R (and thus only abandoning it within the public sphere) for the purposes of pursuing private perfection, whatever that might mean. It might mean that the religious citizen is still privately motivated by R (even though R has met deliberative public defeat) to hold the same view concerning M. However, this religious citizen, in compliance with this Jeffersonian compromise, advances only non-religious reasons in the public square for the same view concerning M. For example, a religious citizen might be privately motivated to oppose abortion for religious reasons yet voice only non-religious reasons for banning abortion when involved in public deliberation. Whether the religious citizen abandons or merely privatizes R, pursuing an *ex post* separatist strategy will lead the religious citizen, in light of the fact that R with respect to M has been defeated, to bracket in the public square her R relevant to M and employ only non-religious reasons for her public policy proposals with respect to M, with the understanding that she might be able to refine her R such that it becomes assertable in future deliberation.[2] In the meantime presumably, she should not allow R to be the determining factor when voting with respect to M, given the deliberative defeat of R concerning M.

Another option available to religious citizens in the face of deliberative defeat is to try to resuscitate R (in the light of its defeat) by pursuing some variation of an *ex post* reconstructivist strategy. One variation of this strategy will lead the religious citizen to reinterpret and recast semantically those elements of her religious system of beliefs which pertain to and inform R so that R_r (where R_r means R after sufficient semantic reconstruction) can be advanced in a way that is no longer open to defeat. This means that the language and terms used in the expression of R (such that R_r could be achieved) would be interpreted metaphorically/symbolically/poetically. For instance, let us imagine a religious citizen who advocates a certain foreign aid policy on the basis of a religious line of reasoning—say, "because Jesus tells us to do so"—which somehow gets defeated. This religious citizen may opt for semantically reinterpreting the phrase "because Jesus tells us to do so" to mean roughly "because it serves our human goals to do so." Here, the language of Jesus is simply advanced, at least within the public square, as motivationally potent metaphor.

Another variation of the *ex post* reconstructivist strategy would be simply to adjust one's theology/religion itself such that it systematically expresses an altogether different line of reasoning (i.e., an altogether different R) with respect to M. In either case, the *ex post* reconstructivist strategy is pursued by the religious citizen with the understanding that the presently defeated R might be further refined and/or perfected such that it is no longer defeated, thereby suspending the need for a continued pursuit of an *ex post* reconstructivist strategy.

I do not mean here to be advocating any one of these strategies over and above another. I simply mean to sketch these as *potential* options (among others, perhaps) for the religious citizen in the face of deliberative defeat. Which option or variation is pursued will, in large part, depend upon the particular situation. In any case, it is crucial to notice that, in both of these post-defeat scenarios, the separatist and reconstructivist strategies would be *pursued* by the citizens themselves. That is, the *ex post* separatist and reconstructivist strategies I have sketched are not coercively *imposed* upon religious citizens prior to entering the public square. If an *ex post* separatist or reconstructivist strategy is pursued by a religious citizen within the public square, it is pursued as a conscientious response to a forum of deliberation that has heard and engaged the religious citizen's R. On this open model of the public square, inclusion acts as the default; exclusion or modification of religion comes as a result of deliberative defeat. Whereas *ex ante* separatist and reconstructivist strategies are oppressive insofar as they seek to impose *prima facie* gag rules and qualitative constraints which are not justified to religious citizens, *ex post* separatist and reconstructivist strategies in fact do offer reasons and justification to religious citizens for the restraint and reconstructivism to be pursued. In short, religious citizens should pursue these strategies precisely because, as a result of deliberation, the religious reasons offered have been defeated.

7.3 Socratic Engagement and Respect

This model of an open public square, then, does not require religious citizens to bracket their religious doctrines *prior* to entering the public square. Rather, citizens are invited to participate in public deliberation with whatever reasons they see fit to bring, with the understanding that further deliberation may, in the end, defeat the line of reasoning they initially bring to the public domain. As such, citizens are allowed to *engage* one another at the most fundamental level within the political sphere. This level of deep engagement is prohibited by the restrictive model of the public square advanced by *ex ante* separatists and reconstructivists. Yet, only when the public square is open to citizens as they choose to come can those citizens actually engage one another deeply and thereby participate in the "kind of public deliberation necessary to test the plausibility of contending comprehensive moralities—to persuade others of the merits of our moral ideals, to be persuaded by others of the merits of theirs" (Sandel 1998a, 211). I call this model "Socratic" precisely because it seeks to position Socrates as an exemplar of one participating in public discourse. Throughout most of Plato's dialogues, Socrates is presented as being committed to engaging his interlocutors as they come—i.e., complete with their commitments and convictions—in the hope of involving those interlocutors in truth seeking inquiry. Participation in this sort of inquiry, Socrates understands, opens him up to the possibility of not only refuting his interlocutors but also being refuted by them.[3]

Interestingly, it can be said that Socrates expresses toward his engaged interlocutor an attitude of respect, one that is distinctively at odds with the liberal conception thereof. On the neutralist liberal view, citizens respect one another by justifying their political positions according to reasons that are not drawn from their own comprehensive doctrines. Thus, under this Rawlsian view, showing respect for others requires that a citizen not only bracket her own deep comprehensive doctrinal convictions but also ignore those held by her interlocutors, at least as far as justification of public matters are concerned. As such, the liberal conception of respect expresses itself as a process of leaving others alone and refusing to engage them as they come. Gag rules and conversational restraints imposed upon religious citizens, Rawls suggests, help us achieve this form of respect in the public square by forcing us to offer "public reasons." But, for Socrates, this process of ignoring his interlocutor (by means of ignoring his deeply held convictions) is precisely a form of *disrespect*. Consider, for instance, the manner in which Socrates uncharacteristically disengages (by means of silence) some of Plato's dramatic characters like Cleitophon in the *Cleitophon* and the Eleatic Stranger in the *Sophist*. Socrates does not try to engage these individuals, and hence refuses to show them respect, precisely because they willingly refuse to allow for the possibility of actual engagement. In the *Cleitophon* (as in the *Republic*), Socrates has nothing to say to Cleitophon who, as seen in the *Republic*, rejects the distinction between truth and falsity.[4] In the *Sophist*, Socrates refuses to participate in discussion with the Eleatic Stranger who seeks to "lay unfilial hands upon that pronouncement" (242b) of Parmenides concerning the law of non-contradiction, thereby putting such a law "to a mild degree of torture" (237b).[5] In both cases, Socrates refuses to engage those interlocutors who choose to undermine the necessary logical conditions for truth-seeking inquiry. Involving others in inquiry for Socrates is the greatest manifestation of respect precisely because doing so takes that interlocutor seriously and implicitly accepts the risks of doing so: Socrates' interlocutor might be right and thus Socrates might be refuted. It is only when others would prevent that inquiry from taking place by undermining or rejecting the logical conditions for inquiry that Socrates writes them off and does not engage them. In this manner, the Socratic conception of respect is consistent with the "deliberative mode of respect" advocated by Sandel.

> [W]e respect our fellow citizen's moral and religious convictions by engaging, or attending to, them—sometimes by challenging and contesting them, sometimes by listening and learning from them—especially when those convictions bear on important political questions. There is no guarantee that a deliberative mode of respect will lead in any given case to agreement with, or even appreciation of, the moral and religious convictions of others. It is always possible that learning more about a moral or religious doctrine will lead us to like it less. But the respect of deliberation and engagement afford a more spacious public reason than liberalism allows. It is also a more suitable ideal for a pluralist so-

ciety. To the extent that our moral and religious disagreements reflect the ultimate plurality of human goods, a deliberative mode of respect will better enable us to appreciate the distinctive goods our different lives express. (1998a, 217–218)

Not only does this model of an open public square facilitate this Socratic conception of respect, but it also facilitates the level of Socratic engagement necessary to prevent the doxastic polarization effect affiliated with enclave deliberative groups. As we have seen in Chapter Five, separatist models of public discourse tell religious citizens that their most deeply held religious convictions have no place in the public forum. This restriction poses a serious practical threat to the stability of our democracy precisely because, if citizens are told that they cannot discuss their most deeply held convictions in the public square, it is likely that many of them will turn to enclave deliberative groups wherein they are free to do so. The polarization resulting from these sorts of enclaves threaten the sort of extremism, hatred, intolerance, and violence democratic societies should hope to avoid. The Socratic engagement possible within an open public square may do much to diffuse this political threat of instability associated with group polarization.

7.4 Socratic Uses of Undefeated Religious Reasoning

This model of an open public square, then, invites citizens to bring their religious convictions into public deliberation and thereby adopt the risks of doing so. As implied above, a fair amount pivots upon our understanding of what constitutes the deliberative defeat of a line of reasoning. And, to be sure, explaining what constitutes deliberative defeat is not easy. Perhaps it will be useful then to proceed by first saying a little about what does *not* necessarily constitute deliberative defeat.

Simply because a religious citizen's line of reasoning in public deliberation falls short of *convincing* his fellow interlocutors does *not* entail that her argument has been somehow defeated in the relevant sense. Imagine a case where, in the course of deliberation, a religious line of reasoning concerning M does not win anyone over. There may be, for instance, a counterbalancing set of secular reasons with respect to M. However, it might very well be the case that neither line of reasoning definitively defeats the other (nor is either line defeated by any other set of reasons). What then?

In cases where a religious line of reasoning proves unconvincing but undefeated, that line of religious reasoning may prove itself to be useful for democratic deliberation nonetheless. As we saw in last chapter, one of the main difficulties facing Stout's view of public reason is that it advocates prudential constraints on religious citizens on the grounds that (as Stout sees it) religious reasons are mostly unconvincing in our otherwise very secular, public discourse. Thus, it is an act of prudence for religious citizens to employ non-religious modes of discourse in order to avoid resentment of religious pluralism and the consequent secularized public discourse. Of course, as we have seen, these prudential constraints are only prudent if the aim within deliberation is to actually convince interlocutors. But this may not be the goal after all; hence, Stout's prudential constraints seem insufficiently motivated.

So what function(s) might an unconvincing and yet undefeated religious line of reasoning serve? Religious reasoning may very well be useful in *interrupting* the dominant forum of deliberation in such a way as to *challenge* and call into question that forum of deliberation itself. Consequently, religious reasoning takes on a distinctively Socratic function of confounding one's interlocutors. Like the broad torpedo-fish to which Socrates is likened in the *Meno*,[6] religious reasoning might numb the current framework of discussion and bring its participants to a critical state of *aporia*, or perplexity, with respect to the values, terms, topics, and assumptions implicit within the current framework of discourse. And, operating as a sort of Socratic gadfly,[7] religious reasoning might thus stimulate a second-order *inquiry* into the appropriateness of the *status quo* implicit within the first-order deliberation.

As I demonstrated in the last chapter, this second-order inquiry may act to disambiguate the values, terms, topics, and assumptions implicit in the first-order deliberation (6.3). Or, by virtue of being challenged by the religious reasoning, the result of this second-order inquiry might be the reconsideration, reinterpretation, or redefinition of those values, terms, topics, and assumptions such that deliberation at the first-order level can be entertained differently in the future. This may mean that the religious line of reasoning is no longer unconvincing at the first-order level. Or, it may just mean that the values, terms, topics, and assumptions implicit in the first-order deliberation stand unchanged but are rather now made *explicit* as a result of the second-order inquiry prompted by the religious contestation. Making terms explicit may be a good in its own right precisely because doing so effectively abandons any overly ambitious claim that the current framework of discussion is "neutral" in some Rawlsian sense. This pushes the forum of deliberation beyond the politics of hypocrisy towards a politics of honesty. In any case, the second-order deliberation brings about inquiry concerning not only *how* to deliberate at the first-order but also *what* to deliberate about at the first-order. Thus, religious reasoning may be useful in the following respect: religious reasoning might pose a Socratic challenge to the current framework of discussion, which leads to *aporia*, which prompts further inquiry and deliberation, thus promoting the politics of open engagement and honesty. In short, religious reasoning may serve democratic deliberative forums well simply by allowing, facilitating, and sometimes forcing the road to inquiry to remain open, as C.S. Peirce would have it (Peirce 1899, 54). Thus, affording space within the public square for religious reasoning helps evade the problems related to the crippling of deliberation haunting Rawlsian separatism (See 5.3.2).

Perhaps one of the most important and telling historical examples of this sort of gadfly-function of religious reasoning and participation in the public square comes to us from Martin Luther King, Jr. during the civil rights movement of the 1960s. King advanced overtly religious arguments and advocated religiously motivated non-violent protests in order to create what he referred to as "constructive, non-violent tension" in the city of Birmingham, Alabama. Yet, as King explains, the goal was not simply to create turmoil for the sake of turmoil or retaliation against an unjust government. Rather, as he writes in his famous *Letter from a Birmingham Jail,*

> Just as Socrates felt that it was necessary to create a tension in the mind so that individuals could rise from the bondage of myths and half-truths to the unfettered realm of creative analysis and objective appraisal, we must we see the need for nonviolent gadflies to create the kind of tension in society that will help men rise from the dark depths of prejudice and racism to the majestic heights of understanding and brotherhood. The purpose of our direct-action program is to create a situation so crisis-packed that *it will inevitably open the door to negotiation* (King 1963, no page, emphasis added).

King's use of religious reasoning and religiously motivated direct-action campaigns were aimed at prompting second-order deliberations about how deliberations and negotiations at the first order (concerning race-relations in the Birmingham) were being conducted. It was hoped that this inevitable second-order deliberation would ultimately expose the values, principles, flaws, biases, and limitations of the deliberations and negotiations at the first-order—namely, that African-Americans were being systematically excluded from good-faith negotiations with city leaders. And, so King suggests, it was necessary to prompt this second-order deliberation (by means of this constructive tension) so that negotiations at the first-order could take place properly and in a way that was democratically inclusive of African-Americans.

7.5 Deliberative Stalemate and Temporary Modus Vivendi

Let us imagine for a moment that religious reasoning executes within a particular forum of deliberation this Socratic torpedo-fish/gadfly function outlined above. In other words, let us assume that the non-defeated yet unconvincing (at the first-order) line of religious reasoning provokes enough contestation of the current framework of deliberation to prompt a second-order inquiry. Let us imagine further that the religious line of reasoning is unable to resolve/determine the second-order inquiry and thus remains unconvincing at the first-order. Despite the fact that the religious line of reasoning remains unconvincing, the end result may be the disambiguation, clarification, and explicit articulation of the values, terms, etc. previously implicit within the first-order forum of deliberation. Now, in addition to the fact that the religious line of reasoning remains unconvincing, let us imagine that it still has not been definitively defeated. There is no clear-cut winner or loser in this forum of deliberation, even though many of the values, terms, assumptions, etc. have been clarified through second-order inquiry. I shall call this scenario *deliberative stalemate*. What will we do in the face of deliberative stalemate?

One way of trying to answer this question is by first getting clear on exactly what our goals might be at this point. At this juncture, Rawlsians would have us simply accept this present state of disagreement as an inevitable fact of reality. Rawls might have us cite the present state of deliberative stalemate as evidence for what he calls "the fact of reasonable pluralism" (1996, 4). However, simply because there is a stalemate at this particular juncture in deliberation does not entail that there will be stalemate tomorrow or the next day. The truth is: we simply do not know what the future of deliberation holds. As Sandel reminds us, contra Rawls, "Whether it is possible to reason our way to agreement on any given moral or political controversy [and thus overcome deliberative stalemate] is not something we can know until we try" (1998a, 211). Thus, one of our goals at this juncture will be to preserve the possibility of further inquiry on the matter at hand such that a deliberative stalemate could be overcome in the future. This is to say, with Peirce, that we do not wish to block the road to further inquiry in pursuit of the truth. Perhaps some religious line of reasoning is right. Perhaps it is wrong. In any case, we need to preserve the notion that deliberative defeat is possible on either side of an issue. And, this means that inquiry and deliberation needs to persist so we can determine if one or more parties in the deliberation can be eventually defeated. Thus, one of our goals in the face of deliberative stalemate should be to promote the conditions for the possibility of further deliberation and inquiry.

Unfortunately, though, the nature of politics is at times such that some decisions *must* be made and be made in a timely fashion. Crudely put, we do not always have the luxury to wait deliberation and inquiry out with respect to certain issues. Some political issues are so time-indexed, severe, and salient that they demand that we *do* something even as we wait out further deliberation and inquiry on the matter. Thus, in the face of deliberative stalemate, one of our goals will surely be that we enable ourselves to make certain sorts of political decisions, even though we would rather wait until deliberation and inquiry definitively tell us what we should do.

Clearly, then, we have these two goals in the face of deliberative stalemate: 1) to preserve the possibility of further deliberation and inquiry such that defeat (and ultimately victory) can be established; and 2) to preserve our capability to make certain sorts of decisions when situations demand us to do so. So our question becomes roughly this: how do we devise a politics that is attuned to the preservation and furthering of public deliberation which is nonetheless capable of addressing important and timely political matters? Obviously, there is no easy answer to this difficult question. However, I attempt to sketch out a response below that takes into account the two goals outlined above.

Let us imagine a deliberative stalemate concerning a political matter M. If it is the case that the political situation around which M revolves does not require immediate and timely action, then it is safe to say that deliberation should simply continue until all defeatable lines of argument are eliminated and the victorious line is identified. However, if the situation *does* require immediate and timely action such that a decision cannot wait out the trajectory of further deliberation and inquiry, we have a different situation on our hands. Let us call these cases *act-now deliberative stalemate situations*.[8] In these cases, perhaps the best we can do is pause deliberation momentarily and, in a manner of speaking, hash out a *temporary modus vivendi* with respect to M. That is, we might simply try to come up with some sort of second-best compromise to which all parties can agree until such time as deliberation is able to decide otherwise, whenever that may be. Of course, this means that concerning M, no one deliberative party will get exactly or entirely what it might desire. This sort of *modus vivendi* will be at best a bargaining of interests and a carving out of policy and public strategies of action in accordance with that bargaining process.

How might this temporary *modus vivendi* be reached? We might take a vote, whether that be a vote of the relevant legislature or a referendum. But, that too might be outside the range of feasibility given the timely nature of the situation. In such cases, then, the courts will likely need to act as the conductor of the *modus vivendi* formation. In any case, the goal will be to assess the disagreement at hand within the act-now deliberative stalemate as it currently stands concerning matter M, weigh the competing interests involved on all deliberative sides, and try to gerrymander some sort of policy which is maximally sensitive to as many interests as possible. Presumably, this gerrymandered policy will be one that makes certain sorts of concessions to involved parties. So, for instance, the *modus vivendi* policy will attempt to make as many concessions as possible to the undefeated and unconvincing religious line of reasoning in the act-now deliberative stalemate situation. This prompts a distinctly different non-deliberative—albeit *expressive*—function of religious reasoning within the public square: to *express* the deeply held convictions of religious citizens such that they can be taken into account in the formulation of a temporary *modus vivendi*. Because religious citizens are afforded the space within the public square to voice their religious convictions and reasons, we have not only a way to assess what their interests are in forming the *modus vivendi* but also some indication of the fervor with which those interests are held. Making these sorts of assessments will better enable us to understand how and to what degree to tilt the distribution of privileges and obligations of the *modus vivendi* agreement.

It is important to note, however, that this hashing out of a temporary *modus vivendi* policy needs to take place within a constitutional framework. Such a framework acts as *de facto* guide when deciding what sorts of concessions can be made and to what extent. Such a framework will institutionally prevent us from making horribly regrettable mistakes in the formation of *modus vivendi* policy. So, for instance, we might be able to make certain sorts of concessions to the religious parties involved in an act-now deliberative stalemate concerning M, but we would not be willing to make those sorts of concessions which would violate the schedule of rights insured within a constitution framework. Of course, this constitutional framework will tend systematically to bias the nature of the *modus vivendi* agreement in a fairly liberal direction. However, this is not to say that the constitutional framework within which these agreements are made is itself closed to revision. It may be the case that deliberation ultimately defeats some tenet of that framework such that future *modus vivendi* agreements should be formulated differently. This, of course, will be a difficult feat—*but not impossible.*

Another significant task of hashing out a temporary *modus vivendi* in the case of an act-now deliberative stalemate will be to come up not only with certain legal policies with respect to *M* but also with certain public strategies of action aimed at designing institutions which would prevent, or at least diminish, the need for such legal policy in the first place. For example, it may very well be the case that we are currently in an act-now deliberative stalemate with respect to euthanasia in this country. However, hashing out certain temporary *modus vivendi* legal policy with respect to euthanasia may prove less helpful than coming up with ways to avoid the *need* for euthanasia altogether. Many elderly and terminally ill patients seek euthanasia as an escape from suffering, hopelessness, and loneliness. We can at least start to diminish the demand for euthanasia greatly by implementing certain practical strategies of action aimed at improving palliative care and strengthening the bonds between the elderly and their families and communities. Similarly, with respect to the abortion issue, we might pursue a public strategy of action aimed at encouraging and facilitating a culture of adoption so as to lessen the demand for the abortion of unwanted pregnancies. By diminishing the demand for euthanasia and abortion, we can take at least some practical steps toward making certain non-legislative/non-policy concessions (by means of these strategies of action) to those who oppose euthanasia and abortion with undefeated/unconvincing reasons within the act-now deliberative stalemate situation. Effectively, these strategies of action are aimed at lessening the extent to which legal policy would even be relevant with respect to *M*. The hope is to dissolve the conflict in some sense prior (not necessarily chronologically) to policy. Again the expressive function of religion in the public square emerges: the expression of deeply held religious convictions within the public square will help tilt the table when it comes to deciding what strategies of action to pursue and how to pursue them.

I call this *modus vivendi* "temporary" for an important reason. This *modus vivendi* is not a compromise made at the terminus of all possible inquiry concerning *M*. It is simply one which is hashed out with the concomitant understanding that deliberation concerning *M* will continue in hopes of overcoming the present status of stalemate. Given that the fact of sociological disagreement present within a stalemate situation does not entail that the stalemate will persist, it may be the case that deliberation can inform us as to the truth (or the true good) concerning *M*. If this is the case, the *modus vivendi* agreement concerning *M* is abandoned and a new policy coined in accordance with the outcome of deliberation takes its place. Or, it may be the case that continued deliberation and inquiry only inform us (at any given moment) that certain positions with respect to *M* have been defeated. In such cases, the *modus vivendi* is revised; we adjust the sorts of concessions made and the distribution of privileges and obligations present within the *modus vivendi* agreement accordingly. In either case, continued deliberation is crucial to the maintenance and checking of the temporary *modus vivendi* agreement. This is to say, then, that a temporary *modus vivendi* with respect to M is only as permanent as, and thus contingent upon, the conditions of the deliberative stalemate concerning M.

As mentioned above, given the constitutional framework within which a temporary *modus vivendi* is to be hashed out, it will likely be the case that any given temporary *modus vivendi* will look roughly liberal. But notice that this is not tantamount to *liberalism* as such. Insofar as the *modus vivendi* agreement is temporary to the degree that it (along with the constitutional framework itself) is contingent upon the trajectory of further deliberation and inquiry, a defining feature of liberalism is abandoned. Effectively, the fact that open square deliberation and inquiry constantly checks the *modus vivendi* (and even the constitutional framework within which this occurs) means that the right is not thought to be prior to the good in the manner suggested, for instance, by Rawls (1996, 173ff.). In theory, we can adjust the schedule of rights operative both within a *modus vivendi* and the constitutional framework in accordance with the outcomes of deliberation.

7.6 Deliberative Defeat

Admittedly, most (if not all) of this model of an open Socratic public square hinges upon the idea that deliberative defeat is a possibility within the course of public deliberation. It is therefore necessary to say something about what deliberative defeat might look like. As we have already seen, deliberative defeat does not mean simply that a line of reasoning concerning M is unconvincing. For, it may be the case that the unconvincing line of reasoning is, in fact, unconvincing precisely because the framework of discussion into which that argument is introduced is itself systematically biased against the conditions under which such reasoning would be persuasive in the first place. This does not, however, rule out the possibility that such a line of reasoning is in fact correct.

Most clearly, an argument would be defeated in the course of deliberation if it could be shown that it is invalid, i.e. that there is some incoherence, contradiction, *non-sequitur*, or other fallacy in the reasoning from the premise(s) to the conclusion(s) of the argument. Of course, it is possible that competent deliberators will have already ironed out any such inconsistencies, contradictions, *non-sequiturs*, and other fallacies prior to advancing their lines of reasoning in the course of public deliberation. Leaving aside the question of whether the argument is sound, it is possible that religious citizens already advance internally consistent, coherent, and valid arguments within the public square. Thus, it may not be very likely that there will be any problems pertaining to the validity of the argument to expose such that deliberative defeat is made manifest.

Another avenue to establishing deliberative defeat would be to show one's interlocutor that his line of reasoning commits him to other things which would be unpalatable. Given that these collateral commitments are, in fact, unacceptable to him, he is prompted to abandon the initial line of reasoning advanced. However, it is at least possible, if not entirely probable, that a deliberator might simply "bite the bullet," so to speak, and own up to those collateral commitments, so as to avoid admitting deliberative defeat.

Deliberative defeat might come about by being shown that there is either too little or too weak evidence in support of either the premises or conclusion of a deliberator's line of reasoning. Of course, the assessment of evidence is a tricky thing. Exactly what constitutes evidence for premises or conclusions such that sufficiency is either attained or not is itself at times open to legitimate contestation. Religious citizens may feel that some aspect of their experience or revelation should count as sufficient evidence for religious premises, while atheists might reject the same as insufficient. Thus, given the difficulties of evidential assessment, it may be quite difficult in some cases to demonstrate deliberative defeat along these lines.

It may be the case that deliberative defeat is demonstrated by pointing out that the consequences of a deliberator's line of reasoning are themselves undesirable. So, for instance, we might try to point out that the consequences of a policy proposed by a religious line of reasoning are negative, and hence that the line of reasoning is defeated. Of course, it may very well be the case that the advocate of a particular policy may again "bite the bullet" and simply deny that the consequences are, in fact, negative as his interlocutor claims. As such, consequentialist assessments will be a difficult way to demonstrate deliberative defeat.

But, the above is all just to say that deliberative defeat is, indeed, *difficult* at times to demonstrate within the public square—not that deliberative defeat is itself impossible. It may turn out, for instance, that the doctrine of ensoulment can be shown to be true and hence that it should inform our decisions about abortion policy. Of course, that same doctrine might prove to be false. Right now, we do not yet know definitively. However, it may be the case that, in the course of deliberation, we can definitively conclude that the doctrine of ensoulment is, indeed, false. In such a case, then, this doctrine will have faced deliberative defeat.

Of course, there remains this problem: what if the course of deliberation and inquiry has definitely established a religious line of reasoning, R, to be false and, meanwhile, advocates of R remain unmoved and continue to hold that R? Can there be deliberative defeat even when all parties are not convinced that defeat has occurred with respect to R? Here, perhaps a distinction between *objective* and *subjective* deliberative defeat will be helpful. On the one hand, if deliberation and inquiry has definitely established R to be false, R has faced *objective* deliberative defeat. But, just because objective defeat of R has occurred does not mean that proponents of R will in fact abandon R, i.e. acknowledge that R has been objectively defeated. (And, conversely, just because R has been abandoned by a proponent does not entail that R has in fact been objectively defeated.) To acknowledge that the R which one has advanced has been objectively defeated is for R to be *subjectively* defeated. In any case, the practical question lingers: what do we do when R has been objectively defeated but not subjectively defeated, abandoned, or otherwise appropriate altered by its proponents? There is, of course, no easy solution to such a problem.

In any case, the concept of objective deliberative defeat outlined above will no doubt leave some wanting and waiting to hear more. For instance, one might wonder how we can establish with confidence (and hence without reasonable contestation) if and when a position has been definitively defeated in course of public deliberation. In order to answer this sort of question fully, though, one would need to spell out a criterion or set of criteria in the light of which some position could be definitively falsified. Of course, the difficulty here is that such falsification criteria would be contingent on some underlying conception of truth. And, given that there is still considerable debate among philosophers concerning competing theories of truth, what gets to count as *the* criteria for deliberative defeat is indeed a matter for further investigation and deliberation, particularly for epistemologists. That being said, whatever criteria of objective defeat we might eventually wish to adopt—and whether they are established by community agreement or by some heavenly Platonic form or rooted in a pragmatist, coherence, correspondence, or some other theory of truth—it is not necessary that we solve these obviously important epistemological problems before we make use of the concept of deliberative defeat as a placeholder of sorts within a normative model of public deliberation. That there remain unsettled epistemological problems need not be an indictment of my model of public deliberation. For, whatever criteria of deliberative defeat we might find appropriate to adopt, we still stand in need of having some workable concept of deliberative defeat in place for any model of public deliberation to proceed. In fact, that my model of deliberation remains uncommitted to any robust philosophical and epistemological theories can be seen as a virtue, for the function of deliberative defeat as a concept within my model of deliberation can accommodate any number of epistemological accounts.

7.7 Meeting the Fallible Inquiry Requirement

In any case, perhaps the most significant problem for any potential deliberative scenario may very well be that a citizen—religious or non-religious—*is simply not open* to the possibility of acknowledging the defeat of the position she advances in the public square. That is, perhaps a citizen holds her beliefs with respect to M in such a way that is *prima facie* closed to any further inquiry. In other words, perhaps a citizen holds her beliefs with respect to M so tenaciously that she does not (and will not) entertain the possibility that those beliefs could be refuted in any way, thereby refusing to acknowledge the possibility of both objective and subjective deliberative defeat with respect to M. Ought religious citizens who hold their religious belief with respect to M in this way introduce their religious lines of reasoning into the public square with respect to M?

I think not. If it is the case that a religious citizen holds her belief with respect to M in such a way that, by virtue of the utterly non-fallibilistic manner in which that belief is held, she is unable to acknowledge or own up to the objective deliberative defeat of that belief (i.e. such that subjective defeat would be impossible), then that religious citizen ought not to attempt to introduce her religious belief with respect to M into public deliberation. For, public deliberation presupposes the possibility of deliberative defeat. Therefore, if a religious citizen denies the possibility of the defeat of her religious belief with respect to M, then that religious citizen logically denies the possibility of her religious belief participating in deliberation and inquiry with respect to M. Consequently, the religious citizen in this case cannot rightly advance her position with respect to M into a forum of public deliberation precisely because she refuses to accept the risk of defeat implicit in doing so. She refuses both to be engaged as an interlocutor participating in public deliberation concerning M and to engage others concerning M. In refusing to engage others, she refuses to show respect for others, at least with respect to M. Thus, for this religious citizen to advance her religious belief with respect to M in the public forum, even though she refuses to engage in actual deliberation concerning M (and thus to show respect for others in the public forum), is for her to violate the virtues of good citizenship, at least with regard to M.

This view above commits me therefore to saying that the civic duties of good democratic citizenship presuppose what I shall call a *fallible inquiry requirement* incumbent on religious (as well as secularist) citizens in the public square. If a religious citizen wishes to participate in the public square concerning M, she should be willing to participate in inquiry with other citizens not only with respect to the truth of other viewpoints concerning M, but also with respect to the truth of her own religious view as it pertains to M. This means, then, that the religious citizen must be willing to hold her religious line of reasoning with respect to M in a fallible manner when entering the public square concerning M, implying that she opens herself up to the possibility (and the risk) that her belief might be defeated. If it is the case that a religious citizen is open to the possibility of defeat and thus in compliance with this fallible inquiry requirement, then that religious citizen does not violate the duties of good citizenship simply by introducing her religious lines of argument with respect to M in the public square. For, that religious citizen is attempting to participate in deliberation and thus to engage and to be engaged, to show respect for and be respected by her interlocutors.

But, what exactly justifies this fallible inquiry requirement? Clearly, meeting this requirement positions a citizen such that she is open to deliberation with others. But, what justifies the requirement that one be open to deliberation in the first place? Some political theorists, like Amy Gutman and Dennis Thompson, argue that citizens have some sort of deliberation-independent moral duty to give and exchange reasons with others (2000, 172; cf. 2003, 43). But, note that this sort of argument assumes that we *already* agree that liberal values like reciprocity and accountability to one's fellow citizens should trump other values that one might have (Talisse 2005a, 105). When trying to justify something like the fallible inquiry requirement, Cheryl Misak is right:

> We can't simply rest on the appealing thought that deliberation, conversation, and taking seriously the views of others is the right way to proceed. We must not beg the question in favor of the liberal democratic values [such as reciprocity or openness to inquiry] we may hold dear. (2004, 10–11)

So, what then justifies this fallible inquiry requirement? Misak's Peircean theory of deliberative democracy (2000; 2004) provides a nice answer here. As she points out, there is an organic connection between holding a belief and the obligation to participate in inquiry with others. For one to say that she believes (or to assert) that *p* is for her to hold that *p* is true. And, for one to hold that *p* is true is for her to hold that *p* cannot be further refined and could henceforth meet any challenges brought forward. For one to maintain all of that is for her to be engaged in the process of justifying her held belief to others—to giving and exchanging reasons concerning *p*. Thus, when someone says that she believes that *p*, she is thereby committed "to defending *p*—to arguing that [one is], and others are, warranted in believing *p*" (Misak 2004, 12). Of course, in order to defend *p*, she must be *willing* to entertain challenges to *p*, such that her belief that *p* is "responsive to or answerable to reasons and evidence" (2004, 12). And, this means, of course, that a believer of any variety is tacitly committed to participating in deliberation and thereby owning up to the risk of deliberative defeat. This, of course, does *not* entail that all citizens will actually meet the justificatory demands to which they are committed in virtue of embedded epistemic norms. Yet, it does entail that the fallible inquiry requirement for proper participation in the democratic public square is itself justified, given the organic connection between holding beliefs and the tacit commitment to being responsive to reasons in a deliberative forum.

I should pause here to emphasize what makes my view distinct from the increasingly high-profile defense of religious participation in politics advanced by Christopher Eberle (2002). Unlike Rawlsian liberals, Eberle seeks to accommodate religious participation in the public square by easing the public justificatory requirements of liberalism. While Rawlsian liberals claim that citizens should show respect to their fellow citizens (as free and equal) by successfully offering public reasons sufficient to justify their coercive policies, Eberle argues that respect for fellow citizens simply requires that citizens *sincerely attempt* to offer convincing secular reasons (2002, 84–151). Thus, for Eberle, even if one fails to produce this corroborating secular rationale in support of her position, she has met the duties of good citizenship if she *pursues* it (2002, 10). The implication of his view, of course, is that religious reasoning is perfectly acceptable in the public square, as long as the citizen puts forth an earnest effort to provide non-religious reasons to others by "conscientiously engaging" her compatriots in such a way as to hear objections and, potentially, to change her mind.

On the surface, it might appear that my view above is quite close to Eberle's in that we are both permissive of religious reasoning, as long as citizens meet minimal justificatory responsibilities to engage in deliberation with other citizens. That being said, there are at least two key differences that are worth mentioning here. First, whereas Eberle permits religious reasoning, he thinks that it is necessary for citizens to pursue some distinctly non-religious rationale, even if it is not found. Given the suspicions expressed earlier (in Chapter Five) concerning the possibility of neutral public reasons, I avoid making this demand. Rather, my model of the public square simply asks citizens to be willing to hold their religious lines of reasoning in a certain manner—i.e. in such a way that is open to the possibility of objective deliberative defeat and hence the exchange of reasons. Second, my view is distinct from Eberle's insofar as it provides a non-question-begging answer to the following: Why engage in truth-seeking inquiry with others in the first place? It seems to me that Eberle's view relies too much on the happy coincidence that any particular religious view will or can countenance his ideal of conscientious engagement. For instance, we can imagine a religious citizen asking the following question of Eberle: Why should I be interested in respecting others by even attempting to offer *any* rationale for the positions I advocate? Here, like other liberals mentioned above, Eberle seems committed to begging the question about what justifies the requirement of fallible engagement in inquiry; my Peircean view above provides an epistemic argument as to why they should.

Now, of course, someone might find this Peircean argument suspicious and want to object to it by claiming that there are cases where a citizen could believe p to be true and yet *legitimately* refuse to hold p fallibly and in a manner that positions her to meet the justificatory responsibilities of exchanging reasons with others. For instance, one might say that there are certain beliefs that no reasonable person could possibly call into question. Take, for example, the belief, S, that "sexual abuse of young children is morally bad." No one in her right mind, so it seems, would say that sexual abuse of young children is morally unobjectionable. However, when someone asserts S, she may very well be confronted with an interlocutor who calls S into question by objecting to the assumed definition of sexual abuse implicit in the expression of S. It might be asked, for example, if any physical contact below the shoulders counts as sexual abuse. Now, the proponent of S is put in a situation where she needs to consider what her definition of sexual abuse ought to be. And, it is precisely at this point that she needs to be prepared to offer reasons in support of her favored definition—and hence her belief S, as she interprets it—when objections are leveled. And in order to consider reasons when faced with an objection, she needs to be willing to recognize that her definition of sexual abuse might be wrong. Note, of course, that the same could be said of any belief that we might otherwise think to be beyond the scope of reasonable objection. Once we are challenged to flesh out the details of what we mean by this or that belief, there emerges room for reasonable objections and hence the need to answer them through the exchange of reasons.

Another sort of objection to my Peircean argument for the fallible inquiry requirement might run as follows: there are certain social contexts wherein one might take p to be true and yet not have a duty to hold p in such a manner that it is open to deliberative defeat and hence the free exchange of reasons precisely because doing so would make her especially vulnerable to either ridicule, manipulation, or some other form of mistreatment. Thus, in such a context, the interest in avoiding ridicule or mistreatment would overrule the responsibilities of holding p fallibly and exchanging reasons in light of objections. For example, consider someone who believes G, that "the state should legalize gay marriage." We can imagine a situation wherein if she voices her actual reasons for holding G, she might face extreme opposition in the form of chastisement and dismissal due to the unpopularity of some of her views concerning homosexuality. In this case, the fear of alienation or harsh treatment by her interlocutors might motivate her to conceal her actual reasons for believing G and, hence, not to offer them for critique or objection. But, clearly, this sort of case represents a situation wherein one's interlocutors are acting in bad faith as far as inquiry is concerned, for their aim may be nothing more than to poke fun at or to twist words of or simply to hurt persons with whom they disagree. And, this case is not a properly deliberative scenario. Consequently, one's civic obligations under these conditions may change. There may be some need for what David Estlund calls "countervailing deviation" from ideal deliberation in order to achieve a situation wherein constructive deliberation can occur (Estlund 2007, chap. 12ff); for instance, there may be a need for some form of activism (Young 2001, 676ff.). But, my Peircean argument above simply demonstrates that believers are tacitly committed to participating in actual inquiry when and where it is available. In other words, my view is a normative view that applies to citizens within the scope of properly deliberative circumstances.

7.8. Religion in the Public Square?: A Conditional Response

In many ways, the discussion in this chapter so far has been leading back to fundamental question of this book: Can religion properly play a role in the public square? My response is a conditional one. If a religious citizen is able and willing to hold her religious belief with respect to M in such a way as to meet the fallible inquiry requirement outlined above, then I can see no reason why we should ask that citizen to bracket her religion upon entering the public square. A religious citizen who meets this requirement with respect to the belief she holds concerning M does not violate the duties of good democratic citizenship when she employs her religious reasoning in public deliberation concerning M, at least until the point of deliberative defeat of the religious line of reasoning in question, if and when that occurs. Likewise, a citizen who meets the fallible inquiry requirement with respect to the religious lines of reasoning she holds concerning M does not violate the duties of democratic citizenship when she votes on the basis of that undefeated religious line of reasoning with respect to M. If a religious citizen is not able or willing to meet this fallible inquiry requirement with respect to her religious beliefs held concerning M, then she violates the duties of democratic citizenship when she voices her religious beliefs in the public forum with respect to M. Whether or not this same religious citizen (who refuses to meet the fallible inquiry requirement) can vote on the basis of her religious beliefs with respect to M is a trickier question. If her religious belief has met objective deliberative defeat, although not subjective deliberative defeat (precisely because she refuses to acknowledge objective defeat), I think we would want to say that the she acts as a bad citizen when she votes in accordance with an objectively defeated line of reasoning. Of course, in her eyes, she is not doing anything wrong precisely because her position, so she thinks, has not been defeated. As such, the practical problem remains: How do we convince this citizen to fulfill her duties as a democratic citizen? In cases where both the fallible inquiry requirement has not been met and where defeat of the same belief has not occurred, the issue gets a bit cloudier. My inclination is to suppose that she violates the same duties of citizenship when she votes according to a non-inquiry-ready yet undefeated religious belief. But that judgment may be too quick. For, although this citizen holds her religious belief with respect to M in a non-fallibilistic manner, her belief might nevertheless be correct. If so, it seems that we have a case of true but unjustified (and unjustifiable, at least as far as the religious citizen in question is concerned) belief. Should we commit to saying that a citizen who holds a true belief, though in the wrong way, stands in violation of the duties of good democratic citizenship when she votes on the basis of that true belief? Here, it is just not clear to me what to say.

In any case, I should be fair to note the potential danger involved with my conditional view as presented above. An objection might run something like this: Does meeting the fallible inquiry requirement of the public square require religious citizens to semantically reconstruct their religion prior to entering the public square? The fear represented by this sort of question is that the manner in which someone holds a particular belief (i.e., either in a non-fallible or fallible manner) bears upon the content of the belief held. So one might object: to ask a religious citizen to hold her belief with respect to M such that the fallible inquiry requirement is satisfied is to ask her to reconstruct the content of the religious belief actually held with respect to M. If this objection is correct, then to claim that the religious beliefs actually held by citizens are being accommodated within my model of the public square is at best misleading. For, so the objection might run, it is not the actually held religious beliefs that are being allowed into public discourse but sufficiently reconstructed religious beliefs. As such, the hypocrisies of reconstructivism (outlined in Chapters Two and Three) pervade my model of the public square.

If this objection above is correct, then my model of the public square will not have room enough to accommodate those religious citizens it was designed to include. For, it might be the case that a number of religious citizens find that they do not and cannot hold any of their religious beliefs in a fallibilistic manner (such that the fallible inquiry requirement could be met) without compromising the beliefs actually held. If this is the case, it will indeed be difficult to find room for religion in the public square on my model. Of course, it must be added that the same sorts of exclusions obtain with respect to secularist citizens as well. If secularists are unable to hold their views and convictions in a fallibilistic manner in such a way as to meet the fallible inquiry requirement, then they will be likewise excluded from my model of the public square. What this means then, in the end, (if this objection is correct) is that my model of the public square will be able to accommodate perhaps only a small circle of deliberators with respect to M, who find that they can meet the fallible inquiry requirement without having to reconstruct (and thus compromise) the views and convictions that they really hold concerning M. And, this narrowness may be a problem in its own right.

But, I think this sort of objection to my model jumps the gun. It may be true that any number of the beliefs held by a religious citizen are held in a non-fallibilistic manner such that meeting the fallible inquiry requirement with respect to those beliefs would require the reconstruction of those beliefs prior to entering the public square (which would mean that *that* citizen's religion has no room in the public square). But, perhaps this is not as frequent as some might suppose. Perhaps it would behoove us simply to slow down and work on a case-by-case basis when making these sorts of determinations. It might be true, for instance, that many of a religious citizen's religious beliefs as they pertain to relevant political matters are held in a properly fallible manner such that meeting the fallible inquiry requirement would not require reconstruction of her religious beliefs. Perhaps with respect to any particular M, a religious citizen finds herself fully committed to a particular religious line of reasoning but is still in principle open to the idea that she might be wrong concerning that religious line of reasoning concerning M. We must not simply assume that this religious citizen is unwilling to exchange reasons about the views that she holds. How would we find this out? I suggest that we start by asking her. For instance, it may appear to us that a religious citizen holds her belief that abortion is wrong in a non-fallibilistic manner when she says she holds that belief on the basis of bible passage such as Psalms 139:13-16 or Jeremiah 1:5, which she considers to be God's infallible word on the matter. But, is it really the case that the religious citizen in question holds her belief concerning abortion in a non-fallibilistic manner? Might we not simply ask her the following: Is there any conceivable way that you might have misinterpreted these scriptural passages on this matter? Would you be open to the possibility of what Stout calls immanent criticism? It may very well turn out that this religious citizen thinks that, in fact, she has the correct interpretation but that she might still be open to the idea that she is wrong. If this is the case, she holds her relevant religious belief, at least with respect to the issue at hand, in a manner that meets the fallible inquiry requirement. As such, no *ex ante* reconstruction of her religious conviction is required prior to entering the public square and the above objection is quelled.

Now, some might want to push me a bit further by claiming that religious believers commonly hold to certain *core* religious claims about which they either are or should be unwilling or unable to admit defeat.[9] Could a typical Christian, for instance, hold the claim that "all men and woman are created in the image of God" fallibly? Could she meet the fallibility requirement with respect to claims about the lordship of Jesus Christ or other such claims? Of course, the concern raised by these sorts of questions is whether my model of the public square is, at the end of the day, simply too restrictive in what it requires for responsible democratic citizenship. It may seem that my fallible inquiry requirement is asking religious citizens to be wishy-washy and unconvicted, i.e. unfaithful, and hence to choose democracy over one's religion.

But, I think the concern here is, again, largely off base. The fallible inquiry requirement does not necessarily require religious believers to hold core religious claims fallibly or to call into question what they take to be their religious source(s) of normative authority. For instance, a religious citizen might properly "stand firm" and say that she takes scripture to be absolutely infallible when it states that persons are created in the image of God. However, when a citizen brings that claim into the public square—i.e., when that claim is used in the justification of policy with respect, say, to civil rights or slavery or whatever—she is now of course interpreting, contextualizing, and applying that core religious claim to *M*. The fallible inquiry requirement can be met in this case if she simply considers the move from the religious conception (i.e. core religious claims and the source of normative authority) itself to the particular political entailment—that intermediate space of reasoning, so to speak—and holds *that* fallibly and in a manner attuned to the justificatory responsibilities of exchanging reasons.[10] Even if it turns out that if she is unwilling or unable to entertain the possibility that she could be wrong about central, core religious claims itself like, say, "Jesus is Lord," those claims *alone*—that is, minus interpretation, contextualization, and application—do not generally entail a particular view concerning this or that public policy.

But what if there were some situation where a citizen's core religious belief—say, "Jesus is Lord"—somehow *itself* lands on the table of democratic discussion concerning *M*? What happens if the religious believer absolutely refused to acknowledge the possibility that such a belief could be defeated in an argument? What should we say about that? Indeed, this is a difficult case. As implied above, I think that a religious believer could probably find some room in which to remain a fallibilist. But, if not, what then? In such a case, it looks like we may have—in that particular case—a situation where this citizen has to make a choice between being a good religious believer (as she sees it) or being a good democratic citizen with respect to *M*. The choice, in this *particular* case, is between religion and democracy. And, with respect to this particular case, the citizen might very well go either way to say, "So much the worse for democracy!" or "So much the worse for religion!" But, to be sure, I do not think things need to come to this. In most cases—nay, probably every actual case—one can be a fallibilist about the political implications of one's religious beliefs without even raising the question about whether we must be fallibilists concerning what might be an otherwise unassailable core, religious belief.

In any case, it may be true that my model of the public square will still leave out some, perhaps many, religious persons at particular moments with respect to particular issues. However lamentable this may be, it is not necessarily an indictment of my model of the public square. My model is *not* necessarily aimed at including all religious persons, *no matter what*. Rather, I am merely trying to present a model of the democratic public square which does not exclude those religious persons who may already find (or in the future come to find) themselves minimally predisposed to deliberative democratic participation. That is, my model of the public square, unlike the *ex ante* separatist and reconstructivist proposals, seeks to bring into the fold those democratically predisposed religious persons who wish to be included. It is my suspicion at the end of the day that there are more democratically predisposed religious citizens than some would have us believe. And, my model of the public square is merely geared toward erring on the side that attempts to include those religious citizens who are.

Of course, the case-by-case approach advocated by my model of the public square requires that all citizens be willing to practice the deliberative virtue of charity within the public square—i.e., that we be willing to hear the religious citizen out and consider the possibility that, with respect to any given *M*, this religious citizen is holding her relevant line of reasoning in compliance with the fallible inquiry requirement. How do we find out if this is actually the case? We ask her questions and try to engage her in inquiry. And, by doing so, we extend to her the first sign of respect. Then we see what happens from there.

7.9 Conclusion

In this chapter, I attempted to imagine what a democratic public square might look like if the restrictions upon religious reasoning are dropped. To introduce religious reasoning into public deliberation implicitly commits the religious reason-giver to the risk of deliberative defeat with respect to that religious reasoning (7.2). I attempted to sketch out several strategies to be pursued by religious citizens in the face deliberative defeat (7.2). By allowing religious citizens to voice their religious convictions, my view of the public square allows for deep Socratic engagement. I claimed that the willingness to accept the risk of deliberative defeat when engaging in public discourse manifests a distinctively Socratic conception of respect for interlocutors—the willingness to hear them out and consider their reasons seriously. Doing so within the public square helps avoid the threat of doxastic polarization associated with enclave deliberation (7.3). I suggested that undefeated yet unconvincing religious reasoning within the public square may be useful to the degree that it acts Socratically to prevent the calcification of deliberation by stimulating second-order inquiry concerning the terms, values, and assumptions implicit with current first-order frameworks of deliberation (7.4). In the face of what I call act-now deliberative stalemate, I proposed the strategy of hashing out a temporary *modus vivendi* which is revisable in light of the progress of further deliberation on the matter. At the level of orchestrating a temporary *modus vivendi* agreement, undefeated religious reasoning takes on the role of expressing the religious interests such that the negotiation of that *modus vivendi* can be tilted accordingly (7.5). I recognize the difficulties involved in establishing deliberative defeat. Despite these difficulties, it is possible that a position might be objectively defeated, even though it remains subjectively undefeated (7.6). Ultimately, I proposed a conditional response to the question of whether or not religion could legitimately play a role in the public square by suggesting that: if religious citizens meet an fallible inquiry requirement with respect to their religious reasoning concerning a political matter such that objective defeat could be acknowledged and thus subjective defeat attained, then there is no need to restrict their use of religious reasoning in the democratic public square (7.7–7.8).

Notes

1. Hereafter, I will make significant use of the variable M to indicate a *particular* matter. This is not to be needlessly abstract or redundant. Rather, my intention is merely to draw attention to the manner in which this discussion is meant to obtain with respect to individually specific matters and not more generally than need be.

2. The religious citizen's R may be defeated because of the formulation and articulation of that R. However, it may be the case that simply refining and perfecting that R in the light of certain objections allows that R to be formulated again in a way that is no longer open to defeat by those objections. If such refinement takes place, then the religious citizen might bring that refined R out of privatization and into the public square. Here, I think it is important to understand that refining one's R is not the same as semantically reinterpreting one's R.

3. Socrates steadfastly admits his willingness to be refuted during a conversation in order to obtain truth. This willingness to be refuted is actually one of the ways that Socrates both identifies himself as a philosopher and distinguishes himself from the sophists. In the *Gorgias*, Socrates says that he is more than willing to carry on more conversation with Gorgias if he is the "same kind of man as I am." Socrates goes on further to describe this "kind of man" in the following way: "And what kind of man am I? One of those who would gladly be refuted if anything I say is not true, and would gladly refute another who says what is not true, but would be no less happy to be refuted myself than to refute, for I consider that a greater benefit, inasmuch as it is a greater boon to be delivered from the worst of evils oneself than to deliver another" (458a). Hereafter, all citation to the Platonic dialogues will simply make reference to the specific dialogue and the appropriate Stephanus numbers. All citations are made to the translations in Plato 1989.

4. Recall that Cleitophon tries to bolster Thrasymachus' argument against Socrates in Book I of the *Republic* by suggesting that justice is what *seems* to be the advantage of

the stronger as opposed to the milder form of relativism advanced by Thrasymachus which states that justice simply *is* the advantage of the stronger (340b). Thrasymachus, though, does not heed the suggestion of Cleitophon and ends up being refuted by Socrates. Interestingly, Socrates would not have been able to refute Cleitophon's reformulation of Thrasymachus' argument precisely because Cleitophon effectively rejects the truth/falsity distinction when he rejects the distinction between what *is* the advantage of the stronger and what *seems* to be the advantage of the stronger. Without such a truth/falsity distinction, no refuting arguments can be formulated by Socrates. At this point, Cleitophon simply steps out of the conversation (as he rejects the conditions for such a conversation), never to be heard from again in the *Republic*. See Roochnik 1990, 102, ff. for an interesting discussion of this exchange.

5. The pronouncement of Parmenides here is essentially that one cannot say or think that what-is-not *is*. In order to challenge this pronouncement, then, one must effectively confront a contradiction.

6. *Meno* 80a

7. *Apology* 30e.

8. There are obvious parallels between what I have identified as *act-now deliberative stalemate situations* and what William James calls "genuine options" in his essay, "Will to Believe."

9. I am indebted to Wilfred McClay for posing this objection to me.

10. See, for instance, Perry (2003, 55 ff.) for a helpful discussion concerning how Christians might be able to interpret Biblical passages relevant to homosexuality and same-sex marriage (e.g. Genesis 19:1–29; Leviticus 18:22; Leviticus 20:13; and I Corinthians 6:9) in at least two competing ways, while at the same time not denying the truth of the Bible itself. I am indebted to Justin Cahill for pointing out this example to me.

Conclusion

Since the founding of this country, Americans have grappled with issues related to the interplay of religion and politics. In light of the often controversial mixture of the two, it is perhaps little surprise that the torch-bearers of America's most distinctive intellectual tradition—classical American pragmatists like William James and John Dewey—sought to sooth the apparent tension between religion and democratic politics by suggesting a method of semantically recasting religious beliefs to be compatible with a pluralistic democracy. But, these attempts fall short of sufficiently including the traditional religious believers who constitute the majority of the religious voices our public square actually needs to address. Unfortunately, contemporary attempts to think within this pragmatist framework advanced by Cornel West and Richard Rorty face similar sorts of problems.

Mainstream liberals like John Rawls seek to restrict the public role of religion, emphasizing the obligations of citizens to meet a liberal principle of legitimacy by offering their compatriots public reasons in justification of the policies and candidates they favor. But, this liberal view, too, faces a multitude of difficulties. If good citizenship requires that citizens offer reasons that *truly* remain neutral with respect to their comprehensive doctrinal commitments, it is of course right for us to expect that they be shown where and how these sorts of reasons are to be found. Moreover, the expectation that citizens bracket their deepest convictions in the public square—most often their religious convictions—invites the threat of polarization, extremism, and the failure of the sort of robust democratic deliberation liberals hope to vitalize.

In addition to the various lines of criticism that I have offered in this book, what I hope to have provided here is a strategy for accommodating religious citizens and their modes of reasoning in the democratic public square. My aim is to have made this provision in such a way that does justice to both religion *and* democratic citizenship: to incorporate religious reasoning in the scope of public deliberation in a way that *also* provides a framework for holding religious citizens democratically and epistemologically accountable. Hence, the argument of this book is by no means advanced as an apology for careless citizenship on the part of religious citizens. Rather, I have sought to catalogue the theoretical and practical flaws of restrictive models of political participation while encouraging religious citizens to practice responsible citizenship by offering a conceptual framework wherein that might be possible.

For many years now, the debate concerning religion and democratic citizenship among contemporary thinkers has centered on the *content* of the reasons employed in the activities of the public square. One of the implications of this book is that we would be better served to shift our focus of attention to the *manner* in which citizens hold and employ the various sorts of reasons that actually animate their political lives. To that end, I have provided an open model of the democratic public square that encourages citizens to hold whatever lines of reasoning they hold in a manner that is open to truth-seeking inquiry and, hence, to the possibility of deliberative defeat—that is, to practice what we might think of as the deliberative virtue of humility. Of course, there is still much work to be done; we are still in need of a fuller schedule of deliberative virtues. It is my sincere hope that this book can push us further toward a constructive discussion about what those might be.

Bibliography

Ackerman, Bruce. 1989. "Why Dialogue?" *Journal of Philosophy* 86: 16–27.
Aikin, Scott and Michael Hodges. 2006. "Wittgenstein, Dewey, and the Possibility of Religion." *Journal of Speculative Philosophy* 20 (2006): 1–19.
Allen, Anita, and Milton Regan, eds. 1998. *Debating Democracy's Discontent.* New York: Oxford University Press.
Allen, Danielle. 2004. "A Multilingual America?" *Soundings* 87.3–4: 259–280.
Alterman, Eric. 2002. "Rawls and Us." *The Nation* (online edition). December 5, 2002 issue.
Arthur, John, ed. 2002. *Morality and Moral Controversies: Readings in Moral, Social, and Political Philosophy.* Upper Saddle River, NJ: Prentice Hall.
Audi, Robert. 1997. "Liberal Democracy and the Place of Religion in Politics." In Audi and Wolterstorff 1997.
———. 2000. *Religious Commitment and Secular Reason.* New York: Cambridge University Press.
Audi, Robert and Nicholas Wolterstorff. 1997. *Religion in the Public Square.* Lanham, MD: Rowman and Littlefield.
Baghramian, Maria and Attracta Ingram, eds. 2000. *Pluralism: The Philosophy and Politics of Diversity.* New York: Routledge.
Barber, Benjamin. 1999. *A Passion for Democracy.* Princeton, NJ: Princeton University Press.
Barry, Brian. 2001. *Culture and Equality.* Cambridge, UK: Polity Press.
Beiner, Ronald. 1998. "The Quest for a Post-Liberal Public Philosophy." In Allen and Regan 1998.
Benhabib, Seyla. 1992. "Models of Public Space." In *Habermas and the Public Sphere*, ed. Craig Calhoun. Cambridge, MA: MIT Press.
———, ed. 1996. *Democracy and Difference.* Princeton, NJ: Princeton University Press.
———. 1996. "Toward a Deliberative Model of Democratic Legitimacy." In Benhabib 1996.
Berlin, Isaiah. 1969. "Two Concept of Liberty." In *Four Essays on Liberty.* New York: Oxford University Press.
Bohman, James. 1996. *Public Deliberation.* Cambridge, MA: MIT Press.
———. 2003. "Deliberative Toleration." *Political Theory* 31.6: 757–779.

Bohman, James, and William Rehg, eds. 1997. *Deliberative Democracy.* Cambridge, MA: MIT Press.
Boxx, William T., and Gary Quinlivan, eds. 2000. *Public Morality, Civic Virtue, and the Problem of Modern Liberalism.* Grand Rapids, MI: William B. Eerdmans Publishing Co.
Bromwich, David. 2004. "Democracy and Normal Life." *Soundings* 87.3–4: 281–300.
Brooks, Thom, and Fabian Freyenhagen, eds. 2005. *The Legacy of John Rawls.* New York: Continuum Books.
Buchanan, Allen. 1989. "Assessing the Communitarian Critique of Liberalism." *Ethics* 99: 852–82.
Buchler, Justus, ed. 1955. *The Philosophical Writings of Peirce.* New York: Dover.
Cahn, Steven, ed. 1997. *Classics of Modern Political Theory.* New York: Oxford University Press.
Carrette, Jeremy. 2005. *William James and the Varieties of Religious Experience.* New York: Routledge.
Carter, Stephen. 1993. *The Culture of Disbelief.* New York: Doubleday.
Cohen, Joshua. 1993. "Moral Pluralism and Political Consensus." In Copp et al. 1993.
———. 1996a. "Deliberation and Democratic Legitimacy." In Bohman and Rehg 1997.
———. 1996b. "Procedure and Substance in Deliberative Democracy." In Bohman and Rehg 1997.
Cohen, Marshall, Thomas Nagel, and Thomas Scanlon, eds. 1974. *The Rights and Wrongs of Abortion: a Philosophy & Public Affairs Reader.* Princeton, NJ: Princeton University Press.
Copp, David, Jean Hampton, and John Roemer, eds. 1993. *The Idea of Democracy.* New York: Cambridge University Press.
Dahl, Robert. 1998. *On Democracy.* New Haven: Yale University Press.
Davion, Victoria, and Clark Wolf, eds. 2000. *The Idea of a Political Liberalism: Essays on Rawls.* Lanham, MD: Rowman and Littlefield.
Descartes, Rene. 1984–1991. *The Philosophical Writings of Descartes.* Vols. 1–3. Trans. John Cottingham, Robert Stoothoff, and Dugald Murdoch. New York: Cambridge University Press.
Dewey, John. 1957. *A Common Faith.* New Haven, CT: Yale University Press.
Dombrowski, Daniel A. 2001. *Rawls and Religion: The Case for Political Pluralism.* Albany: State University of New York.
Dryzek, John. 1996. *Democracy in Capitalist Times.* New York: Oxford University Press.
Dunn, Allen. 2004. "The Temptation of Metaphysics: Jeffrey Stout's Account of the Limits of Moral Knowledge." *Soundings* 87.3–4: 301–314.
Dworkin, Ronald. 1985. *A Matter of Principle.* Cambridge, MA: Harvard University Press.
———. 1993. *Life's Dominion: an Argument about Abortion, Euthanasia, and IndividualFreedom.* New York: Knopf.
Dyer, R. A. 2004. "Unitarian Group Denied Tax Status." *Star-Telegram* (Dallas-Fort Worth). http://www.dfw.com/mld/dfw/news/state.8692961.htm?1c. May 18, 2004 edition (accessed September 20, 2004).
Eberle, Christopher. 2002. *Religious Conviction in Liberal Politics.* New York: Cambridge University Press.
Eldridge, Michael. 1998. *Transforming Experience.* Nashville, TN: Vanderbilt University Press.
———. 2005. "Why a Pragmatist May be a Pluralist." *Transactions of the Charles S. Peirce Society* 41.1: 119–122.

Elshtain, Jean Bethke. 2000. "Religion and American Democracy." In Boxx and Quinlivan 2000.
Elshtain, Jean Bethke, and Christopher Beem. 1998. "Can This Republic Be Saved." In Allen and Regan 1998.
Emerson, Ralph Waldo. 1837. "American Scholar." In Whicher 1960.
———. 1838. "The Divinity School Address." In Whicher 1960.
Estlund, David. 1998. "The Insularity of the Reasonable." *Ethics* 100.2: 252–275.
———. 2007. *Democratic Authority: A Philosophical Framework*. Princeton, NJ: Princeton University Press.
Etzioni, Amitai, ed. 1995. *New Communitarian Thinking*. Charlottesville: University Press of Virginia.
Fish, Stanley. 1999. "Mutual Respect as a Device of Exclusion." In Macedo 1999.
Fishkin, James, and Peter Laslett, eds. 2003. *Debating Deliberative Democracy*. New York: Blackwell.
Freeman, Samuel, ed. 1999. *John Rawls: Collected Papers*. Cambridge, MA: Harvard University Press.
———, ed. 2003. *The Cambridge Companion to Rawls*. New York: Cambridge University Press.
Friedman, Marilyn. 2000. "John Rawls and the Political Coercion of Unreasonable People." In Davion and Wolf 2000.
Gale, Richard M. 2002. "A Challenge for Interpreters of *Varieties*." *Streams of William James*, 4.3.
———. 2005. "The Ecumenicalism of William James." In Carrette 2005.
Gaus, Gerald. 2003. Contemporary Theories of liberalism. London: Sage.
George, Robert. 1999. "Law, Democracy, and Moral Disagreement." In Macedo 1999.
———. 2001. *The Clash of Orthodoxies*. Wilmington, DE: ISI Books.
George, Robert, and Christopher Wolfe, eds. 2000. *Natural Law and Public Reason*. Washington, DC: Georgetown University Press.
Goodman, Lenn. Forthcoming. "Naked in the Public Square."
Greenawalt, Kent. 1988. *Religious Convictions and Political Choice*. New York: Oxford University Press.
———. 1995. *Private Consciences and Public Reasons*. New York: Oxford University Press.
Gutmann, Amy. 1987. *Democratic Education*. Princeton, NJ: Princeton University Press.
———, ed. 1994. *Multiculturalism: Examining the Politics of Recognition*. Princeton, NJ: Princeton University Press.
Gutmann, Amy, and Dennis Thompson. 1996. *Democracy and Disagreement*. Cambridge, MA: Belknap Press.
———. 2000. "Why Deliberative Democracy is Different." In *Democracy*, ed. Ellen Frankel Paul, Fred D. Miller Jr., and Jeffrey Paul. Cambridge and New York: Cambridge University Press.
———. 2003. "Deliberative Democracy Beyond Process." In Fishkin and Laslett 2003.
Habermas, Jurgen. 1995. "Reconciliation Through the Public Use of Reason: Remarks on John Rawls' Political Liberalism." *Journal of Philosophy* 52: 109–131.
Hardwick, Charley D., and Donald A. Crosby, eds. 1997. *Pragmatism, Neo-Pragmatism, and Religion*. New York: Peter Lang.
Hart, William. 1998. "Cornel West: Between Rorty's Rock and Hauerwas's Hard Place." *American Journal of Theology and Philosophy* 19.2: 151ff. Downloaded from *Proquest*, pp. 1–11.

Holmes, Stephen. 1995. "Gag Rules, or The Politics of Omission." In *Passions and Constraint*. Chicago: University of Chicago Press.
Holy Bible. New International Version.
Jackman, Henry. 2005. "Jamesian Pluralism and Moral Conflict." *Transactions of the Charles S. Peirce Society* 41.1: 123–127.
James, William. 1977. *The Writings of William James*. Ed. John J. McDermott. Chicago: University of Chicago Press.
Kinsley, Michael. 2003. "Abolish Marriage: Let's Really Get the Government Out of Our Bedrooms." *Washington Post*. July 3, 2003. p. A23.
King, Jr. Martin Luther. 1963. "Letter from a Birmingham Jail." http://www.nobelprizes.com/nobel/peace/MLK-jail.html
Kymlicka, Will. 1990. *Contemporary Political Philosophy: An Introduction*. New York: Oxford University.
———. 1998. "Liberal Egalitarianism and Civic Republicanism." In Allen and Regan 1998.
Lachs, John. 1997. "Transcendence in Everyday Life." *The Journal of Speculative Philosophy* 11.4.
Larmore, Charles. 2003. "Public Reason." In Freeman 2003.
Macedo, Stephen. 1990. *Liberal Virtues*. New York: Oxford University Press.
———, ed. 1999. *Deliberative Politics: Essays on Democracy and Disagreement*. New York: Oxford University Press.
MacIntyre, Alasdair. 1984. *After Virtue*. South Bend, IN: University of Notre Dame Press.
———. 1988. *Whose Justice? Which Rationality?* London: Duckworth.
MacIntrye, Alasdair, and Paul Ricoeur. 1969. *The Religious Significance of Atheism*. New York: Columbia University Press.
Macpherson, C. B. 1965. *The Real World of Democracy*. New York: Oxford University Press.
Mansbridge, Jane. 1983. *Beyond Adversary Democracy*. Chicago: University of Chicago Press.
Mendus, Susan. 2000. "Pluralism and Skepticism in a Disenchanted World." In Baghramian and Ingram 2000.
Mill, John Stuart. 1859. *On Liberty*. In Cahn 1997.
Misak, Cheryl. 2000. *Truth, Politics, and Morality*. London: Routledge.
———. 2004. "Making Disagreement Matter." *Journal of Speculative Philosophy* 18.1: 9–22.
———. 2005. "Pragmatism and Pluralism." *Transactions of the Charles S. Peirce Society* 41.1: 129–135.
Mitchell, Susan. 2000. *American Attitudes: Who Thinks What About the Issues that Shape OurLives*. 3rd ed. Ithaca, NY: New Strategist Publications, Inc.
Mouffe, Chantal. 2000. *The Democratic Paradox*. New York: Verso.
Mulhall, Stephen and Adam Swift. 1996. *Liberals and Communitarians*. 2nd ed. Malden, MA: Blackwell Publishers.
Nagel, Thomas. 1987. "Moral Conflict and Political Legitimacy." *Philosophy and Public Affairs* 16: 215–40.
National Election Studies Guide to Public Opinion and Electoral Behavior. University of Michigan. http://www.umich.edu/~nes/nesguide.htm.
Neuhaus, Richard John. 1984. *The Naked Public Square*. Grand Rapids, MI: William B. Eerdmans Publishing Co.
Nozick, Robert. 1974. *Anarchy, State, and Utopia*. New York: Basic Books.

O'Shea, James. 2000. "Sources of Pluralism in William James." In Baghramian and Ingram 2000.
Parker, Kelly. 1999. "James: Experience and Creative Growth." In Rosenthal, Hausman, and Anderson 1999.
Peirce, Charles S. 1878. "How to Make Our Ideas Clear." In Buchler 1955.
———. 1899. "The Scientific Essay and Fallibilism." In Buchler 1955.
Perry, Michael. 2003. *Under God: Religious Faith and Liberal Democracy.* New York: Cambridge University Press.
Plato. 1989. *The Collected Dialogues.* Edited by Edith Hamilton and Huntington Cairns. Princeton, NJ: Princeton University Press.
Rachels, James. 2003. *Elements of Moral Philosophy.* 4th ed. New York: McGraw-Hill.
Rautenfeld, Hans von. 2004. "Charitable Interpretations: Emerson, Rawls, and Cavell on the Use of Public Reason." *Political Theory* 32.1: 61–84.
Rawls, John. 1971. *A Theory of Justice.* Cambridge, MA: Harvard University Press.
———. 1985. "Justice as Fairness: Political not Metaphysical." Reprinted in Freeman 1999.
———. 1993. *Political Liberalism.* 1st ed. New York: Columbia University Press.
———. 1996. *Political Liberalism.* Paperback edition. New York: Columbia University Press.
———. 1997. "The Idea of Public Reason Revisited." Reprinted in Freeman 1999.
———. 1998. "*Commonweal* Interview with John Rawls." Reprinted in Freeman 1999.
———. 1999. *The Law of Peoples.* Cambridge, MA: Harvard University Press.
Raz, Joseph. 1968. *The Morality of Freedom.* New York: Oxford University Press.
———. 1990. "Facing Diversity: the Case of Epistemic Abstinence." *Philosophy & Public Affairs* 19.1: 3–46.
Reidy, Daivid. 2000. "Rawls's 'Wide View' of Public Reason: Not Wide Enough." *Res Publica* 6: 48–72.
———. 2004. "Speaking for the State." *Soundings* 87.3-4: 315–348.
Reutzel, Todd. 2004. "These Stones Will Cry Out: A Critique of Government Displays of the Ten Commandments." *Soundings* 87.3-4: 403–454.
Reynolds, Charles. 2004. "An Appreciation of Stout's Contributions to Religious Ethics." *Soundings* 87.3-4: 481–499.
Roochnik, David. 1990. *The Tragedy of Reason.* New York: Routledge.
Roper Center for Public Opinion Research Website. University of Connecticut. http://www.roperweb.ropercenter.uconn.edu
Rorty, Richard. 1979. *Philosophy and the Mirror of Nature.* Princeton, NJ: Princeton University Press.
———. 1982. *Consequences of Pragmatism.* Minneapolis: University of Minnesota Press.
———. 1988. "The Priority of Democracy to Philosophy." In Rorty 1991.
———. 1989. *Contingency, Irony, and Solidarity.* New York: Cambridge University Press.
———. 1991. *Objectivity, Relativism, and Truth.* New York: Cambridge University Press.
———. 1994. "Religion as a Conversation-stopper." In Rorty 1999.
———. 1997. "Religious Faith, Intellectual Responsibility, and Romance." In Hardwick and Crosby 1997.
———. 1998a. *Achieving Our Country: Leftist Thought In Twentieth Century America.* Cambridge, MA: Harvard University Press.
———. 1998b. "A Defense of Minimalist Liberalism." In Allen and Regan 1998.

———. 1999. *Philosophy and Social Hope.* New York: Penguin.
———. 2003. "Comments on Jeffrey Stout's *Democracy and Tradition.*" Paper presented at the AAR annual meeting in Atlanta, Georgia on November 23, 2003.
———. 2005. "Anticlericalism and Atheism." In Rorty and Vattimo 2005.
Rorty, Richard, and Gianni Vattimo. 2005. *The Future of Religion.* Ed. Santiago Zabala. New York: Columbia University Press.
Rosenblum, Nancy. 1998. "Fusion Republicanism." In Allen and Regan 1998.
Rosenthal, Sandra, Carl Hausman, and Douglas Anderson, eds. 1999. *Classical American Philosophy: Its Contemporary Vitality.* Urbana: University of Illinois Press.
Russell, Bertrand. 1968. "William James's Conception of Truth." *Philosophical Essays.* New York: Simon and Schuster.
Santayana, George. 1957. *Interpretations of Poetry and Religion.* New York: Harper and Brothers.
———. 1962. *Reason and Religion.* New York: Collier Books.
Sandel, Michael. 1982. *Liberalism and the Limits of Justices.* New York: Cambridge University Press.
———, ed. 1984. *Liberalism and Its Critics.* New York: New York University Press.
———. 1996. *Democracy's Discontent.* Cambridge, MA: Harvard University Press.
———. 1998a. "A Response to Rawls's Political Liberalism." Appendix to the second edition of *Liberalism and the Limits of Justice.* New York: Cambridge University Press.
———. 1998b. "The Limits of Communitarians." Preface to the second edition of *Liberalism and the Limits of Justice.* New York: Cambridge University Press.
———. 2004. "Rawls, Liberalism, and Justice." Legacy of Rawls Public Lecture held at Vanderbilt University on January 26, 2004.
Sher, George. 1997. *Beyond Neutrality.* New York: Cambridge University Press.
Sher, George, and Baruch A. Brody, eds. 1999. *Social and Political Philosophy: Contemporary Readings.* Orlando, FL: Harcourt Brace and Co.
Simmons, Aaron. 2005. "Review of *The Future of Religion* by Richard Rorty and Giannit Vattimo." *Philosophia Christi* 7.2: 524–528.
Stout, Jeffrey. 2004a. *Democracy and Tradition.* Princeton, NJ: Princeton University Press.
———. 2004b. "Responses to Five Critical Papers on *Democracy and Tradition.*" *Soundings* 87.3–4: 369–402.
Stuhr, John J. 1997. *Genealogical Pragmatism.* Albany: State University of New York Press.
———. 2003. *Pragmatism, Postmodernism, and the Future of Philosophy.* New York: Routledge.
Suckiel, Ellen K. 1996. *Heaven's Champion: William James's Philosophy of Religion.* South. Bend, IN: University of Notre Dame Press.
Sullivan, Michael, and John Lysaker. 2005. "You Talking to Me?" *Transactions of the Charles S. Peirce Society* 41.1: 138–141.
Sunstein, Cass. 1993. *Democracy and the Problem of Free Speech.* New York: Free Press.
———. 2001. *Republic.com.* Princeton, NJ: Princeton University Press.
———. 2002. "The Law of Group Polarization." *The Journal of Political Philosophy* 10.2: 175–195.
———. 2003. *Why Societies Need Dissent.* Cambridge, MA: Harvard University Press.
Talisse, Robert. 2001. *On Rawls.* Belmont, CA: Wadsworth.
———. 2005a. *Democracy After Liberalism.* New York: Routledge.

———. 2005b. "Dilemmas of Public Reason." In Brooks and Freyenhagen 2005.
———. 2005c. "Deliberativist Responses to Activist Challenges." *Philosophy & Social Criticism* 31.4: 423–444.
Talisse, Robert, and Scott Aikin. 2005. "Why Pragmatists Cannot be Pluralists." *Transactions of the Charles S. Peirce Society* 41.1: 100–118.
Talisse, Robert, and Caleb Clanton. 2004. "Stout on Public Reason." *Soundings* 87.3–4: 349–368.
Taylor, Charles. 1994. "The Politics of Recognition." In Gutmann 1994.
———. 1999. "Atomism and the Primacy of Rights." In Sher and Brody 1999.
———. 2004. *Modern Social Imaginaries*. Durham, NC: Duke University Press.
Tillich, Paul. 1957. *Dynamics of Faith*. New York: Harper and Brothers.
Waldron, Jeremy. 1993. *Liberal Rights*. New York: Cambridge University Press.
Walzer, Michael. 1983. *Spheres of Justice*. New York: Basic Books.
———. 1990. "The Communitarian Critique of Liberalism." In Etzioni 1995.
Wertheimer, Roger. 1974. "Understanding the Abortion Debate." In Cohen, Nagel, and Scanlon 1974.
West, Cornel. 1980. "A Philosophical View of Easter." *Dialog: A Journal of Theology*. Winter 1980. In West 1999.
———. 1984. "Religion and the Left." *Monthly Review*. July-August 1984. In West 1999.
———. 1988. "Introduction: The Crisis in Contemporary American Religion," *Prophetic Fragments*. Grand Rapids, MI: William B. Eerdmans Publishing Co. In West 1999
———. 1989. *The American Evasion of Philosophy*. Madison: University of Wisconsin Press.
———. 1999. *The Cornel West Reader*. New York: Civitas Books.
———. 2004. *Democracy Matters*. New York: Penguin Press.
Whicher, Stephen E. 1960. "Introduction: The Divinity School Address." In Whicher 1960.
———, ed. 1960. *Selections from Ralph Waldo Emerson: An Organic Anthology*. Boston: Houghton Mifflin Co.
Wolfe, Alan. 1995. *One Nation After All*. New York: Penguin Books.
Wolterstorff, Nicholas. 1997. "The Role of Religion in Decision and Discussion of Political Issues." In Audi and Wolterstorff 1997.
Wyatt, Kristen. 2004. "Three Catholic Bishops Bar Communion for Politicians Who Support Abortion Rights" Associated Press. http://www.ap.tbo.com/ap/breaking/MGBZ4WF3IXD.html. Downloaded on September 20, 2004.
Yoder, John Howard. 1997. *For the Nations: Essays Public and Evangelical*. Grand Rapids, MI: William B. Eerdmans Publishing Co.
Young, Iris Marion. 1990. *Justice and the Politics of Difference*. Princeton, NJ: Princeton University Press.
———. 2001. "Activist Challenges to Deliberative Democracy." *Political Theory* 29.5: 670–690.

Index

abortion, 5, 90, 127, 135, 144
Ackerman, Bruce, 5–6, 12, 77–78
act-now deliberative stalemate, 134
African-American churches, 55, 57, 59
Audi, Robert, 78–79, 84

bishops, 5, 6, 12
blood transfusions, 115
Bohman, James, 101–102
burdens of judgment, 66

citizenship, democratic, 6, 8, 11, 45, 116, 142–143
civic republicanism, 85
Clifford, W.K., 22, 40
coercion, 6
Cohen, Joshua, 77
comprehensive doctrine, 3, 8, 65, 87–89, 94–96, 102–103
conversational constraint, 113; ex ante, 82, 98–101; ex post, 127–128

Darwinism, 28
deliberative defeat, 126–128, 136–138
deliberative stalemate, 133–135
democracy, 2, 16, 49–51, 101–102
Descartes, Rene, 17
Dewey, John, 33–34, 64

Elshtain, Jean Bethke, 3, 94
Emerson, Ralph Waldo, 32–33, 59

ensoulment, doctrine of, 47, 137

fallible-inquiry requirement, 138–140, 143–145
Friedman, Marilyn, 96

gadfly, Socratic, 131
Gaus, Gerald, 66, 83, 105
gay marriage, 91, 142

Holmes, Stephen, 21–23, 78
Hook, Sydney, 34
hope, 18, 21–23, 42, 52

immanent criticism, 48, 109–110, 118–119
integrationism, 9

James, William, 15, 91
Jefferson, Thomas, 4, 46
Jeffersonian Compromise, 127
Jehovah's Witnesses, 115

King, Jr., Martin Luther, 58, 131
Kinsley, Michael, 91

Larmore, Charles, 80
Liberalism, 1, 65, 67, 80; comprehensive, 64; minimalist, 86; political, 64, 67, 97

liberal principle of legitimacy, 2, 124, 168

majoritarianism, 3
meaning, pragmatist theory of, 19
meliorism, 21, 27
Mill, John Stuart, 1–2
Misak, Cheryl, 140
modus vivendi, 97, 134–136

Nagel, Thomas, 76–77
naturalism, 32
Neuhaus, Richard John, 97–98
neutrality, doctrine of, 98–99, 102, 104, 107
no-fault divorce law, 87

Peirce, C. S., 131, 133, 141
pluralism, 3, 16, 26–27, 32, 65–67, 112–113
polarization, law of group, 102–104
pornography, 89, 99
pragmatism, 16, 23–25, 34; classical American, 15, 32, 39; neo-, 40, 42, 45, 64
Problem of Indeterminacy, 98–99
prophetic pragmatism, 49–51, 58–59
public philosophy, 3, 11, 86
public square, 3, 8, 15, 64, 70–72, 85, 125

Rawls, John, 63–64, 69, 73–75; fact of oppression, 66–67; fact of reasonable pluralism, 65–67; *modus vivendi*, 97, 134–135; overlapping consensus, 97, 120; political conception of justice, 69, 92; public reason, 68–69, 72, 99; reasonable, concept, 65, 67, 80; respect, concept of, 129, 135, 139
reconstructivism, 32, 59
Reidy, David, 99–100
religious liberty, 46
Roe v. Wade, 90, 105

Roman Catholic Church, 5
Rorty, Richard, 39–41, 47–48, 64; conversation stopper, religion as a, 46–47; on redescription, 57–58; Rortyan Reconstructivist Allowance, 43–44; Rorty's Pragmatic Argument for Separatism, 47–48
Russell, Bertrand, 24–25, 27

Sandel, Michael, 86–87, 90–92
Santayana, George, 33–34
self-reflexive problem, 100
separatism, 72, 85; ex ante, 128; ex post, 127–128; for purity of religion argument, 79
skepticism, 17
Socrates, 129, 147
Stout, Jeffrey, 48, 107–109, 112, 116; immanent criticism, 109, 118, 126; prudential constraint, 111, 113–114; on resentment, 112, 118–120; on respect, 109; on secularization, 112, 117
Suckiel, Ellen, 24–25
Sunstein, Cass, 102–103
supernaturalism, 33–34

Talisse, Robert, 103–104
temporary *mothus vivendi*, 134–135
traditional religious believers, 31, 43, 56–57
truth, correspondence theory of, 25, 55–56; pragmatist conception of, 55, 59
tolerance, 26–28

voting, 8, 69

West, Cornel, 16, 50, 51, 55; pragmatic argument for a reconstructivist strategy, 54. *See also* prophetic pragmatism
Wolterstorff, Nicholas, 92–93 WWJD?, 95–96

About the Author

J. Caleb Clanton is assistant professor of philosophy at Pepperdine University in Malibu, California. Prior to this appointment, he served on the faculty at Vanderbilt University as a lecturer in philosophy, computer science, and engineering management and as a research associate in the Vanderbilt Center for Ethics. His research centers on issues related to social/political philosophy, applied ethics, and American pragmatism. He holds a Ph.D. and M.A. in philosophy from Vanderbilt University and a B.A. in philosophy from the University of Alabama in Huntsville.

BL 65 .P7 C53 2008
Clanton, J. Caleb, 1978-
Religion and democratic
 citizenship

JAN 2 9 2008